REFOCUSING
THE VISION

REFOCUSING THE VISION

Religious Life into the Future

LIVING THE VISION
revisited, revised, and expanded

BARBARA FIAND

A Crossroad Book
The Crossroad Publishing Company
New York

The Crossroad Publishing Company
481 Eighth Avenue, New York, NY 10001

Printed in the United States of America

Library of Congress Cataloging-in-Publication Data
Fiand, Barbara.
    Refocusing the vision : religious life into the future / Barbara Fiand.
       p. cm.
    Rev. and expanded ed. of: Living the vision. 1990.
    Includes bibliographical references.
    ISBN 0-8245-1890-X (alk. paper)
    1. Vows. I. Fiand, Barbara. Living the vision. II. Title.
BX2435 .F48 2001
248.8'94 – dc21   00-012576

1   2   3   4   5   6   7   8   9   10   06   05   04   03   02   01

To
Clare Gebhardt and Catherine Griffiths,
companions on the journey,
in friendship and gratitude

CONTENTS

PREFACE

It has been over ten years since *Living the Vision* was first published. Much has changed for us during that time; much also still remains the same. My reasons for revisiting what I wrote a decade or so ago is largely because the book continues to be used in formation programs as a source for reflections on the vowed life. Some reconsideration and expansion may, therefore, be called for in order to touch base with present-day reality, to help focus us in the here and now, to connect us with the insights and wisdom of today, and to engage us in further dialogue toward transformation. If it is true that, as modern science assures us, there is really nothing permanent except change, it may be that, in the final analysis, reconsidering and expanding our vision are the best ways to be faithful to it.

It is said that Sigmund Freud once tipped his hat to himself when passing a large wall mirror, only to recognize with embarrassment that the one he had greeted was not a stranger but himself. A similar experience was mine not long ago when I was giving a workshop in a stately old mansion whose former owners had generously endowed it with mirrors in every conceivable spot. I was forever peeking in on myself, intruding on my own privacy.

It is a strange quirk of human self-awareness that has us perceive ourselves without instant recognition, see ourselves without immediately knowing it. The fact that we are usually embarrassed when this happens might indicate that somehow we are surprised at it, that we really expect to have better self-awareness, a clearer presence to ourselves. Perhaps we begin to suspect that something is not quite harmonized in our perception, in our vision of who we are. Perhaps also this rather extroverted occurrence uncomfortably reminds us of the much more complex matter of inner awareness and depth perception to which all of us are called, but in which we are all wanting to varying degrees.

Giving this latter insight serious consideration is a painful business, one we would probably all rather avoid. Why is it that we "have eyes but do not see"—at least not as we might? Could one of the reasons perhaps be that so many of us are spending too much of our time and energy reacting and responding to the periphery of reality, be it internal or external, and thus, often unknowingly and with the best intentions, are losing sight of what really counts? The mystic warns us that "God is the circle's center for those who dare embrace Him [or Her]. For those who merely stand in awe, He [or She] is the circle's rim."[1] Are we perhaps so much in awe that we forget to plunge into the center?

The title of this book evolved over a number of years that for me, as for most of us in religious life, were spent rewriting constitutions and reformulating government plans and community policies, in other words, *looking at ourselves*. Like others during these years, I kept wondering about the meaning of it all even as I was engaged in the process. I saw us expend a great deal of energy as we met, planned, and debated for hours. I saw the documents that resulted. They were read and then neatly put away on our shelves or in our drawers as we went about discussing, debating, and rewriting further documents. I found the experience interesting, useful for good organization and management. I kept wondering, however, whether, in *looking* at ourselves, we were really *seeing*; whether, in expecting the questions we were asking about ourselves to be answered, we were really questioning; whether we were in awe of the rim of our lives together and were losing our yearning for deeper vision, our quest for the center. Somehow in our discussions together I kept hearing questions that no one (including myself) was asking aloud; I kept sensing concerns about issues that we were not raising; I kept experiencing a hunger that none of our meetings and documents could satisfy; and I kept feeling that I was not alone in this. And so I decided to write and to probe into the meaning of *vision*.

It is consoling to me and, I am sure, to all of us that in the past ten years the questions and concerns of the late eighties and early nineties have begun to be addressed. It seems to me that we dialogue more easily today and are able to express our doubts and discontent more readily. We clearly continue to struggle and to face difficult issues together. Many of us, however, also prefer to hold on to the escape mechanisms of denial. It is difficult to face the death of traditions that have become sacralized over the years. Creativity and challenge continue to be mistaken for radical liberalism, and holding on to the status quo, doing what "we have always done," still tends to be hailed as fidelity to the vision of the founder or foundress.

My last ten years' encounter with religious life, especially through my retreat and workshop ministry, has deeply enriched me, but it has also increased my sense of urgency to bring things out into the open, to identify disagreements and encourage discussion, to invite us to come together to face the pain and struggle that all of us are experiencing. Writing, at times, is easier than speaking, especially for an introvert. One moves into the quiet of one's self and there lets everything that one has heard and seen play around, dance in the heart of one's very being until a focus is reached and insight breaks through. The pain but also the excitement of writing is in the waiting; in letting the dance be dance, the play be play; in not forcing the process. This kind of writing is the exact opposite of Robert's Rules of Order, to which so many of our discussions, planning sessions, assemblies, and chapters are still, even today (albeit in modified form at times), being subjected. It is different too from working for consensus and not letting anything be tried until everyone agrees. Hence, this kind of writing is freeing. It lets the question be and does not worry about "absolute" or "simple" majority. As a consequence, of course, it cannot provide too many "guidelines," too many final solutions, fixed answers. It rather lets questions move into deeper questions and recognizes the light in what appears to be darkness. It honors the process of emergence. The vision that bears witness to this emergence is much like a child's experience of sunrise. It is filled with wonder, with prayer.

I do not know how often, in the writing as well as the rewriting of these pages, something entirely different from what I had planned came to word. Perhaps a similar experience will grace the reader. What you expect to find (and perhaps even what I would like you to find) in these pages may not be here. My prayer is that you can allow this and thus move into the openness of deeper possibilities; of finding in these reflections what presents itself to *you;* of being with *that* and of someday, as the right moment emerges, sharing *that* with your congregation.

It is my hope that this book will be meaningful to religious of every age group, to men and women alike. These pages do, however, have some areas of difficulty and they, for most readers, will probably be found right at the beginning. Because all modes of conscious life are influenced by the culture in which they flourish, I began this book with a reflection on the "age of change" in which we live our vows. Ours is a time when cultural paradigms are collapsing and the dualistic worldview which served so well for centuries in bringing us not only progress and prosperity but also the spirituality to support them has reached the limits of its own possibilities and is beckoning us from within its own demise to move beyond it and look for deeper, more authentic ways of seeing. An explanation of dualism, of its origin and influence and the spirituality it engendered, can make for somewhat difficult reading, and I wish I could invite the reader simply to avoid these preliminary observations and to look for greener pastures in the later part of chapter 1, where holistic spirituality is discussed. The issue, however, is not as simple as that. Holistic spirituality as the basis for living our vows in contemporary times can be appreciated only when viewed in relation to the dualism in which most of us were reared. The comparison between holistic and dualistic spirituality, their origin and message, is, therefore, of the essence in laying a meaningful foundation for the rest of the book. In order to help clarify matters further, I have added appendixes 1 and 2 to the revised edition of this book. Appendix 1 addresses itself to the needed transformation of consciousness for this our time and to the new way of seeing that is its fruit. It compares individual growth and development with the changes inherent in cultural development and religious thought. Appendix 2 describes more specifically the origin and mind-set of what today we have come to call the "modern" worldview. It also presents some of the discoveries of contemporary science that invite us to change our perspective. Because the topic is vast, a brief appendix can clearly not do it justice. My discussion of this topic, therefore, is restricted to what may be relevant for religious life and its need for transformation. Both appendixes are added to help toward a better understanding of the reasons for, and origin of, the crisis we find ourselves in today, to identify it as broader than merely a crisis of religious life, and to assist us in recognizing vital and necessary areas for growth and change.

Chapter 2 expands and specifies the theme of holistic

spirituality as it explores some of its implications for the self-understanding of men and women religious. It concentrates specifically on issues of ministry, of membership and governance, and explores how our vision changes when we approach each other as a "society of equals," as members of Christ's *basileia*. It stresses the primacy of disposition in living the vows and ideally moves us away from seeking a foolproof ground plan or guide. Its intent is to open up the deeper realities that entice us from the "rim" to the "center" of our lives, from power and control to surrender.

The next three chapters concern themselves with our vows in the order in which we usually profess them: poverty, consecrated celibacy, and obedience. In each case I have attempted to explore the vow first within the context of the holistic paradigm developed in chapters 1 and 2 (and expanded also in appendixes 1, 2, and 3). This, then, is followed by some reflections on the practical concerns that address us in the existential situations of everyday life. What is presented here is intended to be open-ended. I make no pretensions of having the final word on any of the issues raised. That, quite clearly, would betray the main objective of these reflections, namely, to identify consecrated life in particular, and the dedicated life of the believer generally, as a spiraling process of ever expanding vision, of an ever deepening movement into God. No one in this process stands as a solitary prophet or primary wisdom figure. In community, our insights must be shared and challenged toward the deeper vision of the whole. The questions at the end of the chapters are designed to further this. The intention is at all times to expand the reflective process begun through the reading of the chapter and to enhance the involvement of the reader in the vision itself.

By far the most revision and expansion will be found in chapter 4, whose title was also changed. The questions raised there are provocative and may be disturbing to some. I present these reflections with the sincere hope that they will engage us in fruitful, honest, unbiased, and truly necessary dialogue. Ours is a precious way of life that in many respects is in dire need of refounding. No one will be able to do this unless *we* do. For this we need to name what, in fact, we are living; we need to discuss why we are doing what we are doing; we need to do so without feeling defensive and in a forum that is open to us. Those who are interested in our way of life need to see us living it the way we profess we do—for our health and wholeness and for the building up of the Body. My revisions of this book are made in this spirit and plead for reflective openness and conversation.

The book ends with some thoughts on membership. I owe these in large measure to the wonderful women and men from diverse religious congregations who were in the first years of their discernment and who participated in the various programs for newer members throughout the country. I learned much from them: I learned of their hopes and dreams, their willingness to serve, their dedication. I learned to love them, trust them, and respect them. They gave me hope for the future of religious life, but their insights and observations also left me with some concerns. Chapter 6 speaks to both.

This book is clearly concerned with the consecrated life of religious. It is, however, not written exclusively for them. The Body which is Christ has many members and, as Paul tells us (1 Cor. 12:12–27), each member needs the others. The secluded life of religious in the past may have given the impression to their Christian brothers and sisters that they lived their relationship to God apart from the rest of the Christian community. This, if it ever has been true, can be true no longer. Just as religious in the past several years have become actively involved in ministry with married couples and, therefore, had to learn about consecrated matrimony, so, it seems to me, married and single persons also need to support, minister to, and know their brothers and sisters in religious life. Our call is to serve God in diverse ways according to our gifts, always, however, for the unity of the body. For this, interdependence and support are essential. The glory and the brokenness of religious life are offered in these pages, therefore, for the prayer of the membership. "If one member suffers, all the members suffer with it; if one member is honored, all the members share its joy" (1 Cor. 12:26).

There are many whom I wish to thank for their help and encouragement in writing this book. My gratitude goes first and foremost to my own congregation for encouraging the dance within my heart, the play within my thoughts to come to center in the S.N.D. position paper on the vowed life that I wrote several years back. Thanks also to my sisters in Ipswich, Massachusetts, for inviting my first lectures on this topic and, after them, to the many religious congregations throughout the world and especially to the Religious Formation Conference in the United States that kept the issues burning within me. My gratitude, once again, to the publishers, editors, and staff of the Crossroad Publishing Company for their graciousness and their support and to Sandy Lopez-Isnardi for the artwork. To the numerous friends with whom I have shared and reflected, my heartfelt thanks. Finally, in a very special way, I wish to thank those women and men who believe in the call to witness to consecration and mission through religious life. I want to thank you for your faith, for your hope, and for your perseverance.

Chapter One

TURNING POINT

[In the Chinese province of Kiaochau] there was a great drought. For months there had not been a drop of rain and the situation became catastrophic. The Catholics made processions, the Protestants made prayers and the Chinese burned joss-sticks and shot off guns to frighten away the demons of the drought, but with no result. Finally the Chinese said, "We will fetch the rainmaker." And from another province a dried-up old man appeared. The only thing he asked for was a quiet little house somewhere, and there he locked himself in for three days. On the fourth day the clouds gathered and there was a great snow storm at the time of the year when no snow was expected, an unusual amount, and the town was so full of rumors about the wonderful rainmaker that Richard Wilhelm went to ask the man how he did it. In true European fashion he said, "They call you the rainmaker, will you tell me how you made the snow?" And the little Chineseman said, "I did not make the snow, I am not responsible." "But what have you done these three days?" "Oh, I can explain that. I come from another country where things are in order. Here they are out of order, they are not as they should be by the ordinance of heaven. Therefore the whole country is not in Tao, and I also am not in the natural order of things because I am in a disordered country.

17

So I had to wait three days *until I was back in Tao and then naturally the rain came.*[1]

This story, discussed by Jungian analyst Shinoda Bolen in her book *The Tao of Psychology,* speaks symbolically to what she calls a "drought mentality" of the psyche. It signifies a state of dis-ease and anxiety caused by a lack of inner order, a feeling of being severed from the Whole (the Tao). The orientation of this anxiety, claims Bolen, points almost exclusively toward the future, filling the psyche with the dread of insufficiency and being self-fulfilling in its inordinance. To return to wholeness and restore fertility and creativity (rain) requires becoming centered once again—finding one's "quiet little house"—in order to become still, to experience the One.

How might Bolen's story apply to the many concerns and issues that address religious life in contemporary times? My sense is that we can find great relevance in it, and that the call to return to quiet inner ordering so that we might overcome the noise and drought and encounter creativity once more in our lives and our communities will become ever more audible once we allow ourselves to listen to the silence within and orient ourselves toward the One. Religious life as many of us have known it is rapidly declining. Every year an estimated twelve to fifteen congregations that once flourished with life and energy are formally being dissolved.[2] Few are founded to make up for the difference. Talk of new members seems more like wishful thinking than concrete reality to many of us. There are many reasons, therefore, to take the "drought" seriously; many excuses also to adopt a "drought mentality." Nor does the latter afflict only us. Bolen's story points beyond, I believe, to our culture and to the entire perceptive framework of contemporary Western society. No human phenomenon ever appears in isolation. We are essentially with-others-in-the-world. Their vision

affects us. What afflicts them afflicts us, and vice versa. The call
to "leave the world and not allow oneself to be 'contaminated'
by it" may sound plausible to Thomas à Kempis, but socio-
logically it is a fallacy. Religious, like most other humans, are
culturally affected much more than we are counter-cultural.
To understand ourselves, then, we have to understand, at least
in broad strokes, the *what* and *why* of contemporary world
perspectives; how living in and being influenced by them im-
pacts our behavior and provides the explanation we give for
our situation and the solutions we propose for our problems.

Culture in Crisis

We live in difficult times, times of great change and uncertainty,
times of conflict and doubt, of social as well as ethical confusion. Those "who know"—philosophers, theologians, social
and physical scientists alike—tell us that the difficulties we experience are global, that in every facet of our lives we are faced
with insights and discoveries that can no longer be contained
in the concepts and categories with which we were once comfortable, concepts and categories which for centuries assured
us with clear absolutes and gave us the answers we needed
to preserve the present and contain the future with optimism.
Ours is an age of crisis, calling us toward what Fritjof Capra,
the well-known atomic physicist turned mystic, diagnoses as
one monumental turning point of perception, a gigantic shift
in attitude—in the way we have been used to seeing, judging,
as well as responding to reality: to ourselves, to the world, and
to God.[3]

The turning point Capra is suggesting is, of course, difficult to recognize and even more difficult to see as desirable by
most of us, caught, as we are, in the maelstrom of transition.
No civilization lets go easily of the perspective through which

it has achieved its glory and with which it has grown comfortable. Hence rigidity and inflexibility are often the precursors of ultimate crisis and are a major factor in its agony. Capra, citing Toynbee, explains it well:

> After civilizations have reached a peak of vitality, they tend to lose their cultural steam and decline. An essential element in this cultural breakdown...is a loss of flexibility. When social structures and behavior patterns have become so rigid that the society can no longer adapt to changing situations, it will be unable to carry on the creative process of cultural evolution. It will break down and, eventually, disintegrate.

The "drought mentality," in other words, sets in, and starvation is bound to follow:

> Whereas growing civilizations display endless variety and versatility, those in the process of disintegration show uniformity and lack of inventiveness. The loss of flexibility in a disintegrating society is accompanied by a general loss of harmony among its elements, which inevitably leads to the outbreak of social discord and disruption.[4]

One needs little evidence to recognize these phenomena as of our time. Discord and disruption exist everywhere. Psychologists call ours the age of alienation and write volumes about anxiety. National as well as international inflexibilities insist that there is only one way, one's own way, and so billions are spent on "weapons for peace" and the "New World Order," and mistrust of anyone who speaks of dialogue and of living with differences is widespread—always, of course, "in the interests of national security." Within the church this phenomenon is echoed. Here our inflexibility rises "in defense of the faith" and of the authority of the magisterium. It stifles any and all creative rethinking of "tradition," is suspicious of interdisciplinary let alone interfaith dialogue, and holds a rigorously punitive stance toward every kind of scholarship that calls for discussion where dogmatic finality has been declared.

Symbolically speaking, it seems that Western civilization needs to withdraw into its "quiet little house" and silence itself into harmony with the universe once again, in order to be able to take hold of the opportunities which light up for it in this time of crisis. We might note that the Chinese term for crisis (*wei-ji*) speaks of both *danger* and *opportunity*.[5] The philosopher Martin Heidegger, known so well for his depth insight into our contemporary dilemma, speaks in the same vein when he assures us that "where there is danger there deliverance thrives as well."[6] Crisis appears as a dimension of transformation. "We live today in a globally interconnected world, in which biological, psychological, social, and environmental phenomena are all interdependent."[7] To describe this world correctly and begin to understand its dilemma, Capra sees the need for an "ecological perspective," a perspective which I would prefer to call *holistic* in order to distinguish it more clearly and more immediately from the dualistic worldview which, I believe, has brought our society and our culture to this point in history and to this crisis.

Dualism

Dualism, the cornerstone of Western thought for millennia, might in its systematic articulation be traced back as far as Greek idealism and the Greco-Roman worldview, though modern analysts frequently give it a more modest beginning in Descartes, ascribing the mechanistic worldview flowering from it to Newtonian physics. For our purposes its Greco-Roman beginning will have more meaning, for the Greeks and their passionate preoccupation with permanence in the midst of change were responsible for first systematically dividing the world of reality into spirit and matter, soul and body, the sacred and the profane, certainty and illusion, the superior and the inferior, good and evil, the masculine and the feminine— with the former to be sought after, the latter at best to be avoided, at worst to be endured.

Most interpretations of reality spring, I believe, from some form (fair or foul) of self-awareness and consequent self-reflection, with subsequent projection outward. It was so with the primitive's fertility rights and continues to be so, consciously or not, in most contemporary theories, from economics to psychology and even criminology. We are, therefore, not too far afield if we imagine that our Greek ancestors did the same. Looking at themselves and their relation to time and change, they became convinced that much pain and loss (hence evil) accompanies transitoriness, while permanence brings with it stability and trustworthiness (the good). Their own embodiment spoke, of course, of change. It was matter (in later Latin times not only theoretically but, in fact, etymologically linked with woman: *mater*—mother; *materia*—matter). That which held their identity intact even as their body decayed they called "soul"—"spirit." Matter became the principle of change and illusion; spirit became the principle of permanence and truth.

We are all familiar, at least somewhat, with dualistic metaphysics, for it became the hallmark of Western Christendom. From Augustine and Augustinianism through Anselm and medieval scholasticism, it permeated Christian thought to the point of exclusivity and virtual canonization. (Many a mystic was condemned for straying from it.) Ultimately, of course, it led to "Ockham's razor" and to universal skepticism, only to be revived again in Descartes and modern enlightenment. In contemporary times we meet its reverse side in materialism and encounter its results in almost total nihilism: the death of all values, the theater of the absurd.

Dualistic spirituality, which is dominant in our church even to this day, holds within it both the hierarchical as well as the patriarchal view of the sacred. The hierarchical springs naturally from the dualistic, for if one half of reality is seen as good and the other as evil, if one half can be trusted and must be sought after and the other must be avoided, it is easy to conceive of an inbuilt perceptive framework where "better than," "higher than," "more noble than," "holier than," are naturally placed in opposition to the other half, and qualities are even divided internally and ranked according to their proximity to spirit and remoteness from matter. The exact origin of patriarchy seems unclear. What is not unclear, however, is its dualistic orientation. As Jungian analyst Edward C. Whitmont points out:

> The religious trends which characterized the era of patriarchal ego development were based on the devaluation of natural life and matter, of mundane existence, and of the body. Concrete reality, as we encounter it, was increasingly devoid of the spirit and opposed to it. The inwardness of being in the world, which is the realm of the Feminine, was rejected.
>
> Misogyny [hatred of woman] and androlatry [male sidedness], then, are indissolubly intertwined with the religious convictions and beliefs that were held during the last two to four thousand years or more.[8]

We face today the results of a dualistic, patriarchal, and hierarchical spirituality. It permeates still, even after Vatican II, our liturgies and prayers, our ecclesial structures and mandates, our church's official presence in the world, and many of the structures of religious life. We were all reared in it, trained as religious to see through its set of glasses, judge with its measuring sticks, weigh with its scales. So used to it are we that many of us might balk in disbelief and consternation at the suggestion that there can be another way of interpreting reality, another way of experiencing ourselves and our relation to each other, the world, and God—a way equally valid and profoundly Christian, but holistic rather than dualistic, incarnational rather than disembodied. The reason for this disbelief and dis-ease is that spirituality, as Anne Carr says so well, is "all encompassing and pervasive.... [It] reaches into our unconscious or half-conscious depths. And while it shapes behavior and attitudes, spirituality is more than a conscious code. In relation to God, it is who we really are, the deepest self."[9] We dwell in our spirituality much more than we profess it. It is the ambiance—that which allows us to see, to reflect on, to interpret, and ultimately to respond to the depth questions of our existence. It colors our seeing, our hearing, our speaking, even our breathing.[10] Little wonder, then, that questioning what has been the predominant spirituality of an age— the guiding spirituality of an individual—can cause insecurity and upset.

> Spirituality is expressed in everything we do. It is a style, unique to the self, that catches up all our attitudes: in communal and personal prayer, in behavior, bodily expression, life choices, in what we support and affirm and what we protest and deny....
>
> [It] is deeply informed by family, teachers, friends, community, class, race, culture, sex, and by our time in history, just as it is influenced by beliefs, intellectual positions, and moral options.[11]

It is our deepest myth, the energy that supplies our imagination and our feelings and directs our understanding. Our involvement with it and in it is intense, therefore, although not necessarily always conscious. To feel shaken in it is to experience tremors in the very depths of one's being, and these are intensified in direct proportion to one's unconsciousness. Just as our deepest self may be partially hidden from us, even though it energizes our actions and informs our world perspective and our values, so our spirituality can remain quite ' hidden from conscious awareness and, therefore, remain unexamined. Larger and deeper than speculative theology, it lacks theological specificity and speaks rather from within the wider cultural, racial, and sexual mythos that inspires theological articulation and in turn gets nourished by it. It is the soil, if you . will, from which theology sprouts; a soil, however, that, for the sake of theological clarity and specificity, has been tilled and cultivated in our Western tradition, leaving much of its originality unthought.

Thinking into Our Myths

To think into and bring to consciousness our myths means that we can "affirm and deny them, accept parts and reject others, as we grow in relationship to God, to others, to our world."[12] Thinking into our myths has us, therefore, move beyond them even as we stand within them. It frees us to respond in ever greater depth to their message concerning the ultimate questions of our existence. It empowers us to take their answers and move with them into still deeper questions about our origin and our end: where we came from and why, who we are and how we should live, where our home is and how we might return there. Thinking into our myths in contemporary society means, however, more so now than ever before, doing this also within the context of other disciplines: of archaeology and anthropology, of psychology, sociology, biology and

physics, of linguistics, philosophy and history. This is so because thinking into our myths today means facing the crisis of
our culture and accepting its mandate toward transformation.
This requires honesty, integrity, and courage. We can no longer
be satisfied with religious isolationism or authoritarian absolutism precisely because both of these originate within the very
culture and myth that is in crisis and needs to be transformed.
To think into our myths, therefore, requires an openness to the
possibility of a radical regrounding of our spirituality, a "revolution of consciousness," as Beatrice Bruteau calls it, where
we take the risk and allow for a genuine "gestalt shift in the
whole way of seeing our relations to one another so that our
behavior patterns are reformed from the inside out."[13] This
is no easy task. It asks for a courageous facing of what will
no longer do, and a rethinking of everything that perpetuates
dualism in its divisiveness, elitism, isolationism, and exclusivity. It means bringing to the surface, to conscious reflection,
the fundamental questions which undergird all spirituality and
which for most of us have remained, with their roots generally
unthought and unquestioned, within the realm of blind faith:

- Who is our God?

- Who are we?

- How are we related to our God—in authenticity and
  righteousness, or in alienation and sin?

- How can we return home? What is redemption?

Thinking into our myths means probing the answers to these
questions in their effects on our values and our behavior. It
means regrounding them within the ecological and holistic perspective which may help us through the crisis of our times back
into harmony with the One.

We all know the God of dualism. At the risk of appearing simplistic, one might present the following synopsis:* The God of dualism is a patriarchal ruler, different from a parent in his wrath and remoteness (though called, Father), exacting love, holding obedience as primary. He (and there is no doubt about his gender) made the world out of nothing in six days, and on the seventh day he rested, obliging all of us (under pain of sin) to do the same in imitation and worship of him. The God of dualism is a "mighty fortress," a "bulwark," Lord of lords, King of kings. Only consecrated ministers (men) can approach his sanctuary, and consecrated fingers touch him. His love for us is an issue of faith. He sends suffering as chastisement, for "our own good," and because he loves us. When good things happen to us we are grateful to him, though we also look anxiously toward tomorrow because these moments are usually "too good to be true." Paradoxically, we can also reject this God (lose our faith) for his interference in our lives, since "an all good God would never allow us to suffer so much."

A dualistic interpretation of reality also clearly identifies *our* place in the scheme of things. Ours is a divided humanity: man was made in God's image. Eve, his helpmate, was a secondary creature. Thomas saw her as an "incomplete male"; Augustine wondered whether she had a soul.[14] Humans, from the first sin onward, have been depraved. We are originally sinful. Our relation to God was cut off. We inherited our depravity through the intercourse of our parents. (This view is consistent with a general rejection of the body, of pleasure,

---

*It is important to note that in presenting this we are not primarily concerned with strict orthodoxy. Our interest lies rather with the mythos and its sphere of influence: how it infiltrates our broad self-understanding vis-à-vis the Holy and our overall value orientation and behavior. It is clear that for many of us the picture presented here no longer holds. Others among us are, however, still bound at least by parts of it—if not consciously, then in our unconscious which provides much fodder for guilt and self-deprecation.

and of human sexuality.) Our body is viewed as distinct from our soul (its prison, in fact) while it sojourns in the "valley of tears." The primary sin was that of disobedience and pride—a desire to be like God. The contrasting virtues, therefore, are obedience (preferably blind and quick) and humility, seen as self-debasement and abnegation and judged frequently through external acts symbolizing this. As religious we remember well our "acts of humility" and self-abnegation, as well as our overall "punishment" of the body.

Redemption, in a dualistic-patriarchal system, is achieved through restitution, through suffering in order to "pay the price for sin." It is an "opening of the gates of heaven" through retribution offered to an offended deity—retribution which, because of the enormity of the sin against God himself, had to be paid for by God also. Only God can appease God. Dying for our sins was willed by God and submitted to by Christ in perfect obedience to the Father as a peace offering restoring us to grace. Through Christ's death we became a "holy people," unworthy though we are.

The paradigm fleshed out here may appear rough and, for the sophisticated reader trained in post–Vatican II theology, it may even be somewhat offensive. What needs to be remembered here is that refinements in theology have little effect on the average believer if the foundational myth remains unthought and unquestioned. Thus, for example, it may be true that today few of us remain concerned about mortal sin associated with Sunday work, and we may even be familiar with an up-to-date exegesis of the creation story and have studied contemporary theology concerning sin, yet who of us has really replaced the previous preoccupation with sin with an understanding of the meaning of creative celebration, of work as cosmic liberation, and of rest as joy-filled contemplation of goodness and harmony?

One might dismiss this sort of challenge as impossible in our times and in our culture. Ours is the age of workaholism. If we are not at our jobs, we work at relaxing and worry when we have nothing to do. That, of course, is precisely the point. The roots of workaholism are the same as obligatory rest on the Sabbath. Neither flow from obedience to one's own integrity and one's creative unity with the cosmos, from listening there to the goodness that calls us into a celebration with all of creation. Both of them, rather, are externally induced and are effective because of a fundamental distrust of self. The one obliges under pain of sin, exacting worship—the official surrender of time to the spiritual over against the material concerns of life. The other springs from the need to "make it" in a world where material gain identifies one's status, one's worthiness, and spirit has been dismissed as irrelevant. That the coercion in either case comes from different sources—one from religion, the other from the broader society and culture; one from spiritualism, the other from materialism—is irrelevant. Both are grounded in a split worldview that needs reconciliation.

The "acts of humility" cited above are another case in point. If self-abnegation and the general rejection of the body is no longer an issue today, the self-aggrandizement and the craving for success, prestige, and recognition which is so prevalent in its stead (and as religious we are not immune to this), is merely its other side. What underlies both is a profound sense of personal insignificance and a need to acquiesce to external norms.

As a final example to illustrate that what we are concerned with here is foundational rather than merely speculative, we might briefly turn to a consideration of the issue concerning God's gender. Experience seems to confirm over and over that explanations and argumentation about the theological incorrectness of attributing gender to God have little effect on removing the masculinized orientation of ecclesial regulations and language still operative today. They often merely upset men and women alike, since they profoundly disturb the mythos. "Woman power" does not appear capable of removing the stigma of sexism in our church either. Frequently it only enhances it, for it is often merely a reaction to it, caught in the same cultural dichotomy that has afflicted our imagination for thousands of years. *Who* has power is, after all, not the point. That power is used to *overpower* and exclude is what needs reflection and subsequent healing. The matters we are dealing with here are beyond the intellect alone. They touch us at our very deepest sensitivities. Sandra Schneiders puts it well when she points out:

> A healthy spirituality requires a healing of the *imagination* which will allow us not only to think differently about God but to *experience God differently*. The imagination is accessible not primarily to abstract ideas but to language, images, interpersonal experience, symbolism, art—*all the integrated approaches which appeal simultaneously to intellect, will, and feeling*.[15]

Refounding Our Myths

We have found ourselves for years now, both culturally and ecclesially, trying to straighten things out in isolation from each other and piecemeal, somewhat like the Catholics, the Protestants, and the Chinese in Kiaochau before they joined together and called for the rainmaker. Our answer lies in entering the "quiet little house" and becoming one with each other and all of creation. This clearly calls for a different paradigm than the one we are used to. Our worldview seems to have reached its "limit-situation."

For individual development and maturation, coming to a limit situation means that one has reached that level of growth where the old perceptions and ways of responding will no longer do and new levels of insight are imminent but have not as yet broken through. There is, therefore, for the individual a general sense of confusion and chaos, and even of helplessness while she or he can do little else but wait for a "new dawn":

In a limit-situation, [one] loses [one's] foothold...becomes suddenly aware of the fundamental limitations of [one's] existence, and discovers the radical contingency of all beings encountered. In a limit-situation [our] familiar world loses its solidity and its obviousness, and begins to disintegrate as the ultimate anchorage of [our] existence. A limit-situation reveals the fundamental limits of any and all particular things and situations. It points within these situations to a possible transcendency, indicating thereby that there is something more fundamental, without revealing what that something more fundamental really is.[16]

Individuals experience limit-situations every time their maturation reaches the end of a particular level of consciousness and a breakthrough into the new becomes necessary. When they have grown to the fulfillment of a developmental phase, they become disenchanted and bored. Their world seems to be imploding, for what they have valued in the past no longer holds their interest. They want more but do not seem able to find it.

Limit-situations open up desert experiences for us and invite us to wait for the breakthrough of the new, the challenge of transcendence. The latter comes to us always, however, in its own time—as gift. It opens up new vision and the potential for growth. John Shea clarifies this process for us in his *Stories of God: An Unauthorized Biography* and takes us even deeper:

> When we reach our limits, when our ordered worlds collapse, when we cannot enact our moral ideals, when we are disenchanted, we often enter into the awareness of Mystery. We are inescapably related to this Mystery which is immanent and transcendent, which issues invitations we must respond to, which is ambiguous about its intentions, and which is real and important beyond all else.
>
> Our dwelling within Mystery is both menacing and promising, a relationship of exceeding darkness and undeserved light.[17]

The cultural parallel to this deeply personal event of human transcendence should not be difficult to see. Cultures, we all know, are made up of human beings. If the latter experience the pains of growth, so will the former—only much more slowly, with much greater agony, and often after a much longer wait. Individuals have a lifetime to mature; cultures and the diverse institutions engendered by them can take centuries, if not millennia. (For a more detailed discussion on the implications for religious life, see appendix 1.)

It seems to me, that our cultural limit-situation—the crisis of our age—is ripe at its very core for a "new dawn," for a transformation of perspectives, for the revelation and encounter with Mystery. Students of social change speak of our age as an age of transition. They talk of the demise of the modern era, of the industrial or the mechanistic age. They laud the advent of post-modernism, post-industrialism, the post-mechanistic era. They speak of the collapse of old ways of seeing and doing things, of changing trends. Few, however, seem yet able to tell us much more. The question for us, therefore, is wide open:

What can we hope for in this "possible transcendency"? What will light up for us out of this "new openness"?

I do not think that what will grace us, as we attempt to gather ourselves in the silence of our "quiet little house" and open ourselves toward reconciliation with all of creation, will be anything *new* as such, if "new" implies "totally foreign." Heidegger tells us that our future, paradoxically, comes toward us out of our past. And so it is, I believe, with our call from dualism to wholeness. Fundamentally it is a homecoming to that which has always been there at the root of our Christian heritage and is now simply drawing us out of our forgetfulness and lostness into awareness.

Though Greco-Roman dualism has been with us for so long now that we can hardly conceive of anything other, scholars assure us that, despite theology's attraction to it throughout the ages, it was anything but the power behind the Christian inspiration. Jesus was a Jew and his movement was part of the Jewish history of his time. His concern, like the concern of all other Jewish movements prevalent in his day, was with the reign of God (God's *basileia*), and Israel's role as God's holy people. "However, the Jesus movement refused to define the holiness of God's elected people in cultic terms, redefining it instead as the wholeness intended in creation."[18] Inclusive wholeness, not a division between the sacred and the profane, pervades the vision of Jesus, who sees the *basileia* of God as already present (realized eschatology), even as our eyes are opened and our hearts are softened to acknowledge it.

> The central symbolic actualization of the *basileia* vision of Jesus is not the cultic meal but the festive table of a royal banquet or wedding feast.... None of the stories told by or about Jesus evidences the concern for ritual purity and moral holiness so typical of other groups in Greco-Roman

Palestine.... [H]e does not share their understanding that the "holiness" of the Temple and Torah is the locus of God's power and presence.[19]

God's power was with God's people and was evidenced in Christ's healing mission, his inclusion of the sick, the poor, the broken, prostitutes, tax collectors, men and women alike— a "discipleship of equals," as Elisabeth Schüssler Fiorenza identifies it:

> The God of Israel is the creator of all human beings, even the maimed, the unclean, and the sinners....Wholeness spells holiness and holiness manifests itself precisely in human wholeness. Everyday life must not be measured by the holiness of the Temple and Torah, but Temple and Torah praxis must be measured by whether or not they are inclusive of every person in Israel and whether they engender the wholeness of every human being. Everyday-ness, therefore, can become revelatory, and the presence and power of God's sacred wholeness can be experienced in *every* human being.[20]

Edward Schillebeeckx in his reflection *On the Christian Faith* reiterates Schüssler Fiorenza's position when, citing the church father Irenaeus, he insists that "God's honour lies in the happiness, liberation and salvation or wholeness of humanity." Our belief in the creation *means* "that God loves us without conditions or limits: undeservedly on our side, boundlessly."[21] This Christian trust was grounded in the experience of "Jesus' career: from his message and his life-style which matched it, from the specific circumstances of his death, and finally from the apostolic witness of his resurrection from the dead."[22] The early Jesus movement lived in the energy of Christ's vision, standing against dehumanization and the oppression of the patriarchal culture and time in which it arose. The *basileia* included everyone. Its concern was the wholeness of all. Jesus' "announcement of 'eschatological reversal'—many who are first will be last and those last will be first...applies also to women and to their impairment by patriarchal structures."[23] His vision, therefore, spelled the death knell to patriarchy and hierarchy alike. He neither experienced nor addressed God as patriarch. Though the cultural constraints placed upon him as teacher and proclaimer of God's plan for humanity in a particular place and time rendered it necessary to present God as Father,[24] Jesus, in no way, exemplified a patriarchal relation with his God. In fact the very opposite is true. A patriarch is not addressed as *Abba*. Jesus completely purified the Old Testament father-son metaphor of its "patriarchal overtones," says Sandra Schneiders. He "drew his God image from the non-patriarchal presentation of God as the deeply offended but infinitely forgiving father of Israel."[25]

Time and purpose do not permit us to explore this matter further. Much has, anyhow, already been written on this topic with greater expertise. The question that, for our purposes, we need still to ask ourselves, however, is why this ancient heritage did not survive.

Schüssler Fiorenza's historical interpretation, which sees the Christian missionary movement expanding the early Palestine community and reaching out to, yet at the same time becoming infiltrated by, the Greco-Roman culture, is perhaps the most easily understood explanation.[26] No missionary ever remains unaffected by the society to which she or he proclaims the Good News. To "go forth and teach all nations" always will also mean being taught and influenced by them in turn. Social, psychological pressures, as well as time and constant interaction, wear on the original intent of any vision; thus adaptation is inevitable. From Paul's catechetical use of the "altar to the

unknown god" to Nicea and Chalcedon, Greek metaphysics
(not only with simple concepts, but also with its tendency to reduce intellectual [faith] movements to systems and bring unity,
clarity, and permanence where there had been diversity and
process) moved steadily into the Christian tradition. Often this
subtle takeover was enhanced through the church's efforts to
meet dissenters from the faith on their own turf. If that turf, as
was generally the case, turned out to be metaphysical, a defense
of the faith became metaphysical; hence the conflict-resolving
dogma that was finally pronounced to the whole church was
clothed in metaphysical language as well.

Joseph S. O'Leary explains this intermeshing well. The primary hope of the Greek fathers, he points out, had been to
"take captive" Greek intellectuality for the use of Gospel explanation and defense. "But there is perhaps no such thing as a
one-way conquest, and it can be said as well that the Gospel of
Christ was taken captive by Greek intellectuality."[27] As here-
sies multiplied, the common use of concepts and terminology
increased, since the church, in order to preserve the integrity
of the Gospel, became ever more specific in its identification
of the elements of the faith. Thus,

> As the basic principles of philosophy were increasingly
> redefined in Christian terms—so that cosmology was
> founded in the biblical doctrine of creation, theology,
> and theodicy in the doctrine of the Father and his Logos,
> ethics, and psychology in the doctrines of sin and grace—
> a process of intellectual transfusion occurred whereby
> Christianity was enabled to replace metaphysics as the
> supreme intellectual system of the West.... The creeds
> and the dogmas which were originally forged to defend
> Christian identity against absorption by Hellenistic cur-
> rents of thought and religiosity, became after Nicea the

instruments of the exclusive establishment of Christianity as the true philosophy abrogating all others.... Dogma may have been counter-metaphysical in so far as it preserved the identity of the faith against metaphysical absorption; but by its emphasis on definition and certitude and its claim to be treated as a first principle dogma betrayed its own purpose and became the instrument of the strongest assumption of a metaphysical identity of the Christian faith.[28]

The matter was not improved either with the switch from Greek to the more tightly logical medium of Latin where the doctrines of the early fathers "were assembled in a rather petrified system, in which the margin of vagueness or mystery they retained in Greek was mercilessly lopped away."[29] The influence of Augustine here was powerful. Metaphysics under him became the ground-plan for all experience: "a systematic geography of love and desire, joy and suffering, sin and virtue."[30] There was in the Christian West ultimately but one religious vocabulary, the terminology of Augustine's Latin, geared to control and hold all movements of the Spirit within its concepts:

> Thus in whichever direction one pursued either religious experience or theological speculation after Augustine one came up against the all-embracing structures of his ground plan, which seemed the definitive institution of the boundaries of the Christian truth. Nor could an escape be found through a return to Scripture, since Scripture was automatically read (even by the Reformers) through Augustinian eyes.[31]

The relevance of these observations for a depth understanding of religious life and the interpretation of the vows will,

I hope, become evident in the succeeding chapters. For the present we might end this brief as well as somewhat complex reflection on the reasons for our "forgetfulness" of the earliest traditions—our seeming separation from our roots—with one further and also deeply alarming observation by O'Leary: "If the Church today is vulnerable to the critiques of Marx, Freud, and Nietzsche," he points out, "it is largely because of an Augustinianism insufficiently overcome." He sees this as a "metaphysical institutionalization of the Gospel, which does not allow it to deploy its liberative challenge in concrete interplay with social and psychological situations, but tries to inscribe its message in a systematic code."[32] The pertinence of this insight for religious seems obvious, especially after the long and often painful struggle many of us have experienced in seeking approval for our constitutions as expressions of *our* experience and of *our* hopes. Whenever liberation language and concern for justice threatens the establishment, the establishment has become top-heavy. O'Leary insists (and this is certainly not new to any of us at this point) that for an authentic living of the Gospel today we need to "overcome metaphysics." We need to return to the roots, to open up to new paradigms in order to allow Christianity to become credible once again for our age. It is clear that contemporary liberation theologians—those concerned with the equality and dignity of women and of any other oppressed group, Christian ecologists and those who with them proclaim the goodness of all creation, as well as mystics everywhere—strongly agree with these observations. We are concerned here, it seems to me, with an ecclesial equivalent of Newtonian physics and our responsibility as God's people to think beyond its absolutes into our beginnings—into the energy of the Christian tradition as it emerged in its earliest times. If James J. Bacik is right and contemporary society is experiencing an "eclipse of Mystery,"[33] then it will be our task to open ourselves up once more to the possibility of its reappearance. Nothing less than that is worthy of our heritage.

In the world of physics the quantum theory did this for scientists. It exposed them to mystery beyond Newtonian "solutions" and allowed them ultimately to present to us new foundations for an understanding of our world and for approaching reality. Its discovery, however, took them through a profound intellectual crisis, which involved them in an intense emotional and existential experience of reality as paradoxical, as fundamentally dynamic and organic. This, because of its revolutionary difference from previous assumptions, almost led them to despair.[34] We will want to look at some of their theories later on in our reflections (see appendix 2), since the quantum vision offers an interesting perspective which profoundly influences the post-modern worldview and has striking implications also for our revisioning of religious life. To accept reality as essentially paradoxical necessitates a radical shift in one's attitude. It did so for the scientists, and will do so for us. One must learn to approach one's world with different questions. The one-sided certainty of a mechanistic, dualistic worldview no longer holds, and a holistic, ecological approach seems much more meaningful. "The spirit no longer appears to us an intruder in the realm of matter; we begin to suspect that we should rather welcome it," writes James Jeans, while Lincoln Barnet postulates "an ultimate, undiversified, and eternal ground beyond which there appears to be nowhere to progress."[35] The biologist Adolf Portman speaks of a " 'non-spatial abyss of mystery' which opens out behind the living organism, or at its origin."[36]

Taking our cue from the world of science, then, we might, for now, in our quest for a new paradigm, begin with a surrender to the mystery. Our answers, we are told, will not come in calculable clarity, and we remember John Shea's promise that our experience will be one of ambiguity, of "exceeding darkness" as well as "undeserved light." The depth spirituality which we are seeking as we return to our roots within an atmosphere of open rather than blind faith and attempt to think into our myths there will be one with no final solutions. Questions will most likely lead to deeper questions as intellect yields precedence to heart, and we, in our thinking, leave room for the existential and experiential, for the mystical, the paradoxical.

Toward a Holistic Paradigm

We have already certain indications of the milieu out of which holistic spirituality arises: from our earliest traditions in the Jesus movement we know that God is essentially lover, nurturer, parent. The mystics who kept this insight experientially alive throughout the history of the church expand it for us. They draw their understanding of divine love quite naturally from their own experience of authentic self-giving. Love, they tell us, is love only if expressed toward another. No one can love in isolation. Love in its very essence speaks of outreach, of otherness, of sharing. God's love cannot be different here, only infinitely more so. In its reaching out for the other it, therefore, almost of necessity "breaks out" into creation. Creation is the love act of God.

The terms the German mystic Eckhart uses to describe this divine activity are filled with the exuberance and energy of the *dabhar*, the divine Word: in God's "pleasuring-forth" the universe, God is the "great underground river that no one can damn up and no one can stop." The divine creator "finds joy and rapture in us." The lover of humankind is "ever green, ever verdant, ever flowering. Every action of God is new.... God is the newest thing there is, the youngest thing there is. God is the beginning.... God is voluptuous and delicious."[37] For Hildegard of Bingen "all creation is gifted with the ecstasy of God's light." God is "the resounding Word, the It-Shall-Be." Poetically reflecting on God's creative activity she hears God speak: "With my mouth I kiss my chosen creation. I uniquely, lovingly, embrace every image I have made out of the earth's clay."[38] A more contemporary mystical experience has T. S. Eliot refer to God's creative energy as a "dance at the still point," drawing our attention to God's dynamic paradox:

> At the still point of the turning world. Neither flesh nor
>   fleshless;
> Neither from nor towards; at the still point there the
>   dance is.
> But neither arrest nor movement. And do not call it fixity.
> Where past and future are gathered. Neither movement
>   from nor towards,
> Neither ascent nor decline. Except for the point, the still
>   point,
> There would be no dance, and there is only the dance.
> I can only say, there we have been; but I cannot say
>   where.
> And I cannot say, how long, for this is to place it in
>   time.[39]

In God's divine act of love infinite diversity becomes manifest: "Everything that is is bathed in God, is enveloped by God, who is round-about us all, enveloping us. Being is God's circle and in this circle all creatures exist. Everything that is in God is God."[40] Holiness, therefore, pervades creation. "And God saw that it was good" (Gen. 1:4, 10, 12, 18, 21, 25, 31). God's creation is God's echo, an act of infinite wisdom, grace, and playful joy: "from of old I was poured forth.... I [wisdom] was God's delight day by day, playing before God all the while, playing on the surface of God's earth; and I found delight in the children of humankind" (Prov. 8:23, 30, 31).

The perspective I am here describing may appear new and perhaps foreign to some but is, as I mentioned already, quite rooted in our earliest traditions. When one reads the creation accounts, much depends on where one wishes to place the emphasis. Thus, a God rejoicing at the goodness of all is simply a God not frequently mentioned in dualistic spirituality, which chooses to place its emphasis elsewhere; but one can hardly deny the fact that in Scripture this God is duly represented. Incidentally, the same God of the first creation account cited above is also the God beyond patriarchal dualism, if one allows oneself to see this: "God created man in his image; in the divine image God created him; *male and female God created them*" (Gen. 1:27). The image of God cannot be contained in one-sidedness. Elsewhere I have discussed the attempts to do precisely that, to suppress the God of diversity (symbolically at home in both genders) through the translation of the term *Elohim* (used for God in this text and composed of a feminine plural with a masculine suffix) in purely masculine terms.[41] Scripture was written and is read by human beings. The writers were inspired, yes, but were writing *within* a culture and worldview. To understand and appreciate the Word necessitates knowledge of this and critical reappraisal at every turn in the human journey. "No text written by human beings is without its shadow side, which the passage of time may throw into deeper relief. Theology is largely a struggle with these shadows."[42]

Now if creative love cannot be contained in one-sidedness, neither ought the human being that issues forth from God be divided against himself or herself. For Eckhart the human being is essentially the love response to the divine; the one who, as creation come to consciousness, in a multitude of ways gathers God's infinite diversity in worship and in praise; the one in whom the universe is brought to word, to prayer, to meaning; the psalmist in whom all of creation praises God; the mirror in whom God is reflected back to God; the virgin mother whose emptiness receives God and births God back to God in gratitude;[43] the spark where in the eternity of time and the infinity of space the love of God breaks forth, lights up, bursts into song:

> God is always flowing into the soul and can never escape the soul. But the soul can easily escape God. As long, however, as a person remains under God, that person receives the unmediated divine influx.... The masters say that the soul receives light from light.[44]

> Seize God in all things for God is in all things.[45]

> The prophet says: "[God] has stretched forth [God's] hand" (Jer. 1:9). And he means by that the Holy Spirit. Now he goes on to say: "[God] has touched my mouth" and means by this that "[God] has spoken to me" (Jer. 1:9). The mouth of the soul is the highest part of the soul and this is meant by saying "[God] has put [God's] word in my mouth" (Jer. 1:9). That is the kiss of the soul: there mouth comes to mouth; there the Father [Mother] gives birth to the Son in the soul, and there is where the soul is addressed.[46]

The tenderness and passion of these passages is striking. Sue Woodruff, writing on Mechtild of Magdeburg, Eckhart's foremother, identifies similar themes:

> She touches on themes as old as the book of Job, the Psalms, the Song of Songs. Her writings abound in images

of light, fire, reflection, love, longing. She sees the soul in these images and God in the same images. We are the spark; God is the fire. We are the fire; God is the light. We are the light; God is the moon. We are the moon; God is the sun. We are the sun; God is love. We are love; God is compassion. We are compassionate; we resemble God.[47]

The call of the mystics is a call to creative fidelity, to a response out of a diversity of gifts, in utter releasement, for the glory of God. "We—body, soul, male, female, young, old—mirror the splendor of creation. We are the ground, the humus, where the God-seed can germinate, root and flower forth in our day."[48] But we can also choke this seed and thwart the creative effort of God. If the primary virtue in this holistic approach to our traditions is surrender to the creative activity of God in and through me; if I am called to releasement—the creative letting-go of personal presuppositions, assumptions, expectations, prejudices, in order to let be what is as it is in its original divine intent—then the primary vice is precisely the refusal to do this. The will to power (overpower rather than empower) refuses to let God be God in creation. It blinds itself to the giver and posits itself as the origin of meaning, imposing concepts, personal projections and interpretations on others and even on the self. I call it the "Cartesian affliction": "I think, therefore, *it is*" (i.e., What *I* think ought to be). Rather than allowing divinity to be born in one's depths, one imposes it on oneself and lords it over others; one dominates the world. "Why is it," asks Eckhart, "that some people do not bear fruit? It is because they are too busy clinging to their egotistical attachments."[49]

The self-emptying required for creative authenticity is one of the primary themes in the Gospels. But it is, I believe, never simply recommended for the sake of emptiness itself, but always in order to be filled. The "virgin womb" is significant in its emptiness only because it is ready to receive life and to bear it forth once again into the heart of God.[50] We empty ourselves to find ourselves—our wholeness, our authenticity, our freedom—in the love of God.

In contemporary thought an echo of these themes of divine love and human surrender is beautifully found in Rahner's theology of grace. Grace, for Rahner, is the living presence of God—God's indwelling within the human person. Human beings are destined for God and gifted with a unique openness toward this end from the moment of their creation. The presence of God pervades their being. They are transcendence, an active openness (though not always consciously so) to the infinite and absolute.

> God wishes to communicate [God's self], to pour forth the love which [God] himself [herself] is. That is the first and the last of [God's] real plans and hence of [God's] real world too. Everything else exists so that this one thing might be: the eternal miracle of infinite Love. And so God makes a creature whom [God] can love: [God] creates [the human being]. [God] creates him [her] in such a way that he [she] *can* receive this love which is God himself [herself], and that he [she] can and must at the same time accept it for what it is: the ever astounding wonder, the unexpected, unexacted gift.[51]

We are at all times "addressed and claimed" by God's love. We are in fact created for it; we are loved into being for the sake of Love. This call moves beyond membership in any institutional church. It belongs to humankind. God's self-communication is "offered to all and fulfilled in the highest way in Christ." It is "the goal of all creation." It stamps and determines our nature so that a rejection of it brings us into profound contradiction with our deepest being. Whenever we truly and completely accept ourselves, we are held in God's grace for it already speaks within us.[52]

Limit situations where the call beyond is felt especially keenly in the here and now are where Rahner localizes the experience of grace with particular poignancy:

> Grace is operative in the experience of infinite longings, of radical optimism, of unquenchable discontent, of the torment of the insufficiency of everything attainable, of the radical protest against death, the experience of being confronted with an absolute love precisely where it is lethally incomprehensible and seems to be silent and aloof, the experience of a radical guilt and of a still-abiding hope, and so on. These elements are in fact tributary to that divine force which impels the created spirit—by grace— to an absolute fulfillment.[53]

One is reminded here of Eckhart's observation: "the divine countenance is capable of maddening and driving all souls out of their senses with longing for it. When it does this...it is thereby drawing all things to itself....Every creature— whether it knows it or not—seeks repose."[54]

And yet the will to power persists and with it sin and alienation. Our unwillingness to recognize the goodness in which we are held and to respond with releasement and gratitude has brought us already from the first moment of creation into radical contradiction with our roots, our deepest self. We stand in need of redemption—to be re-membered into the Christ, God's love incarnate. This, then, is our salvation: the love of God in our midst, who came to show us our way home into the heart of God; who became human so that we might be divinized— returned into our own depths where God is.

Holistic spirituality sees eternal life as already begun and as realized ever more by our moving into the Christ event in which we are already held. What matters is *vision* and our *living into that vision*. With the early Christians we see Jesus as the Wisdom of God, the "child of Sophia sent to announce that God is the God of the poor and heavy laden, of the outcasts and those who suffer injustice."[55] Our salvation, then, lies in compassion. "Those who follow compassion find life for themselves, justice for their neighbor, and glory for God."[56] They live in the fullness of time. The redemptive task of Jesus was precisely to show us this. His suffering and death cannot be understood in cultic terms, as atonement for sin, nor was it understood that way in the earliest Jesus tradition, though this interpretation soon took over.[57] The God whom Jesus came to proclaim did not need or desire restitution. "Jesus' execution, like John's, result[ed] from his mission and commitment as prophet and emissary of the Sophia-God"[58] who holds open a future for the broken and rejected and offers God's gracious goodness unconditionally to all. Jesus was killed by the ruling powers of his day because of his freedom and the integrity toward which he called his followers. When freedom encounters the need to control, power will always rise up and try to destroy it.

This interpretation of Jesus' death here presented in no way lessens its redemptive character, nor for that matter does it need to do away with the view that Jesus "took on sin," that he "died for our sins," and so forth; for was not the very sin which crucified him—the will to power, to control, to dominate, to oppress—the sin of the world that needed to be overcome? And here also lies the power of the resurrection, for in it sin and its dominance was nullified. The "abandoned" prophet was raised and his message vindicated, namely, that the Lover-God will not be denied, and that the freedom that this opens up for God's people is real. God has loved us with an everlasting love.

We are precious to God; we are the beloved of God; we are held in the palm of God's hand. Any oppressive imagery of God and its concomitant guilt died with Jesus. As Paul tells us: "We have been released from the law—for we have died to what bound us—and we serve in the new spirit, not the antiquated letter" (Rom. 7:6). And later: "The law of the spirit, the spirit of life in Christ Jesus, has freed you from the law of sin and death" (Rom 8:2).[59]

Sebastian Moore in a poetic meditation on the redemptive power of the resurrection expresses these thoughts powerfully in the words of a disciple who has encountered the risen Christ out of, and within, the experience of emptiness left by his death:

> I think, in retrospect, that I saw him *with* that emptiness I spoke of, as though the emptiness were a kind of second sight....
>
> Since then, life has consisted in growing in the vision. Not without words—exciting new words which, we know, are changing forever the religious universe. God is this man. This man had come to epitomize finally all our hope and all our emptiness; and when that space became alive God became alive. God is this man in us.... We have come into this man and feel with his heart and look through those eyes. God we know as Spirit, as the heart of that equation between God and life which no religiousness ever quite dares to make for fear of losing touch with guilt. As we have now! It is all washed away by the blood which we now drink.[60]

In Christ Jesus we stand in the fullness of time *loved*. Our salvation consists in moving ever more authentically into this vision and bodying it forth existentially through compassion.

It is clear that the dualistic-patriarchal tradition to which all of us are accustomed may find the above reflection disturbing. It has, from the beginning of its contact with Christianity, laid stress on the fact that our redemption needed to be won in the face of a deity whose wrath demanded to be placated by human/divine sacrifice and that Jesus' crucifixion paid the "price" for our being reinstated into divine favor. Through it we interpreted the agony of the garden, to mention just one example, not as a struggle with one's own integrity in the face of persecution, but as a struggle with patriarchal decrees. Through it we saw the gates of heaven thrown open with the last drop of blood shed in bloody atonement. It may be difficult and emotionally upsetting for some to shed this image. Thinking critically into our myths often can be just that. The question we need to ask ourselves, however, is whether such an interpretation, given our meditation above on the salvific will of God, is in fact even plausible. Does an *Abba* demand crucifixion? No human parent who truly loves his or her child would. Why must we then contort our own understanding of love with such an interpretation of God's, and reassure ourselves and others, in the face of doubt, by relegating it all to the "divine mystery beyond our experience"?

The experience of a dualistic-patriarchal world, which was ultimately responsible for introducing the cultic dimension into Christianity, was of fatherhood in a general *paterfamilias* context where life and death decisions over children were the patriarch's prerogative. This no longer is our understanding of fatherhood and parenting. Why, then, must we persist in using these concepts for God? Besides, as I have suggested above, this was also not the interpretation of Jesus, who worked hard at bringing the mercy and tenderness of God into our experience. If we are held in the unconditional love of God from the moment of creation, why should the God of sinners be any different from the "prodigal" father of the parable, or from the

shepherd looking for his sheep, or from the woman who lost
a silver piece (Luke 15), or from numerous other examples of
forgiveness and compassion which Jesus presented to us? Why
would Jesus even have told these stories if he had not intended
them to be representative of his God? Sandra Schneiders in
analyzing the parable of the Prodigal Son speaks explicitly to
this issue: "In the parable of the prodigal son (Luke 15:11–
32) Jesus presents the fatherhood of God as the very antithesis
of patriarchy." While the older son through his unquestioning
obedience and loyalty is the perfect spokesperson for the patriarchal structure, "his younger brother, by assuming autonomy,
has rebelled against the very principle of patriarchy according
to which there is only one adult in any family."[61] The father,
according to Jesus, sides with the younger son. Just as he had
enabled his earlier rebellion and quest to venture forth on his
own, so now he not only refuses to punish him but in fact
rejoices at his return. He rejects the older son's demands for
vindication—a "patriarchal principle"—and will not "hear"
the younger son's offer to reenter the patriarchal household as
a servant in restitution for his offense.[62] The father sees the
younger son, as he has always seen him, as his *beloved* son.

> God's forgiving love, not human evil, determines God's
> relationship to humanity. The father, far from asserting
> patriarchal superiority and privilege, seems to recognize
> the younger son as his equal, i.e., as an adult. To the father
> the son's return to the household, like his leaving, is an act
> of adult freedom. The relationship between them is not
> one of offended domination to rebellious submission but
> of freely offered love asking and accepting love in return.
> The prodigal son, like the sinful woman who entered the
> house of Simon to wash Jesus' feet (Luke 7:36–50), is one
> in whom loving repentance and loving forgiveness meet

in total defiance of the patriarchal model of justification through law.[63]

The God of Jesus, our God, is infinite compassion and love. We are drawn into God through Christ Jesus. As we assume responsibility for the Christification of ourselves and of the world, Christ's incarnation continues in us. Our call is to let God be God in us, to surrender our will to dominate in grateful releasement. This is why God became human: to show us how to live, how to fulfill our destiny as lovers of God and of each other, how to find our way back to authenticity. In the death and resurrection of Jesus, God triumphed over all sin— our willful rejection of our own integrity. In Christ all things are made whole; all things are made new. Holistic spirituality invites us to take seriously this Good News and to make it our own.

Conclusion

We live in the turning point, in an age of crisis where the dualism of our past no longer empowers or gives life, and where a more ancient tradition calls us to remember. Who our God is, who we are, and how we are related in authenticity are questions that may not remain speculative any longer. We are asked to live into our myths with the passionate involvement of our very existence. Ours is the choice. We can either wither in the drought and die of dehydration, or face the challenge of "our quiet little house" with all the terror that this may initially bring, and thus move into new life.

The journey through this chapter may have been arduous at times. I did not intend this to be discouraging, however, but rather presented it in the hope of providing a necessary backdrop for our subsequent reflections on the vowed life. Never so much as now in my own life, in my studies, and in my own reflective experience have I been convinced of the need to make choices—personal and congregational decisions—that are supported by wider perspectives than merely one's here and now, or even one's community traditions and specific mandate, one's personal or group interests in immediate issues of the present, important though they may be. Today we are impacted globally and find ourselves within a space-time continuum that makes simple cause and effect decisions laughable. We can no longer trust ourselves to current ways of doing or seeing things—trends, be they psychological or theological or sociological—without thoroughly probing into their "why"; nor can we simply make provisional decisions for the sake of getting the job done, without looking at the wider implications.

Today, living into our baptism through the vows moves us far beyond the given set of rules or constitutions that affect us personally or congregationally. Our very existence is at stake: the credibility of Gospel living and personal maturation through religious commitment. Can women and men become whole as vowed members of a religious congregation in the twenty-first century? Is our life a viable Christian option for our time? Without some depth perspective on the crisis which affects our century's worldview generally and Christian self-understanding in particular, I do not believe we can answer these questions either adequately or meaningfully no matter how strongly we believe in an affirmative response. This chapter's discussion of dualism and of a possible holistic Christian response to it was intended to prepare us for this task in the considerations that follow, to provide, if you will, the soil for the hidden treasure we seek as we turn now to the particular task of reflecting on living the vows in an age of change.

Questions for Focus, Reflection, and Discussion

1. Do you see religious life in our time suffer from what Bolen identifies as a "drought mentality"? How so?

2. How, in your experience of our culture, our church, and religious life, can you identify the relation between dualism, hierarchism, and patriarchy?

3. What is your reaction to the invitation to think into our myths? Does it excite or frighten you? Why?

4. To which paradigm of spirituality do you see yourself belonging, the dualistic model or the holistic one? Why?

5. Have you, in your personal experiences, ever encountered a limit situation? Are the descriptions by Boelen and Shea realistic?

6. What is your reaction to the teachings of the early Jesus movement and the understanding of church as *basileia*?

7. Was your attitude to church dogma and doctrine affected by this chapter's discussion of the missionary movement in the early church and the effects of Greek metaphysics on the formulations of our beliefs? If so, how?

8. What in the holistic paradigm do you find most difficult to accept? What do you find most liberating?

Chapter Two

WHAT MATTERS IS VISION

In the first chapter of Brennan Manning's *The Wisdom of Accepted Tenderness* he explains that "all changes in the quality of a person's life must grow out of a change in his or her vision of reality."[1] The holistic approach to spirituality of the preceding pages attempted to offer just that: a new paradigm, an alternative vision of reality to the one that has dominated our perception for centuries.

1. God's reign is realized in our midst, we said, yet is also still in process, calling us to accept and live into the fullness of time.

2. The Christian community is a "discipleship of equals"—of friends—all of whom are loved and are gifted in diversity and for the glory of God.

3. Creation—all of it—is holy and needs to be encountered as such.

4. We are the breakthrough of God's creative activity and are called to respond to it in releasement and gratitude.

5. Original sin is our refusal of this call, this heritage. It is the will to domination, the will to power.

The question which now concerns us is how this new paradigm, this alternate vision, might affect the quality of our lives as religious, what it can offer us and of what it will ask us to let go as we attempt to live and to draw meaning from our vows and the religious life which flows from them.

Most of us (especially those trained in religious life prior to Vatican II, but also those schooled during that time and those educated later, but by those who could not let go of pre–Vatican II categories) would, I think, agree today that the dualistic paradigm in which we were reared created in us a tendency to reduce any reflection on the vows to an identification and explanation of what we promise and what we subsequently do or do not do to live up to the evangelical counsels or the "consecrated life." It is a paradigm that thrives on regulations that many of us memorized in our early years of training and that still to this day haunt some of us at various times. Much of the prescriptive legislation of canon law regarding the hierarchy of governance or concerning the disposal of property in our present "approved" constitutions is also of this dualistic mind-set and vision. There is a certain order and regularity here that can be quite attractive. Its discipline is reassuring.

The concern that arises for us within a holistic perspective, however, goes beyond the "oughts" of doing. It calls us to let go of safe moorings and to plunge deep. It invites us to probe into who we are and how we are *as vowed*. It asks what it means *be* vowed, to *be* consecrated. It stresses vowed life as a way of *being*—a disposition—leaving the dimension of prescription or prohibition on a secondary plain, safe in the knowledge that the latter must flow from the former or ultimately perish for lack of energy and motivation. It cannot be externally imposed and remain life-giving.

No Longer Set Apart

What, then, does it mean to be consecrated by vow? At this point of our reflection it is clear, I believe, that a holistic paradigm can no longer accept a view of consecration that implies "having been set apart," nor a lifestyle that encourages this concept. Because Jesus came to proclaim the holiness of all of creation, the holiness, therefore, of every human being, because in this way he affirmed our universal mandate to give glory to God simply by being *who we are,* no one needs to be set apart. The world as the breakthrough of God's creative energy is sacred. God, through the incarnation, shows us that there is no division between the world here and the world "above." As God becomes human, humans enter into the divine. There is, therefore, no need for the individual or group to be "consecrated"—in the sense of being made "superior"—in order to bridge the abyss between the sacred and the secular. We—all of us—are called into solidarity, into intimacy with God in Christ, called also, because of that, to cosmic hospitality. Sandra Schneiders speaks clearly to this new vision:

> In the synoptic gospels Jesus insists that nothing that is created remains profane; nothing requires to be set apart but only to be used rightly (cf. Mark 7:1–23). The Sabbath is for humans, not humans for the Sabbath (Mark 2:27). The veil of the Holy of Holies is rent as men and women are drawn into the heart of God by the sacrifice of Jesus (Matt. 27:51). A simple meal of friendship between Jesus and his disciples replaces all sacrifices....
>
> ...[C]onsecration in the community of the New Testament involves neither separation nor superiority.... To be consecrated is to be holy, to be united with God in the love poured forth in our hearts by the Holy Spirit of Jesus (cf. Rom. 5:5).... We have been sent into the world

as Jesus was sent into the world—to bring salvation by solidarity with, not by separation from, those to whom we are sent.[2]

Taking vows, therefore, can no longer be interpreted in terms of making more sacred what already is sacred. It simply cannot mean anything different from what Jesus declared all of creation to be. All of life is holy, and it might be easier for us if we were to understand different vocations as complementary calls to contextualize and bear witness to this holiness, rather than to interpret them "above or below each other" on the hierarchical ladder. In the light of our holistic approach, then, it will make more sense to see religious vows as one sees matrimonial vows: both give a particular shape to, and address a particular way of living out, our baptismal consecration.[3] Thus, through our choice to live celibately in community, as sharing with and listening to one another, we bring our baptismal consecration to maturity in a different way than, but not in a superior way to, others who choose to work out their consecration in other ways.

> Religious and other Christians are equally called to witness to the infinite love of God, but the richness of that mystery requires a variety of expressions. The witness different Christians are called to give is not distinguished by location on a scale of comparative excellence but by the aspects of the mystery of divine love which come to special expression in their various lifestyles. The witness of each Christian vocation is rich but limited; therefore, adequate witness to the mystery of divine love can only be given in mutuality and complementarity.[4]

Because of our inherent finitude, none of us can fully contain and give witness to the breakthrough of God in creation. Each

one of us as we live our calling with authenticity is, therefore, a partial but valid expression of the multidimensional
manifestation of God's self-revelation in Christ.

The vision presented here points directly to the *basileia* of
the early Jesus movement, which we discussed in the preceding
chapter. As Christians we are a community of equals before a
loving God who has gifted us in diverse but complementary
ways and calls us to be for each other out of these gifts, in
gratitude and praise. "The humility by which we simultaneously realize both our limitation and our giftedness opens us
to an appreciation of the mutuality of witness in the church."[5]
Dualistic distinctions which easily arise out of a need to be the
"greatest" in God's eyes will thus give way to genuine celebration as we, in Sandra Schneiders' words, "rejoice in the shared
poverty which establishes us in the lowest place," and has us
find solidarity there with all Christians and even with Jesus
himself, "who is among us, meek and humble of heart, as one
who serves."[6]

Implications

The implications of this perspective for ministry and mission,
as well as for congregational life especially in terms of governance and the initial incorporation of newer members, are
interesting.

Ministry: For starters, it would seem that religious who truly
accept the "community of equals" will find it less difficult to
let go of long cherished congregational ministries and will accept, even enable, the birthing of a church that transcends the
distinctions of lay, religious, and cleric—where people serve
according to their talents, not their "state." Catholic schools
or hospitals are, after all, not more Catholic because sisters, brothers, or priests run them or work in them. Nor do

Catholics have an edge on what is truly Christian. "Defensive separation from the world, and an unconsciously complacent conviction of specialness in the church," as Sandra Schneiders puts it, "must give way to an embrace of all that is human and a cherishing of our solidarity—not only with Christians but with all people."[7]

Of late I have invited the groups I speak to on retreats and workshops to start thinking of their identity not so much by way of clear distinctions, definitions, and the establishment of boundaries—a way of "including by excluding," as a friend of mine describes it—but, rather, by seeking and experiencing at-oneness with each other and with the wider human family. It seems to me that, as we are moving ever more fully into post-modernity, the divides are all disappearing, and that reaching out rather than segregation and separation furthers a way of being that is far more wholesome and consistent with the human condition than we have yet been able to fathom let alone experience.

Welcoming New Life: The welcoming and the incorporation of new members into religious life will, I believe, also be affected when the *basileia* vision of a community of equals truly takes hold among us. It is my hope to address this and related issues in a separate chapter later. I have written about it also and moved it further in part 3 of *Wrestling with God* (New York: Crossroad, 1997). Suffice it to say here that the community of equals for someone seeking the vowed life begins with the first letter of inquiry written by a newer member to the congregation and endures throughout the years of introduction and incorporation until final vows and beyond.

At this time in history and in our contemporary culture it may be necessary, furthermore, for the sake of the Gospel and in fidelity to the vision of equality that concerns us here to broaden our understanding of possible membership beyond the specific three vows as such and to focus our gathering priority, the energy that sustains our togetherness, on our charism and its imperative to further God's reign instead. *All* forms of exclusivism and elitism, from the subtlest to the most blatant, will need to be addressed critically and radically here. This is not an easy task, for most of them are imbedded in the very structure of incorporation ("formation") itself and in our understanding of membership on which the latter is based. They almost universally favor and foster the hierarchical attitude that has been with us for thousands of years as a cultural phenomenon.

Perhaps on the symbolic level it would help to see the needed shift from a dualistic to a holistic process of welcoming membership as similar to moving from an imitation of the structured initiation rites of young men in aboriginal cultures to accepting the more organic movement into maturity of the young women in these same cultures. Persons do not have to be put through a "trial" to prove their belonging or their fitness (no matter how "hard" we had it "when we were novices"). The gift for community and of the charism (as was the gift of womanhood in the young woman of primordial times) is found within and comes forth from those so called in due time. Our development here, if it is authentic, is organic—from the womb of our inner selves, the cycle of our own growth. It need not be imposed or artificially tested but requires nurturance within a covenantal setting sensitive to this. Furthermore, we can no longer expect from newer members what we ourselves are not willing to live. No amount of evaluations and external authority, no matter how subtle or disguised, will bring this about. When they ask us, "Friends, where do you live?" with Jesus we must answer: "Come and see." And what they see will have to be *who we are—all of us*. No person in charge, nor any hand-picked community, can successfully model the ideal life that the members are not living. Nor for that matter ought they to "model" the life the members *are* living, for we are all in this together, co-responsible. New members come to join *us*. It is the community (all of us, not merely a select group) that must welcome them in word and in deed, for it is the community with whom they will embark on the journey. The "hot-house" mentality of "initial formation" simply does not represent this community any longer, nor does this mentality do enough to challenge members to be truly brother and sister to those who come to join us.

In the last several years we have done much to address the vocation crisis afflicting many of our congregations. My experience with these efforts has been as a teacher in a number of intercommunity novitiate programs where I interacted with newer members for the last twenty years. Not being a member of a "formation" team and, therefore, to some extent as an outsider looking in, I gained the impression that many of our ever changing policies regarding incorporation are more like desperate attempts at patchwork than truly holistic and revolutionary revisions. In the unprecedented rethinking of religious life demanded of us by a paradigm shift of the magnitude we are here discussing for this age and culture, nothing short of the radical will do. We remember Brennan Manning: all authentic changes in the quality of our lives must grow out of a change in our vision of reality. We need to return to the roots. Our deepest roots are found in putting on the mind and heart of Christ Jesus and embracing the foundational vision of his *basileia*.

Governance: The effects which a view of universal giftedness and mutuality of witness in a community of equals will have on congregational governance are somewhat complex and easily open to misinterpretation. A later chapter dealing with authority and obedience will probe more deeply into this issue. For now one simple clarification may be all that is necessary: we all know that to be gifted in a community of equals does not mean to be equally gifted. Just as all of us are called but not all of us are called to the same lifestyle or ministry, so all of us are gifted but not all with the same gifts. Leadership, the empowerment of the group to be about what the group discerns to be its call, is a gift. It is a needed gift wherever people are gathered together toward a common end. Discernment of gifts for the good of the group is a community responsibility, and the election of leadership ought to be precisely that. Our gifts are ours for service. Authority is not antithetical, therefore, to a community of equals but must be viewed by, and called forth in, the group not as elevation, but as service. Nor are these observations to be viewed as a return to hierarchy hidden behind the smokescreen of the word "service." (Hierarchs, after all, have been the "servants of the servants of God" for centuries.) Those, however, who are held in the breakthrough of God know, above all else, that all of life is surrender to self-emptying and thus to freedom. They stand in the freedom of their own inner authority which directs their vision and, from this vision, all their actions toward service and mutual empowerment as they experience membership in the body. They call forth and allow themselves to be called forth on various levels of communal involvement. Diversity of gifts does not mean hierarchy of gifts; hence there also is no hierarchy of service.

Although this appears self-evident, and most of us have heard or said similar things, it is my sense that in the living-out of this vision we often are still plagued by a hidden dualistic hierarchism. What, for example, is the reason behind the seeming need in many congregations to have almost all community offices, boards, committees, and task forces open to all—to all volunteers who wish to "serve"? This policy tends to eliminate any meaningful discernment of gifts—any discernment and calling forth by the group. Could it be possible that a hidden and often unconscious motivation for this policy really lies in a sense of inadequacy and a need for inclusion on the part of the membership coupled with resentment of those truly gifted in one or other area of service whose presence—possibly by request—would foster a perceived elitism? Persons gifted to serve in various areas, such as community life, government planning, facilitation, and the like, can, of course, do the job more efficiently and speedily, but they are fewer in number than the volunteers; hence they *appear* special. This is so mainly because in a dualistic paradigm the value of the function is, because of misplaced abstraction, identified with the value of the person performing it, raising and lowering the individual's dignity accordingly. Equality of persons is viewed as dependent upon the right of all to do all regardless of their gifts. Since we are all called, so the argument goes, we should all be allowed to do anything we want to volunteer for. Often confusion and malfunction, not true inclusion, is the consequence of such a way of thinking, and the inadequacy of service that is the result frequently collapses the agency or committee from within, ultimately leading to no service at all.

Essential for an authentic, holistic paradigm is the internalization of the fact that God breaks out in diversity and that both personal and communal discernment of this breakthrough is mandated for true and life-giving creativity. This vision is described beautifully by Beatrice Bruteau as she challenges our culture toward a revolution of consciousness, "participatory consciousness," as she calls it:

When I love with participatory consciousness, I see that what the other *is* is some of my life-energy living there, and what I am is some of the other's life-energy living here in me. I can no longer divide the world into "we's" and "they's." I have an awareness of one large life circulating through all. In some way, my boundary has become less definite in the sense of being less hard and sealed off. My selfhood has become radiant, streaming out from me, and is found participating in the other even as it is found in me. But I am not engulfed by an all-absorbing unity in which my uniqueness is dissolved. Creative love is entirely the protection and nurturance of personal freedom and uniqueness. It is precisely because a person as a whole is absolutely unique that it transcends all the categories by which abstractive consciousness would classify it. The single large life in which I participate is a community of whole unique selves who freely form and constitute this large unifying life by the intercommunication of their creative love energies. So, far from being absorbed or dissolved, I feel that as a member of this community my interior sense of self-possession, or self-being, is more intense and clearer, in the sense of being more luminous and more truly "I."[8]

It is clear that nothing short of a revolution of consciousness will bring about this kind of perception shift, which challenges all jealousy, envy, over-againstness, authoritarianism, as well as subservience. Nothing short of a revolution of consciousness, in other words, will help us truly and unequivocally celebrate our uniqueness and our giftedness while at the same time recognizing our need for the services of others of which authentic authority is one—not a greater one than the rest, just one among them.

The three examples discussed here, though we touched on them only briefly, were intended to illustrate the transcending of dualism that a holistic paradigm necessitates: transcending the dichotomy of the sacred and the secular, of religious and laity; transcending the split between the "ones who belong" and the "ones who want to belong," between professed and "novices"; transcending the division between "superior" and "subordinate." I will deal with many of these issues again, What needs to be pointed out right now, however, is the fact that transcendence does not at all imply "doing away with" or "eliminating" what is being transcended. Authentic transcendence takes up into itself that beyond which it moves and transforms it. Thus, the secular is not done away with, but acknowledged in its sacredness, in its belonging to the holy, to the whole: "All things are yours whether it be ... the world, or life, or death, or the present, or the future: all these are yours, and you are Christ's and Christ is God's" (1 Cor. 3:21–23). The transcendence in this citation from Corinthians is not of the world but of the "worldly"—of the boasting, of the will to power. Religious in contemporary society do not flee the world. Today the word is "immersion." With Eckhart we are called to be free in the world, free for the world, as well as free of it—of its power, its domination.[9] Transcendence lies not in the will to power, but in the will to surrender; not in flight from, but in embracing and transforming.

If we move to the second example discussed above, I once again do not deny that the one who wants to belong is different from the one who already belongs; the new member, from the older professed member. I simply suggest the transcending of destructive attitudes springing from the absolutization of dualism. This transcendence happens through genuine, sustained, and communal welcome; through the humility of our "shared poverty," of our striving *together* toward holiness; through our acknowledgment of each other's contributions and the legitimacy of felt needs; through mutual responsibility.

Finally, the distinction between gifts and the recognition of the gift of leadership, in particular, is maintained also in the holistic approach to community and governance. We accept the wisdom of the past even as we are transcending our past, for there is no time in history without profound insight. But the abuses of the "superior-inferior" syndrome and the misplaced elitism of our past dualistic mind-set is overcome. Transcendence lies in the acknowledgment, the celebration of diverse gifts and in seeing our mutual call to service. Our passion is for the whole, the holy. We are about the reign of God, not our own. Again we must stress that the holistic as such does not oppose the dualistic, as if one were dealing with a simple logical contradiction where the truth of one premise eliminates the possibility of the other. The holistic, as a matter of fact, does not use logic as its essential language and is quite comfortable with paradox. It sees that mere opposition never leads to transcendence, but only gets caught in an atmosphere of conflict. There is, therefore, no "over-againstness" (though distinctions are maintained and diversity celebrated) in the holistic paradigm. It accepts the categories of the past if they empower life and creativity, but avoids all absolutizations. It simply sees with different eyes.

The Primacy of Disposition

Up to this point in our discussion we have laid special stress on what a holistic vision of religious consecration can no longer accept and will have to move beyond. This led to our reflection on the holistic response to dualism with examples of how such a response might affect our vision and our subsequent decisions and actions in specific areas of religious life. The question to which we must now turn brings us back to the beginning of this chapter and asks more directly how we as vowed religious can give shape to our baptismal consecration. A specific concern for me in this investigation revolves around our calling to give glory to God by becoming fully alive. How does religious life effect fullness of personhood? How can we work out our baptismal commitment toward full maturity and, therefore, indeed claim complementarity with sacramental matrimony by means of the vows we take?

I find that when these kinds of questions are asked, the temptation is often most pressing to revert to prescriptions and prohibitions in order to supply the answers. For some reason, whenever we discern what we are, and how we live, it seems to make some of us feel more secure if we can hold on to and point to details; if we can have the "nuts and bolts" of the vows, if you will, hammered out for us and written somewhere. Often we think that religious life would "work" better—maybe we would draw more members—if we had things more clearly put in black and white. Then too, of course, we could see who is truly poor, or chaste, or obedient.

It is my sense that in many of our discussions on these matters our emphasis is placed too heavily on *action*. Somehow it seems to escape us that authentic action is directly proportional to the disposition which inspires it. If the disposition is not ours, neither is the action. It may be automatic, coerced, performed through manipulation—"playing the game," as some call it—but unless what I do arises out of who I am, out of the integrity of my *being*, it is not mine. We are dealing here with issues of maturity that, as will be discussed later, are intimately connected with authentic obedience. For the present, let me simply reiterate that mature and personal choice flows from a mature and personal vision, perception, and disposition. The former is impossible without the latter. Therefore, if we spend a great deal of time discussing what we are doing, ought to do, resolve to do or not to do, we are wasting precious energy unless what is going on is held within a previously developed attitude that grounds our resolve and our actions. Nor does it help to come together first to agree on the attitude. Dispositions or attitudes are not "agreed upon" by consensus. They emerge from insight which is given to us as grace and then flows out of us. They might be discovered in honest dialogue but cannot be willed or resolved or changed either by persuasion of decree. "When insight happens," Heidegger tells us, "we are struck in our very being by the lightning flash of Being. In insight we *ourselves* are *gazed upon*."[10] Dispositions or attitudes emerge in a personality. They are intrinsically connected with the maturation process. A changing disposition, for example, can rarely be talked about or articulated. It appears *in* us rather than being formulated *by* us. It is an event—in the true meaning of the word as "coming out," "coming forth"—that lights up our entire personality from within. Often it even surprises us in our encounter with it: "I used to see things this way, but now I don't any longer, and I don't really know why," we will say, puzzled at the shift and whence it came.

It can, of course, be argued that membership in a particular congregation or, for that matter, membership in the Christian community presupposes the disposition upon which actions are based. But whereas there certainly is validity to this observation, what it ignores is precisely holistic growth. Babies too are baptized and are, therefore, members of the Christian community. This very fact speaks to the recognition (albeit often unconscious in a dualistic system) of the levels of openness on our journey into God. From the lengthy discussion in chapter 1 about paradigm shifts it has to be clear that all Christians do not see the same realities in the same way. Religious are not exempt here. Our growth into depth varies. Even a common charism does not help change that fact. Diversity in religious life, in outlook, in values, as well as ultimately in lifestyle, is a sensitive matter but it is a fact.

How, then, are we to address these issues? What can be said about the vows we take and the lifestyle that we embrace toward full maturity? It seems that any attempt to get some initial specificity has been thwarted. If discussion about actions—about what we do or should do—is useless unless a prior disposition is recognized and respected, and if this disposition is grace rather than resolve, emerging in time rather than allowing itself to be programmed, there seems to be precious little left for us to say. And perhaps that is exactly how it should be. Perhaps it is precisely in not saying anything—in silence and in listening into that silence—that one begins to get insight into these questions. An exhortation of Karl Rahner comes to mind, one that he wrote in a brief little essay of the 1970s entitled "Experiencing God," and one which I believe could easily be used as the leitmotif, the theme song, if you will, for a depth reflection on the vows:

> Be still for once. Don't try to think of so many complex and varied things. Give ... *deeper realities* of the spirit a chance now to rise to the surface: silence, fear, the ineffable longing for truth, for love, for fellowship, for God. Face loneliness, fear, imminent death! Allow such ultimate, basic human experiences *to come first*. Don't go talking about them, making up theories about them, but simply *endure these basic experiences.* ...
>
> If we do not learn slowly in this way to enter more and more into the company of God and to open to [God], if we do not constantly attempt to reflect in life primitive experiences of this kind—not deliberately intended or deliberately undertaken—and from that point onwards to realize them more explicitly in the religious act of

meditation and prayer, of solitude and the endurance of ourselves,... then our religious life is and remains really of secondary character and its conceptual-thematic expression is false.[11]

What does it mean to live the vows, to consecrate one's life in the spirit of poverty, celibate chastity, and obedience? What was it that happened to us on that day when we spoke our commitment to God in the presence of our community? How did we expect our lives to change with this commitment, and *are* they changing because of it?

"Be still for once," Rahner urges us. Give the "deeper realities" a chance to surface: silence, fear, loneliness, longing for truth, for love and companionship, for God. Don't make up theories about them. Rather, experience them; experience yourself, each other, in the depth of who you are, for without this your life is a sham, whereas *in it* the absolute awaits you.

A question that has become ever more urgent for me during the last several years is precisely about the relationship between these "deeper realities" and the vows. I have wondered for a while now, and Rahner's reflection on how one experiences God has intensified the question for me, whether perhaps our communal or ecclesial attempts to identify and articulate, to clarify, enumerate, and define the hows and whats of our consecration are not leading us dangerously close to losing its heart, its soul.

Rahner is very concrete and surprisingly experiential when he describes what he means by these "deeper realities," the "depth dimension," as I call them. His examples defy theorization. They cannot be verified or categorized. They do not fit into the question-answer format of a catechism, nor would they quite find their way into a book on canon law. They ask, rather, more questions than they give answers. They open up feelings, light up memories, point to possibilities. They speak of life *lived*, of pain endured, of passion and joy. They speak, in the truest sense, of the Christ event, the very focus of our consecration:

> Somewhere, someone seems to be weeping hopelessly. Someone "packs it in" and knows—if he [or she] is now silent, if he [or she] is now patient, if he [or she] now gives in—that there is *nothing more* that *he [or she] could seize on,* on which he [or she] could set his [or her] hopes, that *this* attitude is worthwhile. Someone enters into a final solitude where *no one* accompanies [him or her]. Someone has the basic experience of being stripped even of his [or her] very self. A [human being] as spirit in his [or her] love for truth reaches—so to speak—the frontier of the absolute, . . . which sustains and is not sustained: . . . which is there even though we cannot reach out and touch it, which—if we talk about it—is again concealed behind our talk as its ground [like disposition is to action].[12]

The relationship of these "deeper realities" to the Holy may not be immediately clear. It is, in fact, more intuited than comprehended and often thinking about it hurts—deep down in the heart. That is why so many of us would rather dismiss it and prefer not to deal with it. It does not fit into our accustomed paradigm and, therefore, makes us feel uneasy. It lights up in stillness, in "being-with," rather than through words and explanations. It speaks indirectly of our vows—through loneliness and final solitude, through being stripped and the surrendering of power, through the enduring of silence and the thirst for truth. The acceptance of and dwelling in these "deeper realities" changes one's life. It leads to a change in vision, a change of attitude, and it is here, I believe, where their depth connection to the vows can best be experienced and touched.

What if, for just a brief moment, we would allow ourselves to think of the vows not as things or actions we promise to do or not to do, to give up, refrain from, or engage in? What if we saw them rather as dispositions that we embrace, as a way of being in which we dwell, as horizons that beckon us, as depths into which we commit ourselves to plunge on a life-long journey into the silence and the simplicity that is God? What if we could let the vows light up for us not primarily as modes of action, but primarily as modes of perception—ways of seeing into which we grow, which enable us to encounter ourselves and the world on a deeper, on a sacred plane and, out of the vision won on that plane, lead us to action? What if we could permit ourselves to experience the vowed life as a spiral leading into an ever deepening awareness of the holiness that is life (all of life with its pains and failures as well as its joys), of the sacredness that is creation, every aspect of creation? Would not then the prescriptive or regulatory concerns with which so many of us even today still approach discussions of the vowed life, and which so frequently distract us from the depth of holiness to which we are called, fade into the background, as theory yields to praxis? Would not then also those of us who have become disinterested, tired, and disenchanted with the entire legalistic and dualistic experience which the exploration into the vows has come to mean for us start to become involved again? Would not the vows begin to speak of life lived fully, of yearnings lying in the very heart of our humanity?

I have mentioned already that actions that evolve from visions flow on their own energy, whereas externally induced behavior quickly loses its power and vitality and often can be maintained only through coercion by fear or guilt. What if we could accept the pronouncing of our vows as a commitment to the journey, to the process, as a trust-filled movement into possibilities, not as an accomplished fact that identifies us once and for all in a particular state of perfection that can be clearly measured, evaluated, and verified through predictable behavior? Would not then our strivings and our yearnings gain their rightful place in our life of consecration? And would not our evaluations individually and communally, instead of being merely success oriented, become truly Christlike: "Much is forgiven him, her, us, because we have loved much." The time is ripe at this point, I believe, to move from generalities to the specific. The discussions of the following chapters will attempt to do just that. We begin with a reflection on poverty and its meaning for us as an evangelical mandate. A meditation on celibacy will follow and, I hope, will shed light on the way we live community in covenant and commit ourselves to love one another. I will address some special concerns here, such as our relationship with each other within the context of life's crises and maturation. I will look at the implications of this for community life: how our specific call to face our inner darkness, embrace intimacy needs, and face loneliness finds its shape there. Some thoughts on obedience and authority come next, hopefully to encourage us toward an appropriation of the depth dimension of leadership that transcends old "authority tapes" and moves us to authentic co-listening and responding as the questions of our times open for us ever deeper questions and invite humble releasement as well as creativity. In conclusion I will consider our relationship with our newer members, mention new models of membership, and discuss our responsibility for new life and the very real experience of death and resurrection to which living religious life in contemporary times calls us.

Questions for Focus, Reflection, and Discussion

1. What is your reaction to the observation that holistic spirituality does not see consecration as "setting apart" but sees the entire world as God's creative breakthrough and, therefore, as sacred?

2. The complementarity of different vocations (i.e., matrimonial consecration and religious consecration) is also stressed in holistic spirituality. How does this perspective affect you? Are you comfortable with it?

3. How do you relate to the following observations:

    - "Catholic schools or hospitals are, after all, not more Catholic because sisters, brothers, or priests run them or work in them. Nor do Catholics have an edge on what is truly Christian."

    - With respect to community life and incorporation: "The community of equals [Christ's *basileia*] begins with the first letter of inquiry written by a newer member to the congregation and endures throughout the years of introduction and incorporation until final vows and beyond." (This does not mean, of course, that someone may not leave.)

    - Religious development, "if it is authentic, is organic—from the womb of our inner selves, the cycle of our own growth. It need not be imposed or artificially tested but requires nurturance within a communal setting sensitive to this."

    - "Leadership [is] the empowerment of the group to be about what the group has discerned to be its call."

- "Diversity of gifts does not mean hierarchy of gifts; hence there also is no hierarchy of service."

- "In a dualistic paradigm the value of the function [i.e., leadership] is, because of misplaced abstraction, identified with the value of the person performing it, raising and lowering the individual's dignity accordingly," and often causing ambition, competition, jealousy, and politicking to disrupt community discernment.

- Beatrice Bruteau's reflection on "participatory consciousness" (see p. 63 above).

- "Authentic action is directly proportional to the disposition that inspires it. If the disposition is not ours, neither is the action. It may be automatic, coerced, performed through manipulation—'playing the game,' as some call it, but unless what I do arises out of who I am, out of the integrity of my *being*, it is not mine."

4. What is your reaction to the suggestion that any meaningful discernment on the vowed life needs to be preceded by the experience of silence, by the facing of loneliness, of our ultimate limits, of ourselves, of Rahner's "deeper realities"?

5. How do you feel about seeing the pronouncing of vows as a commitment to a life-journey, a process, as a trust-filled movement into possibilities, not as an accomplished fact that identifies us once and for all in a particular state of perfection which can be clearly measured?

Chapter Three

BLESSED ARE THE POOR

Solidarity with Christ's poor has for a long time now been identified as a specific way in which we as religious through-out the world are called to live out our vowed commitment. Somehow the vow of poverty and our concern for, as well as at-oneness with, God's *anawim* are seen as connected, and the persistence with which many of our community documents stress this connection marks it undoubtedly as central to our way of life in contemporary times.

The Question of Solidarity

We know that the issue of wealth and poverty is one of the most significant concerns both in the Hebrew as well as in the Christian Scriptures. In the Hebrew Scriptures this theme comes second only to idolatry, with which the oppression of the poor is often openly connected. More than five hundred verses (that is, one in every sixteen) in the Christian Scriptures are directly concerned with teachings concerning it, not to mention indirect references found in the actions of Jesus and his followers."[1] Jesus talked more about wealth and pov-erty," Jim Wallis tells us," than almost any other subject, including heaven and hell, sexual morality, the law, or vio-lence."[2] Clearly, the poor are a central concern for Jesus and his *basileia*, and solidarity with them is a membership mandate.

In our time, however, more drastically perhaps than in any

other phase in history, the cruelty of greed and self-interest is evident everywhere. Because of the advancement in media and mass communication during this century, we cannot but encounter it. Daily we receive ever more disturbing reminders of the suffering and evil brought on by a worldwide economic imbalance intentionally created and maintained by those in power for their own purposes. Some call it "the New World Order." The destitution of millions is its consequence.

> Evil is working from ten to twelve hours a day; it is child labour, back-breaking work, the agonizing task, the workaholic obsession—all Evil. Unemployment at the same time as Butter Mountains—Himalayas of butter kept in store and going bad to the tune of millions, Everests of jam flushed down the drain, cattle killed off...and thrown into a common boneyard to keep prices up, the laws of free trade and the Common Market praised to high heaven (while millions die of starvation in the Sahara, in Bengal or the Horn of Africa) and extolled by people who keep our noses to the grindstone so that we can pay our taxes—those taxes with which they finance the destruction of the fruits of our labours—yes, that is what Evil is. Evil is all that is stupid, and the joyful acceptance of stupidity by those who profit by it, and by those who do not suffer because of it.[3]

We are all too familiar with statements such as this observation by Petru Dumitriu in his spiritual autobiography. They disturb us and make us feel uneasy, for we eat butter and jam and meat, and few of us go hungry. How is it, we therefore ask ourselves, that we can be in solidarity with the poor and yet eat well and live comfortably? We claim that there is for us, beyond our baptismal obligation, a vowed commitment to justice. As Gospel women and men publicly professed, we see simplicity of life and exemplary action on behalf of justice as mandatory. We simply may not indulge and live luxuriously (not even with commodities owned in common) as long as the vast majority of the world is subsisting below the level of starvation. The constitutions of my own congregation put it well: We "choose to live with less," they claim, "until all have enough." Yet the problem is that many of us live with more, much more. We live according to the lifestyles of the consumer society that for many of us is our cultural model and that persuasively presents all sorts of luxuries as necessities. In America today, says John Francis Kavanaugh—and I would add, in all countries that share a similar worldview—"the compulsion to consume has become for us as deep as the exigency to survive because the Commodity Form [as opposed to what Kavanaugh identifies as the Gospel Form] of living reveals our very being and purpose as calculable solely in terms of what we possess, measurable solely by what we have and take. We *are* only in so far as we possess,"[4] and in so far as the remuneration for our work renders us capable of acquiring. This kind of cultural dogma can be very persuasive and penetrate deep—way beyond merely conscious levels of value identification and behavior. A radical questioning into the meaning of our vow of poverty, therefore, can be extremely disconcerting. With economic cruelty all around us, however, its persistence, if in the asking it truly breaks our heart, must move us to action.

The stakes are high. We are concerned here with the Gospel's central mandate on behalf of justice. As Jim Wallis puts it, our own "spiritual well-being and our relationship to [God] are at stake."[5] All that evil requires, Dumitriu observes, is the absence of heart. "I have come to suspect," says he, "that a part of God's silence is my own; that a part of God's absence is nothing but the absence of our own hearts, of our humanity, of our friendship. . . . The absences of the human heart sometimes

last a long time."[6] And that may be precisely the issue: the
pain at our seeming impotence in the face of it all, and our
unwilling yet, nevertheless, our real participation in it, in spite
of our well-meant protestations, can also prove too great. We
can thus slip quite easily into a form of dualistic denial. We can
profess one thing and live quite another, refusing ever to face
the inconsistencies of our lives and to embrace courageously
the tensions between our present cultural situation and our
call as religious to live creatively toward personal and societal
transformation.*

I am sure that I am not alone when I confess that I have puzzled much about why it is that so many of us appear so little
moved by the radical demands of our religious profession to
be for the poor (especially, it seems, when they are proclaimed
and interpreted by those in our midst who, for whatever reason, see themselves as more truly representative of this Gospel
mandate and wish to remind us that we should be too). To
what *do* we expect to be committing ourselves when we *vow*
poverty? There is, I believe, a real struggle in this question.
It seems so easy to take back, one at a time, the very *things*
one has given up in a moment of grace and to find all sorts
of justification for this sad retrieval. As the musical *Nunsense*
reminds us facetiously: religious are those who "own nothing
but have everything."

I have agonized, on the other hand, also over the "dos" and
"don'ts" of community stipulations regarding poverty, all presented as guidelines, I know, but possessing little more than

---

*Many of us live in the richest parts of the world and enjoy its goods. As a professor
of mine many years ago told us—a class of struggling graduate students: "Our hands
are also always dirty." Sandra Schneiders explains this well in her book *New Wineskins:*
"[W]e also know that we are constantly implicated in fostering the very systems that we
have analyzed as unjust and exploitative. Every time we go to the bank, buy groceries,
fill the gas tank, we participate in one way or another in multinational systems which
are, at some near or far remove from us, exploiting the poor" (New York: Paulist Press,
1986), 189.

the power of prescription. I have wondered why the guidelines of community directories leave me so cold and, in themselves, fail to empower me. Why do I feel a sour taste in my mouth when I hear discussions on how much gift money may or may not be kept by a vowed religious; when I hear us complaining about signing out cars and about the luxury of those whose work allows them to have one; when the size of allowances is debated; or when I see sisters taking responsibility for monitoring what others own? In those moments it becomes clearer to me why some among us need to move out of community and monitor their own budgets. All frantic attempts at standardization strike me as hopelessly missing the point and having little if any motivational power.

Called to Self-Sacrifice

At times of serious reflection into what poverty might mean for us today, I frequently return to Donald Nicholl's observation concerning the nature of self-sacrifice as the story of evolution and of freedom brought to its highest expression. For few, if any, religious, poverty is an unavoidable affliction, a social evil to which we are bound by economic necessity. We are not destitute, nor should we try to be. All Christians, by virtue of their baptism, are called to eliminate, not to imitate, the poverty in this world. The relation of religious to their vow of poverty, therefore, if it is to be authentic, must resist all artificiality and pseudo piety. It must be one of choice, of free self-gift, of surrender. Nicholl identifies self-sacrifice as "an act of *total* responsibility whereby we take complete hold of ourselves and place ourselves at the disposition of the whole; we cease to be apart and become one with the whole," and thus we "re-present the whole."[7] How might this view help us gain an understanding of our vow?

Nicholl's vision is surprisingly vast and certainly not restrictive to religious consecration. He meditates on self-giving as the leitmotif for the entire history of cosmic unfolding from the first moment of creation, through the formation of the earth, to the appearance of life, the beginning of conscious life, self-awareness, and ultimately self-sacrifice in the Omega Point that is Christ.[8] In the evolution of the cosmos everything that had being, he suggests, gave itself up for the sake of what was to follow—an ever deeper emergence and expression of creative Love—until in Christ the free act of self-gift was brought to total awareness, hence complete freedom, in the fullness of time.

With Dante, Nicholl sees a connection between the outer world and the inner world of the human being, a harmony in the cosmic story. "It is the same Love," he says, "which moves our hearts as moves the sun and the other stars,"[9] as moves the amoeba and with it all subsequent forms of life, as addresses human self-awareness in all its phases of development into openness (see appendix 1), and as ultimately brings creation to the climax of its own movement in utter self-sacrifice. In the evolutionary event nothing can be greater, says he, than the moment of Christ Jesus. In him the "new reality is the act of self-sacrifice deliberately carried out on behalf of others by a self-conscious being. Neither man [nor woman] nor God can go any further than that: *there is no further to go; it is ultimate*."[10] Christianity, Nicholl maintains, lives itself out in the fullness of time bringing to bloom, in Christ, total self-gift.

Because of Christ Jesus, whom we have put on in baptism (and, as religious, once again through our vows), self-giving becomes our foundational "yes." We live in the actualization of this "yes." In us the Love that surges through creation seeks to express itself. We are called as *basileia* people to be for God's ultimate reign—a reign proclaimed by Christ Jesus while

among us, but a reign that is also not yet. Because of Christ
Jesus who gave himself up, and because of the Spirit who sustains us now in this same movement of self-giving, we are
called into the truth of the labor-pangs of creation groaning
in the agony of giving birth (Eph. 1:3–10). We are called into
wholeness, into holiness as the fullness of the creative process.
"Holiness is not an optional extra to the process of creation,
but rather the whole point of it."[11]

Holiness, however, like all of creation, and this cannot be
stressed enough, is in the process, in the birthing, in the growing, in the travail of self-emptying. It flowers in freedom, in
openness, and in vision that leads to action. Holiness, therefore, is not a once-in-our-lifetime decision—not at the moment
of final profession for each of us personally, nor with our
general chapter decrees pronouncing the ideal for all of us collectively; not in the inscriptions and mottos on our walls, nor
in the pronouncements of our directories and news letters. The
Christ vision, even though it is with us in the historical now,
requires our *personal appropriation* in the particular event
of our individual growth into awareness and into vision. If
the culminating point of evolution lies in the self-aware self-
gift springing from the personal freedom and responsibility of
Jesus the Christ, then living in that moment requires for each
of us the same. And it is here, I believe, that we must locate
our vow of poverty. No amount of chapter commitments on
our behalf, valuable though they are, will make us poor; no
amount of external authority will either. We may be vowed
members of a congregation, and our covenant will certainly
affect our way of life, but ultimately the decision to *give all*
is ours, and this decision is the story of a lifetime of personal
responsibility, of guilt, and of redemption. Religious life and
corporate decisions do not absolve us from this responsibility,
nor from the guilt. *We do not vow away our freedom, but*

assume it—a fact sometimes ignored when in corporate pronouncements and regulations we overemphasize the collective and lose equilibrium in the tension with individual choice and responsibility.

A Personal Yes

I do not deny, of course, that as an institution, our corporate orientation on behalf of the poor is important and can be very significant. I personally believe, in fact, that the justification for the existence of any and all Christian institutions is directly proportionate not primarily to their adherence to a particular doctrine but, first and foremost, to their hands-on commitment to justice. Much can be done here through good stewardship, good leadership, and the persistent yet creative anchoring of present community objectives in the charism of the founder. A community's dreams and objectives, however, are, in the last analysis, only as strong as its members. If their acceptance of vision statements does not ultimately spring from their own personal struggle, from their own personal journey into Christ's death and resurrection, from their own personal response to the exigencies of our time, little of lasting value and significance will come about. It is clear that we are here faced once again with the need to embrace those "deeper realities" that Rahner invited us to acknowledge, mentioned in the previous chapter: personal responsibility in the face of utter abandonment, of impotence, of being stripped even of our very self; our experiences of life, really lived fully and maturely, as it moves us into its deepest moments and asks for our total acceptance and surrender.

What if, in the light of the above discussion, we were to embrace the vow of poverty as primarily and essentially (but not by that fact only) an inner attitude, a holy disposition, toward which we come to direct ourselves in ever more profound and sometimes agonizing movements of the heart, filling us with ever deeper yearning even as we recognize our own personal blindness in its regard, our brokenness, and our vulnerability? What if we, in all humility, came to see this inner attitude as grace, as gift, to which we need to open ourselves and for which we must honestly pray each day, which we can never take for granted, never measure or evaluate, not even when we work among the poorest of the poor or when we have given up every last thing we possess? What if we saw poverty as gracing us not first and foremost when we *do* anything but only when we *surrender our power?* Might it not be that then we would be moved by it to a deep solidarity with all of Christ's poor, and to authentic action on behalf of personal as well as global transformation?

Solidarity—being at one with another—is impossible unless one shares in the being of others, in their existential experience. Our stress here must be primarily on *being-with* rather than on *doing-for,* not because the latter is not important, but because the latter without the former is useless both for the receiver and for the giver and can easily become offensive. This is so precisely because, within this perspective, there still *is* a "receiver" and a "giver" and, therefore, solidarity as such has not as yet been achieved. Within a "doing-for" perspective the dualistic-hierarchical mentality of "helper-helped," be it ever so gracious, still rules our hearts. I cannot be at one with someone when I am the exclusive giver, no matter how generous the gift, no matter how hard I work. Only when I can truly let the other's need *gift* me, when I experience the one I "help" as giving me life, and when my services become thanks-giving, do I experience authentic solidarity, at-oneness with the poor. Then I can embrace my sisters and brothers in gratitude for needing me or for being needed by me. Then I am truly poor.[12]

Elsewhere I have meditated on the meaning of Matthew's
"poverty of spirit" (Matt 5:30) and of the virtue of poverty
as primarily a blessed disposition authentically ours in direct
proportion to our mature acceptance of our humanity, our
personhood.[13] The reflection was in no way an attempt to
sidestep the responsibility which is ours on behalf of the mate-
rially poor, but in fact intended to probe the issue of solidarity
without which responsibility remains empty and cold.

> The blessedness of the poor, it would seem (that which
> unites *persons* [in the true sense of that term] . . . and has
> them stand in solidarity with each other), is their *need*
> and, even more so, their *knowledge* of their need, for it is
> *this* that renders them open, receptive, grateful. It is this,
> in fact, which most authentically gives them their essential
> dignity as persons (from Latin *per,* "through," and *sonare,*
> "sound"): those who are open enough and empty enough,
> in need enough, to receive and to give forth (return to
> the giver) what they have received through gratitude. A
> "person" is one *through whom* the sound of creative love
> can flow, one who can receive and respond in the utter
> vulnerability of releasement. As such, [she or he] is blessed
> in a very basic sense; [she or he] is poor.[14]

It is clear that what we are touching on belongs to the depth
dimension of the human personality. Economic advantage or
disadvantage is, as it were, only secondary—not in time so
much as in essence—to this primary poverty that constitutes
us in our being and that, if recognized and accepted, holds us
in solidarity with all of humankind. The invitation to *become
who we are,* to which authentic Gospel living calls us every day,
is a call to recognition, to full consciousness of *self-as-poor.* It is
a call to self-emptying, a stripping of all power fixations, roles,
false symbols of prestige. It is a plea to surrender to all the pain

that this implies, in order to be born into wholeness, into the fullness of time into which Christ Jesus redeemed us. It is an offer to replace our "hearts of stone" with "hearts of flesh," a call to softness of heart. This, I believe, is the first and the most essential mandate of our vow. It does not separate us from other Christians, for they too, through the Gospel, are called to this poverty. It claims us, however, by our specific allegiance to it on the day of our profession. Through our membership in a religious congregation we highlight this Gospel mandate, and we surrender to it publicly. The resulting responsibility ought not to be underestimated. Poverty is from God in Christ Jesus who "emptied himself" to become one of us (Phil. 2:7). When we vow poverty we vow the *movement into God;* we vow to allow ourselves to be changed, to be freed from ego-enhancement and control, and to be faced with the mystery of our own woundedness and sinfulness which, in turn, will enable us to encounter others as our sisters and brothers and to commit ourselves with integrity to justice.

True Poverty

I believe that I am truly poor and, therefore, blessed— energized and empowered by God—only when I can radically stand in my own vulnerability and weakness and proclaim the goodness of God who "fills the hungry with good things and sends the rich away empty" (Luke 1:53), not because God does not want to give them anything but because they are too full to notice any insufficiency. They need to be emptied out first before they can even see the dynamics of holiness and justice. An interesting little story from the East illustrates this Magnificat truth in beautiful simplicity: It is said that the god Shiva decided one day to take on the form of a wise and holy person and to visit humankind. The news of his presence spread quickly, and holy people from everywhere came to him to get an estimate on their chances for salvation. They cited all their achievements and praiseworthy deeds in the hope of being rewarded with salvation as soon as possible. Being generally convinced of their good works, they were usually disappointed when Shiva cited the number of reincarnations that would still be necessary for them to achieve eternal union with him. To one person he gave three, to another seven, and so on. Very last among the long line of seekers was a tiny little man truly ashamed of the insignificance of his life and aware of his many sins. All he had to say for himself was that he loved creation and tried not to hurt anyone. He simply hoped for the promise that someday salvation would be his, for he loved God dearly in spite of the poverty of his achievements. When Shiva, after some hesitation, awarded him one thousand more reincarnations, the man danced for joy and gratitude. It is said that suddenly this man turned into a flame. The energy of his enthusiasm (Greek, *en*, "in," *theos*, "god") and his humble recognition of all as grace had transformed him. Shiva too became pure light. The flames united and moved into eternal bliss.[15] In our own tradition this story brings to mind the parable of the Pharisee and the Publican (Luke 18:10–14). The latter, in the recognition of his need for mercy, went home justified. It is not primarily what we do, but the surrender of our love even as we recognize our own poverty that blesses us.

I believe that I am poor and can, therefore, be hospitable when I know in the very core of my being that everything I have is gift. I believe that I am poor when I can embrace my own darkness as truly mine, and yet know that I am loved, when I can experience the power of compassion within me and through me, because I have known the dregs of the passion and have stood in it and been embraced by God. I believe that I am truly poor when that compassion transforms my world and the needs I experience in it for myself, when it allows me to see the no-thingness in all things and leads me to authentic hunger for justice and for God, when it directs and motivates my actions and radically moves me to embrace others in their poverty.

The Unity of Interiority and Justice

It is becoming ever clearer to me as I reflect more deeply upon the seeming inconsistencies between what some of us as religious profess and subsequently do that the vow of poverty, as well as simplicity, hospitality, and compassion, which are its fruit, will not survive without depth vision. This view is not, of course, shared by all. The dualism of our upbringing can split our world in both directions. In this way, however, holiness and justice will never meet. For the pietist of the "dualistic days" the worry about perfection leaves compassion to those whose designated ministry it is: the missionary, the minister in the "inner city," workers in soup kitchens and shelters for the homeless. But activists of today also can fall victim to this dichotomy. "Concentration on human interiority," in the words of Ann Belford Ulanov, "seems to them inevitably to bring with it neglect of the real problems of our time: the social, the political and the cultural."[16] Concern for personal development, contemplation, and the whole quest for the holy can, by this manner of thinking, be quite easily dismissed as an ivory tower luxury, as navel gazing. "My work is my prayer," they say, and fail to recognize the power of religious aspiration as the backdrop and underpinning of all authentic and truly effective work on behalf of justice. Thus they deprive themselves of its passion and their works of true compassion.

Personal growth and social concerns are not mutually exclusive, nor should the relationship between them be understood

as merely sequential: "once I get my own act together, I will
help others," or "once all my work for justice is done, I will
worry about my own development—go on an extended retreat, pray." The justice of Jesus was held within his holiness
and, as Ulanov points out, "some of the greatest advocates of
the contemplative life did more to move society in the direction of social justice than the most ardent social reformers."
Activists, she claims, often fail to see how "fundamental to social disorder is the disorder within each of us and how much
a re-ordering of society depends upon a re-ordering of individual lives."[17] Today we know that thought is energy. Its
resonance can transform society for peace or further the violence within it. As persons of prayer we need to remember how
significantly we can touch our surroundings. To sit in prayer
and send forth light and healing energy *is* to be about justice. I wrote *Prayer and the Quest for Healing* (New York:
Crossroad, 1999) primarily to highlight this fact and to alert
us to our global responsibility for transformation. Prayer and
the justice agenda are inextricably interwoven. When this is
forgotten, our works can become hollow, our prayer shallow,
and our energy easily dissipated. The story of Kiaochau comes
to mind. Works of justice can also suffer from the drought
mentality.

To be authentically in solidarity with the poor is to stand
in the truth of the human condition and to know that I am
a part. This takes self knowledge and humble self-acceptance.
No social justice theory, no moral philosophy, no fixed doctrine, contains within itself the answer to the injustices of this
world; only the human heart softened by grace and healed
through a life of interiority does so. Holistic spirituality is the
journey toward a soft heart. When I experience in the very
core of my being those who bleed as shedding my blood, those
who hunger as aching with my pain, those who sin as per-

forming my deeds, when I truly encounter the gift which is the human community even in its darkest moments and, deeper still, know myself to hold that darkness as well, then I am at one with humankind groaning for the fullness of creation, the fullness of our redemption in Christ.

The insight described here, however, does not come easily. For it even the most sincere among us need to be "stripped," to be "seared," to experience the desolation and loneliness and defeat that make it possible for us to acknowledge and see our own fundamental emptiness and need and to recognize this as our *glory*. We also need the silence, the space, the inwardness to acknowledge that the stripping constitutes our journey into God, that it is a process which ultimately returns us to the poverty which we are, that it is essential for the experience of Christian companioning and solidarity, that it is the stuff our vow is made of. Nor should the above discourage any of us, for whether we realize it or not, we are held in this process already. It belongs to the birth pangs of creation in Christ. Ours is merely the task of conscientization, of acceptance, and of holding it within ourselves toward personal and communal Christification.

> To go deep within the life of the psyche really unites us with every other psyche. To touch the deep unconscious dimensions of our own personal problems introduces us to that level of association that is really communal.... At this level our own particular problems come to serve as entries into collective human problems: we may even see that our own small solutions contribute a great deal to the ongoing human struggle with these problems.... We recognize as inevitable the connection between self and other, and come to see that our most deeply personal experiences are inextricable from participation in the human

community. As Lady Julian of Norwich says, we are knit into the substance of God, hence we feel knit into one another at the deepest level.[18]

Clearly what we experience here is compassion—a passionate being with the other in his or her passion because we have been there, we are there, we hold it in the depths of our own heart. Ulanov sees "transparency" as a symbolic representation of this kind of compassion. The division between social issues and personal concerns turns out to be illusory, for there is a shining through: "At the most intimate depths of the soul, we see reaching through the communal, and from the farthest reaches of the communal, the deeply personal textures of our own being and of the other's being."[19]

Toward Softness of Heart

In Jungian terms what we have meditated on is called the process of individuation. Whitmont describes it as "always a road, a way, a process, travel or travail, a dynamism; it is never, at least not while one lives in time and space, a static or accomplished state."[20] Much of it fits into the second journey of our life when ego building gives way to the encounter with deeper realities of the Self. The call to holiness, of course, is not denied to anyone, but the movement from an idealistic to a realistic perspective on life happens generally in the second half of our sojourn here on earth. It is its bitter sweetness, its deprivation, its poverty that we are here dealing with.

I find it interesting that today, within our societal context, when and where meditations such as the above have (because of depth psychology and a revived interest in mystical thought and holistic living) finally become possible, a much larger proportion of the newer members of religious congregations, of our associates, and of those generally interested in our life are in, or at least close to, the second journey of life. It is as if, consciously or not, they are involved with these concerns and see religious life as an opportunity to address them. I believe we need to meet them there. The poverty we vow and invite them to join us in, whether through vows or through a simple reappropriation of their baptismal vocation, is a commitment to open ourselves up to a softening of the heart. In this commitment all works on behalf of justice and mercy are guided and supported by a fundamental disposition of at-oneness with the human family. This supplies them with the energy of compassion and of solidarity that they need but that for all of us requires a lifelong process of self-emptying. We cannot invite or plan this process. *It befalls us.* Our vow is our willingness, our trust, our surrender to, and our dwelling in gratitude for, the vision which this process opens up for us: a vision which we know is grace, laced with pain though it may be.

It is my conviction that when we vow poverty we commit ourselves to nothing less than the depth of the Gospel as the Christ event unfolds in us each day anew. Authentic actions flow from this event and, because of it, will be primarily self-motivated and self-energized. Our constitutions, reflections on our lived experience and interpreted at all times out of that existential situation and the societal context of the moment, need, given the above reflection, to be understood not so much as rules, therefore, but as vision statements, love statements, for mutual empowerment.

Some Reflections on
Our Existential Situation

At this point it may be necessary for us to pause in this meditation and to look more specifically for the concrete, for some

of the practical situations and decisions regarding poverty that
address us in our everyday life. We may want to contextualize
what we have reflected upon into our lived reality, asking ourselves how empowerment takes shape or how it is prevented
in our daily lives.*

Clearly, with respect to living the vow of poverty, our discussion has ruled out the element of prescriptive or regulative
goal setting extraneous to the membership. Sandra Schneiders
says it well when she points out that "little is to be gained and
much lost by attempts to standardize the practice of poverty."[21]
This is particularly true in large, sometimes multinational congregations where diversity of lifestyle and ministry is a given
and the relativity of the notion of "poverty" (as it has tradi-
tionally been understood in terms of deprivation, dependence,
and permission to use) becomes especially clear. Furthermore,
on the more individual level, whether we like to admit this or
not, our experience (especially of the more than thirty years
since Vatican II and the emergence of the adult religious) has
demonstrated that we can really write whatever we want into
our directories or constitutions; we can extrapolate forever at
our community meetings and even call this discernment. If the
insight and subsequent experience of our own inner poverty
has not graced us and called us forth, our words will be empty
and our actions without energy. Poverty, quite simply, is not
primarily something we say or do or practice. It is first and
foremost something we *are* and *are becoming*. The tension in
which we are held here is precisely between our covenantal at-
oneness in community on the one hand, and our commitment

---

*The examples and suggestions offered here are by no means exhaustive; nor do I im-
ply that the interpretations given here are the only valid ones. I offer them with the
same intentions as for the preceding: as "gathering-in" material for reflections that I
hope will lead us and our congregations more deeply into a holistic spirituality, into
wholeness.

to maturation as individuals on the other. The very concepts of covenant and community depend on maturity. One assumes the other.

Maturity, however, simply does not happen when adults are kept at dependency status, nor does authentic community. It is "institution" instead and displays all the regressive character-istics that belong to this kind of setting. The problem for us, of course, is that too many of us endured precisely that kind of setting for too long. We were "formed" in it from the earli-est moments of our commitment, and in this "formation" we were given all the answers—answers to questions we had not even asked yet and, therefore, often did not know what to do with. We certainly received the answers to poverty and how, step by step, it was to be lived. With this the process of emer-gence, the movement into personal insight and appropriation, was frequently stifled. We became dependent instead, and that was hailed as humility. The entire process was, to a large ex-tent, external to us, imposed from the outside and accepted blindly. Most things were accessible through permission, and discernment as to their relevance in one's life was left to the (assumed) wisdom—believed to be bestowed with the "grace of state"—of the superior.

After Vatican II it seemed that things drastically changed. The word was "experimentation," and religious all over the country were sent out to study and to learn to think on their own. We attended workshops of every type. The concern seemed to be to move us as quickly as possible from preadoles-cent dependency to the interdependent perspective that, given our chronological age, was expected of us. Emotionally some of us even succeeded, after a relatively brief span of retrieving lost adolescent time. I do not believe, however, that the struc-tures of our institutions ever gave way enough to the need for the adequate economic independence which precedes any mature ability to share.* No one can freely give what she or he has never had. No one can freely share when the sharing is dictated extraneously. The assumption that because we vowed something we willed it simply does not hold up when one considers that what most of us vowed to do without we had not yet experienced.

That one cannot be interdependent without first having moved through independence is a psychological given. The movement through independence will take its own time and will have to be taken seriously if poverty is to be understood holistically. Perhaps the notion of religious life as a lifestyle more specifically for men and women in the second half of life's journey (or at least after independence has been adequately developed and has moved to interdependence) needs to be explored and taken more seriously. What is certain, however, is that the entering of mature persons (by this I mean individuals *aware* of the journey they are on and willing and able to grow) needs to be encouraged. The very lifestyle into which we invite them, however, will then need to speak to their level of maturity. Poverty as dependence is unhealthy for all adults. Our own growth and development, therefore, are also at issue, and the institutional structures which surround these need to be seriously, critically, and openly rethought lest those who join us regress, losing the freedom which has brought them, and we never acquire it.

"Haves and Have-Nots"

A member of the leadership team in my own community asked me some time ago whether I agreed with the statement

---

*Constitutionally for some of us to this day (and also still in canon law) dependence, instead of an adult "commitment to share," is hailed as praiseworthy and as the primary mode of interpreting our vow.

that community life is divided between the "haves" and the "have-nots." This initially is quite a shocking statement for those of us who still live under the illusion of "communal" or "standardized" poverty in which we were "formed." It is an uncomfortable question, to be true, but is it not worth reflection?

To begin with, the lifestyle of the various communities in any congregation certainly varies considerably. What some consider a necessity, others, in their understanding of what comprises a simple lifestyle, have come to see as luxury; yet members of either group profess the same vow. Nor is it necessarily productive or advisable for the congregational or regional leader on his or her official visit to point out inconsistencies and demand change, for even if external compliance does follow, what about the change of heart? Are those who hanker after what is not permitted them truly poor? I am not suggesting that blatant luxuries or the "hamster mentality" acquisitiveness—the indiscriminate collecting of anything and everything one can lay one's hands on—should not be questioned. I am merely pointing out that compliance remains immature unless there is a change of heart and an inner honesty which distinguishes needs from desire.

Our individual lifestyles also show great variance. I do not think that I exaggerate when I say that if any of us truly want something badly enough, we can usually figure out a way to get it, if not through the community, either officially or unofficially for our use, then through our parents or family, or through our friends. Some of us have the fringe benefits of our office or work—we own credit cards—and, depending on our interpretation, use them to "ease the burden" of our congregational or professional responsibilities. Some of us travel a great deal and need the wardrobe of professional life; others do not. Some of us have no family at all and stay home—sometimes alone—

on holidays and feasts. Some of us live alone and manage our own budgets; others live in the motherhouse and never have a chance to plan even a menu. The issue of haves and have-nots, in whatever way one wants to look at it, undoubtedly exists in community life and, when lack of compassion or selfishness is its cause, cannot be ignored. Often, however, the reason for it is simply that the diverse values toward which the vow of poverty directs us cannot always be obtained by uniform practices in its observance: "Our exercise of hospitality in certain circumstances may conflict with our desire to eliminate certain types of food or drink from our diet for ascetical reasons," for example, or "our effective participation in certain political actions for the sake of justice may involve expenditures we would rather not make."[22] The complexity of our ministerial and communal involvements today makes standardization simply obsolete and cumbersome. Our concern here, therefore, is not so much that the issue of haves and have-nots exists in community, but rather that it is an issue and why.

A student in one of my classes one time described her interpretation of the vow of poverty as placing emphasis not on whether we have or do not have things, but on whether *things have us*. She had struggled for a long time, she told me, observing "religious affluence," until this interpretation came to her. Heidegger speaks of the attitude she described as "releasement": letting things "enter our daily life, and at the same time leav[ing] them outside, that is, let[ting] them alone, as things which are nothing absolute but remain dependent upon something higher."[23] We are here, once again, in the realm of disposition, of that poverty of spirit that we discussed at the beginning of this chapter and that alone gives energy to an authentic letting-go and letting-be.

Conformity in possessions is, I believe, a thing of the past and, whether it ever was a fact or not, I do not believe we need to mourn it, for I doubt that it was either realistic or healthy to begin with. Releasement, as Heidegger describes poverty of spirit, is rarely if ever achieved through conformity in this manner. It is achieved through a gradual letting go and through vision obtained in the slow process of life. It is grace. When I hanker after Sister K's computer, I am no poorer than she. When I can let her have it and rejoice in her use of it, I am as rich as she. It is of little value if I sit in shocked silence in front of the community television alone, while my brothers watch their favorite show in their rooms, each owning a private set. What might benefit us all, however, is to explore the reasons why they need to isolate themselves so. Perhaps in some situations we will need to direct our attention, rather, to the one who dominates the community television for, it seems to me, that she or he violates not only community life, but may also need to question her or his sense of poverty. This person *possesses* what we all own.

And what of personal budgets? Some of us have very small ones by choice or by guilt; others have considerably larger ones. Some of us get money from home; others get things bought for them instead. Still others have their family and friends pay for every dinner out and even for vacations. "We are religious," some of us will claim, and look to our community or to others to supply our needs. I believe that the problem here lies not primarily in how much we get or keep, but that we consider consistent "getting" at all as a viable adult way of living. This kind of "poverty" can be an excuse for not growing up. It can also be the reason for once more regressing. And then there are those among us carrying extra jobs for pocket money or spending what little allowance we have on gambling—a rapidly growing addiction among religious these days. What does this behavior tell us about the forced "have-not status" religious have experienced for so long, about the regression

that dependency imposed on adults has fostered, and about
the unhealthy risks this encourages some of us to take in order
to get out from under the unreasonable restrictions on personal
allowances and to gain at least some independence?

An example of this form of regression taken from the society at large can be found in the consequences of what has
come to be called "momism" in the American family today.
In what might now be regarded as a classic work of contemporary social psychology Hendrik M. Ruitenbeek speaks of
the decline in the American male's security and maturity and
of a general male regression as caused by this phenomenon.
To describe it he quotes Robert Odenwald's reference to a
five-year-old's observation that "daddies pay the bills in restau-
rants but...mothers give them the money beforehand."[24] By
the laws of "momism," daddies earn the salary, but mothers
give them their allowance and supply anything over and above,
only to keep the image of adulthood up. Daddies in fact, however, are treated like the oldest dependents. We are not here
concerned with the whys of "momism" in our age, nor with
its validity (in many ways it has already been supplanted by
the much more complex phenomenon of a two-salary family).
We are looking rather at its seeming similarity to the "getting"
mentality of "holy" dependency for men and women alike.
Both cases, I believe, either prevent maturation in the first
place, or encourage an inappropriate return to childishness
later. Neither of them fosters the acceptance of personal mon-
etary responsibility or the development of concern for others.
When one's needs (imagined or real) are taken care of without any significant personal investment or, worse still, when
one's needs are determined by another, one cannot expect to
mature. It is true, of course, as Sandra Schneiders points out,
that contemporary religious "are participating more directly
and extensively in the handling of the finances of their local

communities and institutes and assuming increasing responsibility for the ordinary economic affairs of their own lives."[25]
These are certainly steps in the right direction. Rare still, however, is the religious even today who in her daily choices will
truly be personally affected by this participation in community finances. The growth in awareness here seems slow. And,
whereas I do not wish to minimize the importance of what we
are doing, I for one have not as yet seen it shift us to any large
extent toward an authentic personal and mature sense of fiscal
responsibility. We are as a whole "care-free" and, whether we
are comfortable with this or not, taken care of. It is my sense
that, as holy as some may think this is, it simply is not real.

Personal Responsibility for Justice

I am not out to propose a solution to our dilemma here. It is
serious and needs more heads and hearts than mine. I do not
believe, however, that hiding behind canon law as intransigent
and as opposed to any change in the way we distribute and
handle money can save us much longer from having to deal
with this matter. Institutional compliance to age-old paradigms
of church law may perhaps still work for us collectively. Thus,
as institutes we can even now, with relative success, be "for the
poor" and share community wealth with the oppressed. The
money we may spend as institutes before we need canonical
approval is sizeable. We can also mission those among us who
feel called to work for justice near and far, and we can send
them in our name and with our support. Laudable though this
may be, it can nevertheless dull our individual consciences.
When the institute does it, I can easily take the credit which
costs me nothing. If, however, we are to deal with growth into
personal responsibility for justice and, therefore, a personal appropriation of the vow of poverty by each one among us, we

need to address maturity issues and foster the natural human development pattern from dependence through independence to interdependence. Here church law (which generally disregards, if it is at all aware of, the findings of developmental and social psychology) will be of little help, if not an actual hindrance, to us. Efforts in this area will require tremendous creativity and daring—nothing short of visionaries, who can risk the challenge of thinking into tradition and coupling this with contemporary insight and learning—to bring about transformation. Of course, we always need to balance individual development with the larger congregational concerns, but we cannot ignore it. Since we know that the will of God is not divisive, it is my view that the former generally enhances the latter rather than hurts it. Certain communities (I am told many of noncanonical status but some canonical as well) have tried covenantal sharing rather than the traditional "permission to use," with some surprising (even financial) success. Members in some instances manage their own salaries and give what they can to the common account for the support of those who can no longer work and for the sake of the congregation's justice agenda. Their sacrifice, I have heard, is often considerable. This kind of shift in fiscal management demands trust and the willingness to risk, but also an open and frequent disclosure of congregational needs to all members so that informed pooling of resources can happen.

We all know but, because of the grip past "absolutes" have on us, perhaps we need to remind ourselves from time to time that there is no divinely decreed, foolproof model for the vow of poverty. There is only the mandate to compassionate presence, to sharing, to being for others out of our wealth and our want. The risks of rethinking the way we live out our vow of poverty are high. Ultimately, of course, we do not "live out" our vow anyway, nor do we "practice" it. We rather commit ourselves to live into its grace and to learn from it daily. One can always worry about abuses and in any movement toward responsible freedom there will be abuses, but we can hardly deny that we are free of them now. In the last analysis, our mandate is to foster growth into wholeness; growth toward maturity experienced in community, growth toward compassion both for ourselves and others. Holiness as such cannot be ascribed to an institute but only to its members. Whatever fosters it in them will augment the larger congregation and ultimately bring justice to the whole church.

Questions for Focus, Reflection, and Discussion

1. Have you experienced the pain of your powerlessness in the face of the economic injustice in the world? Can you cite an example? How do you react to the statement that there is for us, nevertheless, an unwilling yet real participation in this injustice, that "our hands are also always dirty"?

2. How can you see self-sacrifice as an authentic expression of your vow of poverty? "We may be vowed members of a congregation, and our covenant will certainly affect our way of life, but ultimately the decision to give all is ours, and this decision is the story of a lifetime of personal responsibility, of guilt, and of redemption." What is your reaction to this statement?

3. "Only when I can truly let the other's need gift me, when I experience the one I 'help' as giving me life, and when my service becomes thanksgiving do I experience authentic solidarity, at-oneness with the poor." Have you experienced this insight? What does it mean to you?

4. How, in your view, can works of justice suffer from the "drought mentality" described at the beginning of chapter 1?

5. Could piety without concern for justice become insipid pietism? Might this be a danger for Christian churches, for religious congregations, for religious?

6. How, in your own experience as a religious, have you seen yourself moving from dependence, to independence, to interdependence? Can you cite specific examples to validate your experience? Do you see a need to address this issue further? What does interdependence mean to you now?

7. How has the "haves" and "have-nots" issue in religious life affected you? What is your reaction? Do you see "releasement" as a fitting response here?

8. Have you experienced the "getting" mentality of immature dependency? How can we as religious foster individual fiscal responsibility?

9. What do you think of the suggestion to change the name for the vow of poverty to "Solidarity with the Oppressed." Does this more closely resemble what we strive to be and do?

Chapter Four

COMMUNITY, CELIBACY, AND INTIMACY

In the preceding chapters I have been primarily concerned with introducing religious vows generally and the vow of poverty in particular within the context of holistic spirituality. I have tried to move away from the dualism of our past and to ask how our way of living into our baptismal promises might help us reach wholeness, maturity, and integrity. The intention of these pages has been to approach the vows as our way of living in the fullness of time, as our way of moving ever more deeply into the Christ event. For this reason I proposed that they be understood not primarily in a prescriptive sense—telling us what we must do and what we may not do—but rather in an attitudinal sense: opening us up to a disposition in which we stand and are held, so to speak, and into which we commit ourselves to grow in ever greater longing for holiness and for wholeness. I suggested that what we vow is open-ended, a process, not a final product at any given or determinable moment. It is a commitment to a depth which takes hold of us ever more fully as we move into our identity as religious.

The present chapter will concern itself with our vowed life in relation to community and intimacy. My emphasis will be specifically on consecrated celibacy, on encountering life—all of life—out of a celibate identity.

Revisiting the Issues

Much has happened to religious life in the last ten years since I first wrote these pages on the vowed life. Much has happened to me as well, as I have encountered many women religious in particular, but also some men religious, and a large number of newer members during the numerous workshops and retreats I have given throughout the English-speaking world. There is no doubt that my understanding of community has been broadened by these encounters, and my hope is that my approach to celibacy has deepened as well. I have attempted to address the former in *Where Two or Three Are Gathered: Community Life for the Contemporary Religious* (New York: Crossroad, 1993). I expanded my reflections on celibacy and intimacy in part 2 of *Wrestling with God: Religious Life in Search for Its Soul* (New York: Crossroad, 1996). It is not necessary to repeat these reflections here, although they are in many respects the foundation for my present thinking. What may be necessary, however, is to identify specifically the emerging areas of struggle that, I believe, are presenting themselves to us on the subject of celibacy and community life today.

Celibacy

As an endnote to this chapter in the previous edition of this book, entitled *Living the Vision,* I made the following clarification:

> With Sandra Schneiders I agree that "celibacy is the determining characteristic of religious life in a way that neither poverty nor obedience can be. Celibacy distinguishes religious life from other forms of Christian life just like taking another person for one's lawful wedded spouse for better or for worse distinguishes marriage from other states

of life" (*New Wineskins* [New York: Paulist, 1986], 69).
Whereas all Christians are asked to follow the will of
God in their lives (obedience) and to embrace poverty of
spirit—to share with others and be in solidarity with those
less fortunate (poverty)—though the way this is done will
be different according to one's calling, the vocation to live
consecrated celibacy is given only to some and identifies
them, therefore, as of a specific life-orientation. This is
what I mean by "celibate identity." (See also Schneiders,
114).

Upon revisiting these observations, I now experience some am-
bivalence that I did not feel when I first wrote them. I reflect
on this here in order to invite dialogue where ten years ago
this kind of an exchange may not as yet have been possible.

I do not doubt that religious life as we have understood it
so far can be identified in the above manner. It is my sense
now, however, that the issue around the celibate vocation and
its association with religious life is simply not as clean-cut as
described there. Although some of us clearly have experienced
celibacy as a vocation, it seems to me that many others among
us did not, and some of us may even have found ourselves
"stranded with it," as it were, many years after we first took
the vow. I would suggest (and conversation with many among
us bears this out) that a great number of religious were, in fact,
primarily drawn to the vision, works, and charism of our congregations and experienced celibacy simply as a "discipline":
something that was required of us and accepted by us with
relative thoughtlessness—depending on our levels of maturity.
Our desire was to become members of a religious congregation. *That* is why we entered. Celibacy was seen as part of that
but not as something that we felt impelled to or even attracted
to as a way of life or as a value in itself.

If this is true, would it be valid, given these motivations, to see consecrated celibacy as our defining characteristic? Might not the "gathering priority" for many religious today—previously identified as the energy that sustains our togetherness—be more realistically placed around the charism of our congregations: something not necessarily clearly definable but something, nevertheless, real; something that speaks to us about the reign of God, that attracted us—consciously or not—and touched us in our longing to serve; something that answered and still answers today our need to be about the mission and to be so with others in a united effort on behalf of justice? I hasten to add that our sense of charism also may not have been as finely tuned for us when we entered as might have been desirable, especially for those of us trained before Vatican II. We wanted consciously perhaps to be teachers, nurses, social workers, and felt that God was calling us to a particular congregation to be about this vocation. Some of us, during our youth, may also simply have *wanted* to be "sisters,"or "brothers," or "priests"—with all the aura that came with this lifestyle. What all of this entailed was not terribly clear to most of us, I believe—least of all the implications of celibacy.

If the above describes the motivations of the religious of the fifties and sixties or before, the desire for community, I am told, appears to motivate those who seek out religious life today. In both cases it seems that celibacy does not appear to be the focal issue—that which draws and compels. Although much may have been written in the past to argue the theological relevance of celibacy for religious life, the existential experience of the membership to verify these theories seems in many cases to be lacking. Many have accepted the discipline, to be sure, but a large number may wonder deep down why. Where, then, does celibacy belong? My question is in no way intended to dismiss it. I ask merely whether we can legitimately see it as the primary mark for religious life, as its essence, so to speak.

The phenomenon of celibacy as such has been with the church from its beginning, and it has not been restricted to the Christian tradition. It is a venerable as well as a mysterious way of life. In *Wrestling with God* I attempted to touch on the mystical dimension in which I believe it is rooted. I tried also to move it away from the grip of dualism and triumphalism that has corrupted its true symbolic significance for ages and, over the years, has turned it into a requirement for all those "seriously striving after holiness"—for all religious, therefore, and clerics as well. I strongly believe that, among religious and clerics, there are indeed some authentically called to bear witness in their bodies to the human heart's unquenchable longing for God that no created love can satisfy. The celibate symbolizes this in a remarkable way, since she or he voluntarily* forgoes the most intimate answer to human longing, the deepest union possible between human lovers, and by so doing speaks poignantly to the "not enough" that marks our hunger for God. The call to this "forgoing" is deeply mystical. It is deeply personal as well.† I wonder whether it can be reduced, therefore, to a general category such as membership in a religious congregation or in the clerical state.

I find it increasingly more difficult to believe, especially in the case of apostolic communities, that our founders' passionate involvement and concern for the works of mercy needed in their time and requiring laborers for the vineyard focused primarily on celibacy (even if it was a vocation for many of them personally). I question the validity, therefore, of a uni-

---

*Though the YES to the call quite often is a process over the span of a lifetime, and not necessarily without struggle and learnings.
†By this I do not mean that it is, therefore, merely private. The testimony given by the celibate is an open statement, a symbol. All the more necessary that the witness be happy and wholesome and real.

versal discipline imposed on religious as a whole which, by that fact, generalizes and thereby quite likely dilutes the truly mystical and personal nature of this vocation.

My observations may, indeed, appear radical to some and be disturbing to others for, were we to give them serious attention, we might find ourselves looking honestly at "Transformative Element 8" of the document "Future of Religious Life," drawn up by the U.S. leadership of both men and women religious congregations in 1989. I have discussed this element and its implications both in *Where Two or Three Are Gathered* and in *Wrestling with God*. It strikes me now that, consciously or not, this joint session of the Leadership Conference of Women Religious and of the Major Superiors of Men intuited what a nondualistic, inclusive model of religious life might require. My suggestion here is that it would require a true honoring of the celibate *vocation* by our movement away from compulsory celibacy.

What all of this will mean for the future of religious life may, of course, be unnerving. At this point in time, the defining role of celibacy keeps our boundaries quite fixed and untouched. It is clear that the culture in which we minister has difficulty understanding celibacy and, with much voiced unhappiness around this issue (especially because of its compulsory dimension with respect to clerics and also a plethora of negative press about sexual indiscretions and abuse by both religious and clerics) the taste for it is steadily declining. It is, therefore, improbable that parents will encourage this lifestyle among their children. Celibacy, quite simply, is no longer seen as a value. There are those among us, of course, who see its asceticism of benefit to them personally for apostolic reasons and, therefore, choose it to allow them greater availability for the mission. Its dualistic mystique, however, has imploded, as it were, and even Catholics today know that there are other equally legitimate ways to become holy. It is highly unlikely, therefore, that the ascetical or the mystical call which, I believe, celibacy is meant to be will produce the numbers that a now imploded church discipline and a Catholic culture brought up on triumphalism and hierarchical states of perfection were able to produce in the past. Given the present situation, therefore, the most likely scenario for religious life as I foresee it, depressing though this may appear to most of us, is a continued decrease in numbers and a future at best of very few but hopefully healthy and happy mystics and those who chose the asceticism of celibacy for the sake of the mission.

But what of the works of the congregation, of the charism that truly energizes us and connects us deeply to the justice imperative of the Gospel and to the human family and that requires workers for the vineyard? With this question, I believe, another scenario for our future opens up. It will require a broadening of our boundaries and an alternate form of membership as "Transformative Element 8" envisioned it:

> In 2010 we will be characterized by inclusivity and intentionality. Our communities may include persons of different ages, genders, cultures, races, and sexual orientation. They may include persons who are lay or cleric, married or single, as well as vowed and/or unvowed members. They will have a core group with temporary or permanent commitment.
>
> ...Such inclusivity will necessitate a new understanding of membership and a language to accompany it.
>
> Religious life still includes religious congregations of permanently vowed members.

There are presently, to my knowledge, only a small number of religious congregations seriously exploring alternate forms of membership. The most realistic among these are, I believe, those who simply have decided to welcome other forms of membership—such as members committing themselves for a limited number of years only rather than forever, married members, those who would choose one or two vows only or who simply make a profession or promise to uphold a Christian value in line with the charism of the institute they are joining, such as service, mercy, hospitality, and so forth. The inviting congregation's plan, in most cases, is to do so simply *by not standing in the way of what may be evolving among them.* They have adopted the organic approach as it were: if the laborers are out there and the harvest is ready, these congregations will invite the laborers—those energized by their charism—to join them. They resist creating structures ahead of time for what may in fact not happen, but they plan to respond to what *may* emerge with gratitude and humility. Triumphalism as to who really, in the final analysis, *belongs* and who does not, is giving way in these congregations to a renewed concern for the mission as primary. Their "gathering priority" is shifting and there is a renewed albeit cautious optimism about the future.

Community

What I have discussed in the preceding observations clearly will call us also to rethink what has been our prevailing concept of community as conventual living. Not only will a broadening and diversification of membership continue to expand the numerous ministry possibilities of religious congregations, but it will also have us deepen our understanding of what community is and how our covenantal bonding might evolve.

Since Vatican II the mandate to foster "community *for mission*" has been given much reflection, action, and energy among us. Holistically speaking this might mean that we have steadily been moving toward internalizing and celebrating in our midst the multifaceted breakthrough of God in the world and that we have attempted to do this particularly by witnessing to God's compassion in many different ways. Diversification of ministries in most religious communities, especially in the United States, has flourished and, although many congregations may still identify themselves in broad terms by the apostolate of their founders (be it education, health care, social work, etc.), their understanding of these ministries in most cases has remarkably expanded, if not always in expressed theory, most definitely in praxis. It has, for example, become clear to many of us that education can take place in many different ways and that for the true educator the world is the classroom. Today we educate as always when we teach in public, diocesan, or private schools, in colleges and universities, but we know that we also do so when we minister to the sick and the dying and share with them the Word of God by our presence and love, or when we rally people on behalf of justice, make music, or paint, when we give spiritual direction, when we counsel and facilitate and organize retreat programs. In the area of health care, as well, we accept today that sickness is not only of the body or of the mind but can be a social phenomenon, and that healing, therefore, transcends the hospital. We work for it also when we counsel those broken in spirit or in heart, when we inspire the depressed, challenge an oppressive system, provide and build houses for the destitute, work to resolve conflictual situations and facilitate dialogue. Ministries of every kind abound in most present-day religious congregations. It seems that we have realized and accepted that our primary vocation is to service where there is the greatest need and that our commonality lies not so much in the *what* of our ministry as in the *how*, in the *why*, and in the *end*.

Not only did we expand our ministries during the more than thirty years since Vatican II; we also have become educated in so doing. This is particularly true for women religious who today count among the most educated women in the United States. We took seriously the call to service in contemporary society. Having returned to the charism of those who founded our congregations, we noted our inadequacy vis-à-vis a world of intellectual as well as practical sophistication. We knew that to be sisters and brothers to the modern man and woman and thus truly to be of service to the church in the modern world, we needed to stand within it, to be educated at the best schools, to minister responsibly and viably as women and men with a contemporary perspective and contemporary faith response. We knew that witnessing does not take place in seclusion or out of an ivory tower mentality, that wholeness, healing, and holiness in this world is achieved when the Christ event can be witnessed in the ordinary, and when every man, woman, and child in any situation, under any condition, can proclaim the Gospel as his or hers. And so we knew why we needed to diversify our ministries.

Our diversification in terms of community living happened much more slowly. For reasons not entirely clear, our conventual style of "being together" (in spite of the fact that fewer and fewer of us worked in the schools and hospitals to which our convents were attached and our schedules were anything but the same) continued to be an ideal. Even where convents were taken over for parish or hospital use and we had to look for alternate housing, our living together stayed for a long time conventual. Often it followed the rhythm of the school year and the horarium of the school day even if none of us taught. There remained the expectation of daily common prayer, and many of us, though our ministries kept us out late into the night, rose early to be there. Our commonality somehow made us feel we were doing it right—according to the values of tradition.

It took years and a great amount of guilt before our living together experienced some significant transformation. In many respects the changes were initiated from the grassroots and happened gradually—one by one. Religious moved away from the larger group. Some wanted a say in their choice of community; some started to live in ones and twos, in apartments or small homes. The reasons for these choices varied, but in all cases the choice demanded personal effort to find alternate ways of bonding and of experiencing togetherness—values that, surprisingly, were often recaptured from the dying embers of discouragement and fatigue and found new meaning with the new lifestyle. It is my sense as I reflect on this that the absence from the larger group did not debilitate the individual's connectedness with the congregation as such. Many involved themselves with the numerous committees and the plethora of meetings these require. Some even found renewed energy for this work, since the distance they created in moving into different living situations gave them the space they needed to regain the desire for involvement. Most of us who were able to watch the grassroots changes I have described here without prejudice have seen a great amount of energy and enthusiasm about forming support groups both to celebrate each other as well as to discuss congregational matters. Generally it is safe to say that a wealth of creativity is emerging.

Yet, while the individual religious seem to be happy with the choices they have made, concern about what is happening with respect to community life continues to be raised. This is particularly so at official meetings, chapters, and congregational assemblies. It seems to me that perhaps one of the reasons community and what it has come to mean to a growing number of us has difficulty being accepted by many religious even to this day (and even while the change steadily continues) is precisely its "grassroots" character. General chapters, for one, do not appear to be used to handling matters such as this nor, I suspect, were they designed to deal with this kind of a phenomenon, and so they persist, chapter after chapter, in calling for a "renewal of community life," without being able to identify, really, where the problem lies. There is dis-ease with what is happening, and quite often, because chapter delegates and the format in which they operate are incapable of addressing it, they commission new leadership teams or special committees to "work at renewal" instead. This kind of mandate usually results in a retreat or workshop on the topic given within the five-year or so interval between general chapters, but it is my experience that essentially little changes. The question, of course, remains to be asked (but rarely is) whether our explorations and concern should not rather be about au-thentic relationality. Perhaps the changes we are experiencing are, in fact, necessary. Perhaps what has happened and continues to happen *needs* to happen in order to lead us to alternate models of relationship, and the form in which the change in community life is occurring—given the often ignored personal nature of the issue—is the only way it can.

At this point in time I think it is accurate to say that our new ways of being together are not just a rare occurrence anymore but are, in fact, a phenomenon that needs to be studied and respected. For a majority of active religious, especially in the English-speaking world, community life the way we experienced it during our formation and for some time after Vatican II is no longer life-giving. What was, simply does not work anymore, and what will be is still emerging. This emergence is happening among us, and the most creative thing we can do about it is to face the issue.

To alleviate our anxiety about this matter, it may help to note that when something does not work any longer it does not necessarily mean that we have done it wrong, and that if only we did the same thing better, things would work again, that we are, in fact, unfaithful and should all return to the fold. When something does not work any longer, it may simply mean that we have outgrown what was good for a long time— for a particular period of history, perhaps, or for a specific cultural setting. It may also mean that we have learned about developmental and social psychology and about the dynamics and complexities of adults living together *as adults*. It may mean that we now know what made us suffer for so long. We may have found out that it was unnecessary, really, and are now resisting it. This realization is often a painful one for religious. When something was part of our tradition for a long time, we have great difficulty letting it go and, even more so, seeing aspects of it as no longer healthy.

The fact that the new is still "on the way," as it were, and that nothing is fixed yet and may, in fact, not be fixed for a long time, is also unnerving. For some of us there seems to be altogether too much diversity in our ways of finding togetherness. So, while the bottom is dropping out of the old ordered ways, the new ways are still emerging and being pri- oritized. The apparent chaos seems to be much too licentious for some of us, and we continue to call for a renewal of com- munity life in the secret hope that things will get back to the way they were. It is clear that in a world where the only thing permanent is change this hope will most likely remain in the area of wishful thinking. Once adults have experienced real life-giving change in which they have been involved and feel invested, the old can be returned to only by coercion or guilt. These, however, are death-dealing tactics hardly to be recommended.

Models for Group Living

As we struggle with these issues, perhaps some understanding of the dynamics and processes of group living may help clarify the *why* of what seems to be happening to us. Desmond Murphy in *A Return to Spirit: After the Mythic Church* identifies the church's and our confusion between "primary *(Gemeinschaft)* and secondary *(Gesellschaft)* groups" in our self-definition (not only ideologically but also structurally) as a major factor in the disintegration of ecclesial institutions. He suggests that the latter *(Gesellschaft)* has been emphasized frequently to the detriment of the former *(Gemeinschaft)*. He uses these sociological terms to identify what might best be understood as organization, society, party, company for *Gesellschaft,* and true community for *Gemeinschaft*. The two entities, although they are mutually dependent, are, nevertheless, exclusive of each other—each having its own aims to be achieved in different ways.[1]

The aim of a *Gesellschaft* is primarily to get the job done. It is "essentially task-oriented. Its skills are instrumental ones." It concerns itself with "business activities, dissemination of information, teaching...counseling, and organizational administration." Efficiency is prized. The primary reason for the group is to be about the task, "not to relate as such." Although it values mature persons with an attitude of responsibility, it does not see itself as needing to further personal growth and development or give nurturance and emotional support.[2]

These latter concerns belong to the *Gemeinschaft* (authentic community). It recognizes basic human needs "necessary for the integrated individuation of the person" and seeks to provide them. "Authenticity, acceptance, affirmation, warmth, nurturance, support, and friendship" are the values of community. They are not luxuries that we hope to get perhaps someday if we are lucky. They are essential elements of primary groups, Murphy tells us. According to humanistic psychology today, we all need some place where, in our interactions, we can experience "congruence, empathy, non-possessive warmth, and non-judgmental attitudes." If they are missing in our institutions, spiritual and personal development cannot happen.[3] We might call what we have created for ourselves a "community," but in reality it is not.

It is Murphy's view that an excessive task orientation has debilitated ecclesial communities. What may have happened all too frequently in our midst is that we *identified* ourselves as communities, but in fact *understood* ourselves and *treated* each other as if we were an organization. We expected things to function as they would in an organization and created the hierarchical structures to support the smooth running of affairs, but we wanted also to *feel* as though we were a *Gemeinschaft*. We dealt with our communities as if they were the concern of an organization and then expected them to work. The ingredients of a community are, however, not "organized." One *grows* into a *Gemeinschaft* if the environment and the openness are there. It emerges out of our togetherness and cannot be legislated, not even with the best intentions.

Our problem, I believe, arose out of the fact that we are in certain respects both a community and an organization—a *Gemeinschaft* and a *Gesellschaft*. Much, for example, of what is referred to as the "common life" entails really the organization of a group, gathered around a sacred task or purpose, under one roof and sharing resources. It has little to do as such with *being* a community even if we call it that, unless the ingredients for a community are present. It is true, of course, that an empowering community is important for the minister, but to assume that the primary "purpose" of community is to enhance our ministries may reduce the former to a means toward action and neglect to see it in its own nature, in its *being* dimension as community. This often has the unfortunate consequence of our addressing it solely in terms of how it can adjust itself to further mission (understood as our work) and tends to subordinate *Gemeinschaft* to *Gesellschaft* needs. We experience community in such a situation more like a "bed and breakfast" place, as Mary Wolff-Salin calls it,[4] and we bring about the exact opposite of what we hope for. A house to which I am assigned or to which I move simply because it is advantageous to my work because of space, location, traveling needs, is precisely that—a convenient place. It may, however, have little to do with community, and unless other issues— issues primary to a community—are also discerned, I cannot expect them automatically to happen. A convenient place does not guarantee that there is anyone at all in the house "with whom [I] have anything in common, whether by age, training, interest, or personality."[5] How can I, therefore, expect to experience empowerment in such a situation?

Means are always evaluated in terms of their appropriateness to their end. If task alone is our end and looms as exclusively important, community will be seen, consciously or not, only in terms of adjusting to it. But we are *persons* in mission, not mere functionaries. As persons we have needs which may differ from our needs as workers. Marx may believe that if our work fulfills us we are fulfilled, but we as Christians know that even Jesus went apart to be with his community and his friends, that he chose his companions and cared for their well-being as persons. He also rested and relaxed and asked his disciples to do the same.

Community is more than a means. It is my conviction that to live as community is, in fact, an essential dimension of religious life as a whole, that one is *called* to it. This may not always mean physical proximity or "life in common," but it does mean that those who share this bonding are also those committed in a special way toward furthering and empowering individuation in each other. This is neither easy nor painless. Mary Wolff-Salin claims that "for the religious, the struggles of life with both God and community suppl[y] the raw materials and the 'obstacles to conquer' for this growth process."[6] Maturity or individuation is a process which enfolds us and challenges us throughout our life. It is "as essential a part of human motivation as hunger, thirst, aggression, sexuality, and pressures toward finding relaxation and attaining happiness."[7] Community is a powerful help toward realizing and furthering this individuation.

To disentangle the age-old intermeshing of *Gemeinschaft* and *Gesellschaft,* of community and our organization around work/ministry (especially because of the "holy" status these have achieved in the name of "tradition") is a mammoth task. It is my sense that a beginning can be made simply by accepting the reality of this enmeshment (which is particularly acute in our large institutions) and by alerting ourselves to the harm and deprivation our past unawareness may have caused.

Some examples of *Gesellschaft* values interfering with community life are quite clear to many of us: presuming that *faith* communities can be formed through guidelines and clearly discernible criteria spelled out ahead of time continues to be a way in which many of us confuse the issue. One can easily think that if *Gesellschaft* issues are dealt with *Gemeinschaft* will happen. A case in point is our continued attempt at creating community (where the above-mentioned depth requirements are met) in huge motherhouses where hundreds of sisters or brothers live—often in retirement. It is clearly one of the greatest problems we face today. This is so, because our motherhouses most often come under the classification of "total institution." Murphy defines these as places "of residence and work where a large number of like-situated individuals cut off from the wider society for an appreciable period of time [because their basic needs are provided for], together lead an enclosed formally administered life."[8]

It is a commonly accepted fact that total institutions have adverse effects on the personal dignity of those who live in them. They tend to bring about loss of self-esteem and further depersonalization. Relationships in total institutions tend to be in terms of roles. There is a negation of affect, while intellect and will reign supreme.[9] As I have mentioned already, however, relating primarily in terms of roles belongs to the *Gesellschaft* paradigm, to a group whose focus is task. It is not difficult to recognize how tragic this can be for many of our elderly. No wonder our sisters and brothers prefer to stay out "in the field" as long as they can, and many religious, when given the chance, voice their resistance to going back to the motherhouses when their ministry days are over. They may not be aware of the sociological data we are discussing here, but they sense what a *Gesellschaft* model of life can do to their soul.

Another example of the community/organization (*Gemeinschaft/Gesellschaft*) mix-up among us is our frequent total overlapping of work roles and living situations, as is the case when entire leadership teams live and work together in the same place, or when those in charge of initial incorporation live with the newer members and at the same time are expected to evaluate them. In the latter case we also have what could easily become a violation of professional ethics—a quasi guidance/dependency relationship mixed in with the standard associational and reciprocal mode of community living. The newer member is expected to live in a peer situation while an in-built role-tied relationship "plays interference," so to speak.

It is clear that until relatively recently few of us knew or recognized any of this. We lived and worked together (albeit

largely in silence) and assumed that since we were all members
of the same congregation, we automatically were a community.
We also assumed that, since institutional life was prescribed
and had been lived for so long and by so many, it was a *value*
in itself and needed to be preserved. Today we know better.
We have become educated in developmental psychology and
relational issues. We are getting in touch with a gnawing discontent in our midst and a longing for affect and intimacy. We
are beginning to see that bodies under the same roof are not
enough. Much more seriously, we also know, although this is
hard to admit, that the fact that we are all members of the
same congregation does not necessarily mean that we can, by
that fact, create an environment where these needs will be met.

Authentic community *needs* conversation and the ability to
connect with one another. It needs depth. Conversation, and
we all know this, is more than talking past each other about
the weather or problems at school or congregational concerns.
Conversation that is life-giving and conducive to *Gemeinschaft*
presupposes some connectedness in the area of education, tem-
perament, interests, vision of life. If none of these are present,
community, even with the best intentions and greatest holiness,
is not going to happen. We are more than silent co-habitants
today. Interrelating is part—a necessary and essential part—
of our being together!

Having said all this, it should be clear why we are having
difficulties, and why all the resolutions and chapter mandates
in the world will not resolve them until we look at old assumptions with the experience and backdrop of contemporary
disciplines and try to understand ourselves rather than con-
demn ourselves. A lifestyle that is not conducive to health
and happiness is not holy. "People," says Desmond Murphy,
"go where their needs are met—unmet emotional needs for
the kind of normal personal interaction that provides the sta-

ble relationships necessary for growth may be an explanation nearer to the mark."[10] He suggests, as I mentioned already, that the disintegration in ecclesial communities can at least partially be explained by the indiscriminate intermeshing of the *Gemeinschaft* and *Gesellschaft* models of togetherness and by the dominance of *Gesellschaft* priorities.

There is no doubt that we all need community. Many of us are choosing today to redefine the term and redesign our relational experiences. Our choices are, I believe, at least in part due to the collapse of former ways of doing and of being, but they are not due to a rejection of togetherness. Human bonding and the covenant we share with one another is precious to most of us. Perhaps the statement: "In order to stay in community I had to leave the type of common life we were living," needs to be reflected on by all of us.

Our Gathering Priorities

Parker Palmer in his groundbreaking reflections concerning the authentic "Community of Truth" may be able to offer us still another way to address the issues discussed above.[11] His interests are in education. The examples he offers, however, clearly go beyond the art of teaching and apply to community in general. Palmer presents two models of community. The first we are all familiar with: it looks somewhat like a pyramid, an organizational or management grid that identifies the group in terms of its leader at the top who speaks for it and is ultimately responsible for whatever happens in it. It was the model of our past. Some of us were trained in it, though, with a growing sense of our own maturity, we have all tried hard to transcend it. God's will in this model is extraneous to us. It is communicated to us by those who speak for God. The model is "hierarchical, linear, and compulsive-hygienic."[12] Nothing is out of place. There is, in Palmer's words, "a conveyer-belt atmosphere about it." On its premises the *Gesellschaft* mode of togetherness is based.

The second model looks more like an atom:

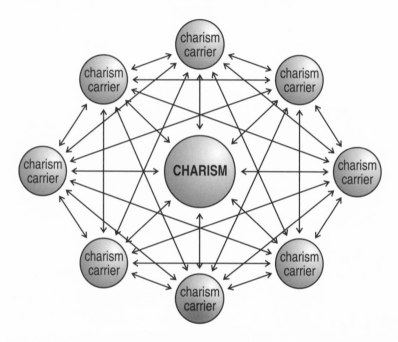

Its nucleus, or hub, holds everything connected and is, in fact, connected to everything. For our purposes I would identify the hub as the charism of our various communities, the energy that draws us and holds us connected to each other and to itself. Paraphrasing Palmer one might say that in this model many are made one because they gather around a common energy (charism) and are guided by a common goal: the mission of Jesus.[13] Whereas the first model concerns itself with objectives to be achieved, the second model symbolizes relationality. The charism in this model is seen, as it were, as a living, growing dynamism that speaks to and receives enrichment from each member of the group. All the members, in turn, charged by their own inner fire, relate to each other in a "circular, dynamic, interactive" way. All are nourished and God is in their midst.

There is in a community based on model 2 a participatory type of awareness that tolerates no *up* or *down* (competition, ambition). There is passion, however, and there can be conflict. "Conflict," says Palmer, "is the dynamic by which we test ideas in the open, in a communal effort to stretch each other"[14] and make the world a better place. In the process of this stretching, we honor the transcendent secret of the charism that is at the center of our togetherness. No one has an edge on it. All, however, are energized by it and give life and vision to it in turn. It carries us along, as it forever reveals and hides itself, drawing us forever into the mystery.

The characteristics of an authentic community of truth described by Palmer are powerful reminders of what true faith communities need if they are to feed their members. True community invites *diversity,* says Palmer, "not because it is politically correct but because diverse viewpoints are demanded by the manifold mysteries" that reveal themselves whenever two or three are gathered in God's name. True community embraces *ambiguity* not because we are confused or indecisive but because we understand the inadequacy of our concepts to embrace the vastness" of the mystery. True community welcomes *creative conflict* "not because we are angry or hostile but because conflict is required to correct our biases and prejudices about the nature" of truth. True community practices *honesty* "not only because we owe it to one another" but because anything else would be a betrayal of the mystery. True community experiences *humility* "not because we have fought and lost but because humility is the only lens" through which truth can be seen—"and once we have seen [it], humility is the only posture possible."[15]

It is interesting that Palmer sees the characteristics we have here adapted for ourselves as essential for an educational community which, as we know, rarely lives and works under the same roof but gathers instead for significant learning encounters. What has been described here, therefore, might be a goal and possibly already a good fit for the various types of covenantal communities that are emerging in our times—however and whenever they come together. Could we say, perhaps, that their gathering priority needs to be the charism of the congregation; that they live in and through its energy as the mystery that connects them authentically and in a powerful way to the Christ event unfolding in contemporary society?

When the mystery of our charism dies, or we lose its "gravitational pull," as Parker Palmer would put it, we "fall out of the communal orbit into the black hole of posturing, narcissism, and arrogance."[16] We lose sight of our at-oneness with one another and with the human family if this happens and become interested merely in our own personal concerns, even as we insist that we are, indeed, about the mission and lecture others on it. The hope for religious life as we move into the twenty-first century is, precisely, our passion for the charism and the love that energizes us in living into its mystery both in our homes and in our ministries. The community we form, however we do that, needs to connect with that passion and be fed by that love.

Relationship and Intimacy

What, then, can be said about community and relationality, about our togetherness and the authenticity it requires? It is my conviction that a community in which each one of us can dwell in his or her own integrity will, first and foremost, have to be a community not only of women or men, but also *for* women or men *as* women or men, that is, a community of adults *for adults as* adults. Sandra Schneiders, I believe, helps clarify this observation by making an appropriate distinction between community styles as lived in what she calls "primary family" and "secondary family" settings.[17] The "primary family" is the community of one's birth. It provides father and mother and often sisters and brothers. In it one is a child related to parents (and other children). The "secondary family" one chooses. In it, as spouses, for example, one is presumed to be an adult. In the primary model of community most members function as children most of the time; they are led and it is presumed that at least initially decisions have to be made for them by the competent authority.

It is clear that this model is not foreign to any of us, not only because we all have had parents, we all were children once upon a time, but also because many of us have lived in religious community before Vatican II. It is also, I believe, clear that this model no longer works for us as contemporary, educated women and men in diverse ministries. Sandra Schneiders puts it well:

> Since all the members of a religious community are at least chronologically adults and ideally psychological and spiritual adults as well, it is counter-productive if not destructive for them to play the role of children at home while trying to function as adults in all other arenas of their lives. This play-acting leads to infantilism, psychological regression, alienation of responsibility, guilt, and malformation of conscience among other things. The appropriate relationship between members of a community, whatever their role in the group, is that of adult to adult. Whatever else it might be, the religious community is not

a two-generation family and the primary family model is
radically inadequate.

Having laid aside the primary family as a model for
religious community living we face the problem of finding
another model which is more adequate. My suggestion
is that the appropriate model is that of *a community of
friends who are co-disciples in ministry.*[18]

A similar suggestion was made now almost twenty years ago
by Joan Chittister when, "futurizing" about religious life and
the disappearance of large institutions, she observed: "This
will affect lifestyle as well as ministry, relationship as well
as work. *Friendship communities rather than work communities* will be more likely to form." Putting her finger right on
the polarities of community and work which we have been
discussing, she follows this observation by an interesting and
certainly hope-filled projection concerning spirituality: "Communal rather than individual spirituality may likely find more
emphasis as well, when groups discover that since they do not
form around common work anymore, they must form around
something of more sustaining value than a simple common
philosophy."[19] The struggle in our present-day reality is, of
course, precisely with these issues, but I do not see that we
as a whole have focused on our gathering priorities as yet. It
is my hope that what Joan Chittister projected is in process,
however. The crisis in which community life finds itself today
may be a sign of this and a holistic spirituality that empowers
those held together in bonds of friendship and mutual support
would certainly do much for authentic renewal here.

But what of the "friendship communities" she anticipates?
What kind of friendship is it that fosters community and
co-discipleship in ministry? What kind of bonding ought to
happen or might be hoped for in our communities if we *as*

women and men, as adults in truly mature ways, are to empower each other to minister for the Gospel? I believe that a
deeper understanding and living of our vow of celibacy can
be of great significance as we attempt to respond to these
questions.

What has fascinated me in reading the constitutions of numerous congregations in the last several years as I prepared
myself for retreat work with them is the stress we seem to
be placing on *communal loving* and *being loved* in our de-
scription of what this vow means to us. It seems to me that
something original is happening here: a vision, not new of
course—Benedict had it way back when[20]—but original for
our time, and after many years of drought.

More often than not in our ecclesial tradition consecrated
celibacy has been interpreted in terms of "giving up." Thus,
the decisions not to marry, not to engage in genital love, not
to have children and enjoy family, fatherhood or motherhood
(always, of course, made toward a greater end) were all primary in the identification of this vow. Books supplementing
our study of it usually went into dualistic-hierarchical details about its excellence; its connection with various stages
of human love, with purity, with chastity; its purpose and end;
its levels of renunciation; its uses and abuses.[21] To be sure, the
asceticism demanded by the vow is not ignored in our documents today, even if it is often only indirectly mentioned (by
reference to apostolic motivations, for example). What is of
interest, however, is the primacy which such concepts as "mutual love," "friendship," "support for one another" receive
in today's constitutions. We all know, of course, that these
modes of relationship also have their sacrificial dimension, but
in this context it does not lend itself easily to analysis, to dis-
section, and is met in "living" rather than in "listing." It is,
at best, described, never clearly defined. There seems to be

a natural invitation, therefore, in our documents to embrace "deeper realities," what Rahner calls the "transcendental"[22]— the "mystery" rather than the measurable, the categorical. Perhaps, then, we need to ask into this depth and wonder what it means for us to "love as consecrated celibates." To what *do* we commit ourselves when we take this vow, and what significance does it have communally?

What if we saw the loving of consecrated celibacy as an *immersing of ourselves into the pain (as well as the joy) of life fully lived?* I have asked myself this for many years now and have stated so publicly on numerous occasions. What if we truly believed that when we promise consecrated celibacy, we promise to journey into the agony and the ecstasy of relationship; into the turmoil, the pain, the revelation of ourselves to ourselves, the revelation of others, and of God which loving nonpossessively will open up for us?* We commit ourselves to love unreservedly for the sake of God's reign.[23] A powerful mandate, this! Nor does it imply that other Christians do not have similar obligations. Their bonding, however, works itself out according to their call. For married persons, for example, this implies the particularized familial setting which is theirs. Ours works itself out with other women and/or men, not so much in a coupled as in a communal and covenantal setting. Community, I believe, is primary to celibate loving, and friendship, bonding, and intimacy among us are, therefore, essential conditions for a healthy and wholesome life.

The question that needs consistently to be faced by all of us around this issue, however, and, it seems to me with increasing

---

*I wish to draw attention to this as a counter-cultural view. Loving today is expected to be smooth, cool, and painless. We fall into it as easily as we fall out of it and, if people do not satisfy our cravings, we can always, as John Francis Kavanaugh points out, "have a Romance with Olivetti," our personal computer, or telephone answering system, or engage in a "Problem-free Relationship" with the latest model car (John Francis Kavanaugh, *Following Christ in a Consumer Society* [Maryknoll, N.Y.: Orbis Books, 1981], 38.)

urgency, is how we might embrace our essential relationality with greater creativity, honesty, and authenticity. The words of Rahner quoted in chapter 2 come to mind again and seem particularly pertinent for many of us in the present experience of refounding community: "Face loneliness."[24] Few religious, I believe, would deny the reality of loneliness in our life. I wonder, however, how many among us can envision the chance of a healthy transformation of this loneliness into an authentic experience of aloneness or solitude. Both are depth dimensions intimately connected to, and in creative tension with, authentic togetherness. They help us address unhealthy needs and the desire to control and open us up to others in freedom and serenity. Rahner warns us, of course, not to envision a quick "fix" for the deeper concerns of our life (and our concerns about relationality are definitely that). In order to probe issues like these reverently, we need to dwell in them rather than to attempt to organize ourselves at the circumference of our lives together and revert, once again, to a *Gesellschaft* solution. We need, ultimately, to let questions *be* questions, even if they hurt. We need to wait. This can mean feeling very alone at times, perhaps even feeling despair. Too often, claims Rahner, especially in Catholic circles, we want neat definitions, tidy solutions. We have not developed the art of midwifery,[25] and so, very frequently, insights get aborted. He warns us that, to move into depth experience, we need to *face* loneliness, to *face* fear. We need to endure *ourselves*. We need to let ultimate, basic human experiences surface. We cannot simply talk about them, but must endure them toward transformation.

Unfortunately one cannot be educated "into" or "out of" issues of relationship. Workshops in assertiveness training and direct communication may help, but individuation—that is, touching the depths of the Self and there reaching out in love— goes deeper than that. Ultimate human experiences of fear

and loneliness, of pain and of growing-needs cannot be programmed out of existence, nor (even with the best intentions)
resolved at community goal setting. Most definitely they cannot be ignored or denied, for pain does not go away if I refuse
to look at it. They need to be *faced,* and they need to be *endured.* For this one needs time and one needs space. It is of little
value for any of us to find escape in our ministries when relational issues are too painful at home, for if we are covenanted
to a group its problems cannot be resolved in our absence. Nor
does what I have come to call the "pilgrim people excuse" hold
up when the mandate is individuation: intimacy and growth
issues take time to surface and be resolved. Whether we like it
or not, they need a certain relational stability where members
commit themselves to the same group and allow for bonding
to occur. For a community whose in and out flow is like a re-
volving door, or for an individual who changes support groups
every few years or whenever relationships begin to make demands, these issues may never surface and certainly will not
be resolved. We take ourselves and our unaddressed conflicts
wherever we go. No one except each one of us, "in patient
endurance" (Rom. 8:25) can work out our redemption (maturation, individuation), and we need a committed community
as our sacred forum for this.

It may console us to recognize that in the struggle for authentic interrelationship we are not alone. Though the ideals of
mature interdependence have been around for a while in the
textbooks of human behavior, their existential reality in our
time and in our culture is extremely rare. The worldview of
our age, as was discussed in chapter 1, is still quite entrenched
in dualistic-patriarchal (hence masculinized) values. Although
this worldview seems to be reaching a limit situation[26] with its
consequent experience of alienation and confusion, the new is
only slowly emerging. The consternation many of us feel when

we find ourselves at our wits' end in the face of communal turmoil and apathy is, therefore, not unique to us. We remember
Beatrice Bruteau's call for a genuine "revolution of consciousness," a "gestalt shift," as she puts it, "in the whole way of
seeing our relations to one another so that our behavior patterns are reformed from the inside out."[27] This is a mandate for
our culture, not one addressed to religious only. We are caught
in the same dilemma as others (married and single alike) whose
drive toward wholeness urges them beyond the very cultural
dysfunctionality in which they themselves flounder.

Unfortunately crises in culture, as well as those of personal
maturation, with which they are intimately connected, do not
resolve themselves immediately upon recognition. They come
upon us and are resolved in their own time. It may help to
understand them as events of "cosmic consciousness," ontological in nature: we do not have them as much as we are held
in them even as we are summoned to deeper consciousness and
consequent transcendence.[28] A certain surrender to the fact, a
gentle honesty which prevents us from blindly claiming im-
munity from global disorder, might be one way of embracing
Rahner's invitation to "endure" ourselves. It will also preserve
us from the illusion that matters are easier, more "together"
in other walks of life.

Called to Vulnerability

Perhaps in this matter of relationship we need also to accept,
once again, the primacy of disposition (something which in an
action- and success-oriented world may be extremely difficult).
I seriously doubt that any kind of community is fostered primarily by what we do in it or about it: whether it is residential
or nonresidential and if the former, where or with how many
persons we live, how often we meet, what we meet about, and

whether there is or is not an agenda for the meeting. Although these issues may be important, our main concern for all models of community, simplistic as this may sound, is whether we trust each other; whether we can be vulnerable, poor, in each other's presence; whether there is, when we encounter one another, a basic stance of openness to the self-revelation of God in this meeting. This will allow for community to happen and, whether we consciously admit it or not, we know that nothing else will. Claiming celibacy as a commitment to love each other finds its meaning and place here also. We are not dealing with rules and regulations, with measurable data as to how one should or should not behave. We are embracing an attitude, an open readiness for encounter, a willingness to be met.

The paradox presented here cannot be ignored: we claim that attitude, disposition, is primary to action; without it no amount of activity is going to bring about successful bonding. Yet it is in interaction that attitude is deepened, pruned, empowered, chastised. In interaction life moves us into mature celibacy, into the depth of bonding and of relationship. Perhaps the reflection-action-reflection model which so many of us have used in discernment processes can serve as a model to explain this. One could say that our initial openness gets deepened further and matures through interaction. We move from openness to action (interaction), to greater openness. This may be illustrated in the following example:

1. *Disposition:* I come to a relationship, into a community with a disposition based on initial faith-filled trust. I have attempted to leave aside those assumptions, presuppositions, prejudices, and negative memories which may be present in me and of which I am aware. I have tried to "bracket them," so to speak, though it is unreal and unhealthy to resolve to forget them. I simply decide not to let them influence me unjustly. I hope for fresh beginnings, for community built on the convic-

tion that growth is and has been in process in all of our lives. Even now, of course, my openness is not total. I, like all of humankind, carry the burdens of my own past—my facticity, my prison walls within. They are often unconscious, buried deep in the denial and repression of past pains: a dysfunctional family, childhood humiliations and abuse, shame of one kind or another, trauma, guilt. Those with whom I relate and interact encounter me out of their facticity also, their openness clouded with unconscious projections, unacknowledged expectations.

2. *Interaction:* We stretch each other. We care for as well as hurt each other. Our trust might turn to distrust. We feel rejection, pain. We are wounded. Here it is that our vow to love each other enters into the picture: we embrace the flood of life to which we committed ourselves by this form of relationship, with all the anguish, turmoil, and grace. We allow ourselves to endure it all, to be with it, to let it teach us. *And we pray!* We pray that we might see as God sees and love as God loves. We do not run away from the flood of pain or busy ourselves with ministerial concerns, but immerse ourselves into a deepened attitude of openness, of trust-grown-wiser.

3. *Deepened Disposition:* And compassionately we walk this earth. Having met, and continuing to meet, our own noonday devil, and knowing how weak we are, we support others in their brokenness. We love.

Taking Ownership of Our Feelings

There may be many different emotions as we move into relationship, into celibate loving, into communal bonding. For those among us who are firmly established in pre–Vatican II training and values, there may be fear, real anxiety. We were never allowed to show our feelings toward others, be they positive or negative. Over the years we have built walls, therefore. We may not even know that we have built them. We may be convinced that our rationalizations are expressions of feelings. Behind them we find ourselves often passively aggressive, obsequious, or gossipy for "sister's or brother's own good." We might come to believe that our silence is virtue while we are like volcanoes that have never erupted. Perhaps our celibate chastity has never been lived. It may have been avoided instead. For us the emptiness of the "virgin waiting to be filled,"[29] the self-sacrifice of total responsibility discussed in chapter 3, was interpreted as abnegation for its own sake. As such it resulted more frequently in a separation from our deepest center—from that part of us that reverberates with passion and with life—than in a life-fulfilling union. Propriety rather than passion was our guiding principle. We did what was expected of us as good religious. Our guiding force was outside of us. When we now hear talk of bonding and intimacy we feel confused and upset. Friendships in our time were frowned upon and regarded with suspicion. Voicing our views was seen as pride and confrontation, the prerogative of the superior. Relational pain is something we may feel or have felt, yes, but we have none of the tools whereby to acknowledge it. Talk of it, therefore, makes us fearful and nervous.

Then there are those among us who are newer in the congregation. We entered, most likely, *for* community with the clear intention of living together. We came to bond, to relate. We now want what we came for, and we want it our way. We find it difficult to comprehend why those we live with may be more reticent. We find ourselves impatient with them at times, and perhaps judgmental. We want to say and show what we feel, when we feel it. We often feel passionately and we may discover, if we have not done so before, that as women we can feel this for women, as men, for men. We may not know why this is happening all of a sudden, and we may feel guilty and ashamed. We may not know what to do with this. We may confide and then feel betrayed by the seeming lack of response, or the fear, or even the failure of confidentiality. These experiences can be bitterly disappointing for us and result in thorough confusion. We may radically question why we are here and may even want to give up.

There are also those among us who are angry (and perhaps these are the majority). We are angry at a community that never understood us or that understood us too late. We are angry at the church that still does not understand nor seem to care. We are angry at our parents who were alcoholic or narcissistic, who perhaps were poor or died too young, with whom we could never relate and who, therefore, never taught us the skills we now so desperately need. We are angry at the choice we made in life for reasons we may now question. We are lonely and we may wonder what we are now doing here, yet see no sufficient reason for leaving. We may desperately want intimacy but may feel that our life-pattern or the reputation we have been "saddled with" in the institute prevents it. Perhaps behind our anger there also is fear of being hurt in the process.

We bring all these feelings—our fears, our expectations, disappointment, and confusion, our anger and our loneliness— with us into relationship. We rarely leave anything behind and ought not deny any of it. We say one to another in the depths of our hearts as we struggle with our feelings and perhaps with our guilt: "I am a vowed religious, a celibate woman, a celibate man, moving into evangelical chastity. I am trying to be (in Henri J. M. Nouwen's words) the *Vacare Deo*,[30] the empty space for the breakthrough of God; the virgin mother, as the mystics would see it; the mirror in whom the divine manifests not only himself but perhaps for the first time at this point in my life—because of my struggle for wholeness—herself as well. I can do this only if you help me, if, as we journey together, as we relate and bond, you help me reveal myself to myself and to you as the crucified and the resurrected Christ.[31] As I am your com-panion, the one who breaks bread with you, be with me in this, as I will be with you, and I vow not to forsake the quest."

This is the stuff, as I see it, of celibate loving, of bonding, the bonding of women, of men, in an honest, insightful, and interdependent way. It has nothing to do with antiseptic sweetness, with perpetual "niceness," with always being in a good mood and never struggling for availability. Nor does it mean liking everyone equally. It has everything to do with integrity, with commitment, with reverence for diversity and willingness to grow. It has everything to do with patience and with waiting and with working out the redemption of our emotions and interactions in the blood, sweat, and tears of our existential nows. "The whole world," says Jung, "is God's suffering, and every individual who wants to get anywhere near his [or her] own wholeness knows that this is the way of the cross. But the eternal promise for him [or her] who bears his [or her] own cross is the Paraclete,"[32] the Spirit of life that groans within us.

A woman in labor waits—not passively, but creatively. Our life is a process of birthing, a movement into God, a deliberate, a quiet, sometimes chaotic, often agonized letting be. There are no quick answers or solutions to learning how to live lovingly. There will be the pangs of birth and the joys of birth, and then there will be the dying and the being born over and over and over again.

Celibate loving, holistic bonding, calls us toward honest, dedicated, mutual empowerment in the life process of maturation and holiness. Anything short of this will, I believe, choke community life and destroy our institutes. If we dare live this love fully, it will, in spite of the contrary claims of our culture, be our vehicle toward wholeness. It will bring us depth and fulfillment, but it will also, and inexorably, lead us through loneliness into the "final solitude" Rahner mentioned, for it will expose us to the radical insufficiency of all human loving and reveal us to ourselves as the living symbols of all of humanity's ultimate and ontological homesickness for God.*

Living the Tension

In an article about the famous American poet May Sarton, Kathryn North meditates on Sarton's "willingness to face the challenges of creative solitude."[33] She suggests that Sarton found the rewards of seeking solitude paralleling the rewards found in facing "the challenges of creative relationship," namely, to "move from a state of mere togetherness to a depth experience of *being with* another: what might be called the moment of vulnerability."[34] North writes: "It is this vulnerability, this nakedness to the other that allows our human relationships to open out into depth communion, not only with one another at the creative level," and for us this is clearly the ministry level, "but with the Ground of Being at the depth level as well."[35]

Perhaps it is this word "vulnerability" once again that holds the key for us in this reflection. We have grown so strong. We are so busy now. We have become so good, so professional at what we do in so many diverse fields. We find ourselves, however, in a functional, efficient world and in a functional, efficient church structure. To be good in it means in many ways to succumb to its values of toughness, logic, certainty, exclu-

---

*For the mystical dimension as well as the symbolic significance of consecrated celibacy see Barbara Fiand, *Wrestling with God* (New York: Crossroad, 1996), part 2.

sivity, ambition, and power. The ways of gentleness, mystery, inclusivity, compassion, and vulnerability do not speak in this world, nor in this church. Yet these are the ways of Christ-filled love, the keys to bonding, to mutual empowerment, to companioning, to life-giving community. We stand in the tension, then, of what appears to be the polarity between the professional and a loving relational life. A "community for mission," if it is to mean anything at all rather than remaining merely a pious platitude, will have to evaluate this tension, examine it holistically in the light of the Gospel, and challenge its possible excesses. Each one of us also, as a member of a religious community and as minister, needs to balance his or her priorities honestly. This challenge is real and it is complex, but it is the challenge of our time. We ignore it only at the risk of our personal and communal integrity.

Some Reflections on
Our Existential Situation

We began the reflections on "Relationship and Intimacy" by suggesting that a community which empowers each one of us to stand in the truth of his or her own integrity will have to be not only of adults, but also *for* us *as* adults. The "primary family" model will not do any longer, whether our parent figures are congregational leaders, pastors, moderators, coordinators, or even just our own sisters and brothers who either appoint themselves or whom we appoint to parent us. Authentic interrelationship demands sensitivity to appropriate emotional distance. Just as depth community is not possible for people who live next to each other without meeting, busy about their separate affairs like atomized apartment dwellers in a metropolitan high-rise, it is also impossible for overdemanding grown-up children who have never learned to stand within and accept the poverty of their own authentic personhood and who, therefore, make the satisfaction of their overblown dependencies the condition for peaceful interaction. I suggested, therefore, Sandra Schneiders' "community of friends who are co-disciples in ministry" as possibly a more appropriate model for adult communities.

The movement, however, into this model cannot be assumed to be easy. It is anything but a simple adult decision. The art of interdependent relating, already mentioned, is "virgin territory" on the map of human development and, though good intentions always help, the day-to-day working out of it is a painful business. The main problem lies, I believe, in the fact that although maturation (individuation) is the business particularly of our adult years, adulthood and maturity do not necessarily coincide. Whereas the former is linear and can be identified with relative chronological accuracy, the latter is a spiraling process which is not so much achieved as it is surrendered to. We are motivated (driven) by the urge to maturation very much as we are motivated (driven) by hunger, thirst, and the desire for happiness. But the stirrings of our urges are not always at out beck and call. With regard to maturation, we can at best be open, willing, and ready. "The wind blows where [and when] it wills" (John 3:8) and with the intensity it chooses. Our experience of it, though it always is grace, can sometimes feel like affliction. And so when we enter into a community even with the best resolutions, the movements of our various journeys may bring with them much pain and conflict, and the call to let be, while "becoming" is happening at all kinds of levels, may often be very difficult to hear. This is particularly true for conventual living or for a living situation modeled after this style of community, because of the physical proximity one experiences there almost continuously. Mary Wolff-Salin puts it well:

We all come into community life, as into marriage, carrying images from the past still insufficiently integrated. Learning not to project these onto others is a long process. Authority figures are the easiest target, but so is any other person who is powerful, gifted, a leader, manipulative, or simply very different from us. It is a long struggle to discover that most of the passions aroused by these issues have to do with my own inner world and conflicts, rather than with the ordinary—or even less ordinary—flesh-and-blood people around me. Few people and institutions have the authority and power our complexes tend to project onto them.[36]

Learning that this is so (withdrawing projections) is, however, an arduous task, and we tend to suffer much, often at our own (unconscious) hands.

Encountering the Shadow

Harsh as it may sound, I do believe there is truth in the statement that in many situations we are as oppressed as we allow ourselves to be, both institutionally and personally. In the former case we can often give the letter of institutional regulations much more power than it deserves, simply because we are not willing to risk the freedom of responsible interpretation. In the latter case, is it not true that the oppression in many of our communities comes from dysfunctionality not addressed? How often does Sister X's pouting, temper tantrum, weeping, complaining, or gossip dictate our individual or group decisions? How frequently do we yield to the one who talks most or loudest or is the pushiest, and then wonder why communal discernment is ineffective? Our fears, anxieties, feelings of inferiority, reluctance to confront, hesitation to speak up, to make decisions, and to take responsibility are, however, as much rooted in an insufficiently integrated past as Sister X's temper tantrum or Brother Y's pushiness. Furthermore, what we see in others is frequently exacerbated by our very own propensity for the same, though it may have been unrecognized or repressed since childhood and often clouded by the intentional cultivation of its opposite. A facilitator friend of mine once shared with me her utter amazement at the frequency of projection in conflictual situations: "I sit there," she told me, "and marvel how it is that Brother M is totally unaware that he is doing precisely what he is accusing his companion of." Jung attests to my friend's observation by a variety of succinct aphorisms recorded by Jolande Jacobi and R. F. C. Hull and well worth our notice:

> Our unwillingness to see our own faults and the projection of them onto others is the source of most quarrels, and the strongest guarantee that injustice, animosity, and persecution will not easily die out.
>
> A person's hatred is always concentrated on the thing that makes him [or her] conscious of his [or her] bad qualities.
>
> A [person] who is unconscious of himself [or herself] acts in a blind, instinctive way and is in addition fooled by all the illusions that arise when he [or she] sees everything that he [or she] is not conscious of in himself [or herself] coming to meet him [or her] from outside as projections upon his [or her] neighbor.[37]

Jung insists, of course, that those upon whom we project our own darkness (or light, for that matter) are not necessarily without blame: "Even the worst projection is at least hung on a hook, perhaps a very small one, but still a hook offered by the other person."[38] Nevertheless, I think it is safe to suggest that our capacity to perceive both vice and virtue in another is directly proportional to our own propensity in their regard. Awareness of this might do much to foster healthy and compassionate communal interaction and constructive rather than destructive confrontation.

The shadow which we encounter through our interaction with others, though its presence appears more often as adversarial, is really, if encountered openly and embraced, a tremendous helpmate toward maturation and integration. Many of those who are walking the mid-life journey recognize in him or her the gate-keeper to the second half of life. To face the hidden and feared dimensions of my personality and yet to survive, even more, to come to know peace in the encounter and to meet, perhaps for the first time in my life, my sisters and brothers as companions in the brokenness pours radiance into the darkness and makes redemption of the sin. It furthers authentic maturation.[39] To be sure, the potentials for growth envisioned here in our interaction do not present our togetherness as a blissful haven of tranquility, but, as Mary Wolff-Salin rightfully points out: "If there is no conflict, no honesty, nothing real can be built. But if I can be able to share with those around me my weakness and pain as well as my strength, my nastiness as well as my love, perhaps it is worth the struggle of a less perfect seeming harmony."[40]

This is not always immediately obvious, of course, to those of us who feel particularly in need of "some peace and quiet" even as, often unwittingly, we may ourselves be contributing to our own as well as communal unrest by the inner "maturation turmoil" we are experiencing. Hence, during times when an understanding community could be especially helpful, the temptation to flee it may be the most intense. There simply is no way around the fact, however, that we encounter our shadow primarily in our interactions with others. The recognition and acceptance of our fundamental co-being is essential here. Wolff-Salin says it well:

> The struggle to withdraw projections and integrate the dark aspects of reality, to find and get in touch with my own authority while recognizing those of others, the work of coming to terms with the contra-sexual—within and around me—all these are necessary steps on the path toward increasing selfhood and openness to the Self deeper and greater than my own. Life together in community can help this process. But it is not an easy way.[41]

Further Reflections on Intimacy

Developing an authentic "community of friends" also carries with it numerous concrete questions about intimacy. To begin with, those of us who live together know that the friendship and bonding to be experienced in our living of the vows cannot be expected to be of equal depth with every person with whom we share community, nor is it denied, of course, to persons with whom we do not live. Either case would be quite unrealistic and, given the human condition, quite impossible, in fact. Personality type, interests, education, background, life experience, culture, ethnic group, and numerous other factors often quite intangible all play a role in drawing persons to each other or keeping them apart. It may be true that we are all members of the same congregation, joined by the same charism, and dedicated to furthering the reign of God, but, beautiful and empowering as this is, it is no guarantee that we all will, therefore, like each other or will like each other equally well. The vow of celibacy, as I have tried to reflect on it in these pages, lays the stress on our willingness to love one another, not necessarily to be attracted to one another.

We are called to immerse ourselves into life with one another: to live it to the fullest, in open responsiveness to relationship with all its beauty and its pain. This immersion will have its dyings and its risings, its closeness and its distance, its positive as well as its negative aspects. Living these means facing them honestly. Openness to relationship does not mean that we can be all things to all people, that we can at all times be present to all members of our community in exactly the way they need or want it. Nor can we expect them to be so for us.

It may be true that in the model of community living in which many of us were trained we used to do everything together, and some of us may in those days even have believed that this implied at-oneness and love. We know today, however, if we did not know then, that there is more to authentic interrelation than doing things together. The physical proximity of my brothers and sisters does not guarantee their presence, just as their physical distance from me does not suggest their absence. Authentic interrelationship points to presence and the gentle intimacy it provides. This is not necessarily obtained according to the mandates of proximity, and may even be curtailed, especially if there is too much of it.

All this seems obvious enough, and one might legitimately wonder whether it needs to be brought up at all. We have lived, after all, for thirty or more years now in settings quite different from those of the early "formation" of many of us. Today, it would seem, we are hard pressed to find even prayer time together. Yet, it seems to me, in the area of emotional needs the tendency to claim togetherness as a right in order to avoid real or perceived exclusion, or to see togetherness as a substitute for intimacy and thus to avoid the hard work this entails, is, nevertheless, still prevalent today. The reality is that living life to the fullest means embracing intimacy issues honestly and freely. My community is not my home if I cannot work out at least some of my affective needs there. Our journey into wholeness includes the working through of our relational issues and should make this possible for us at least to some extent in the company of those whom we have joined in covenant. Yet it is a fact that what all of this will entail in the concrete is rarely explored by us collectively and to its roots. Somehow these matters still seem too painful or too complex for us to address, and it is, therefore, easier to dismiss attempts at new ways of bonding by holding up what was as normative and resisting creative critique.

What, for example, are we really saying when we urge a return to residential community living with the observation that "newer members today are looking for community"? Do we honestly believe that their major motivation for religious life is the desire to live under one roof in order to "pray and share household tasks," as Mary Johnson puts it, and that in so doing empowerment for ministry will be enhanced?[42] Would that things were as simple as that! Might it not benefit all of us to explore seriously whether, in fact, living together *truly* enhances the mission, rather than simply taking for granted that it does? Might one ask, without prejudice, what the desire for living in community actually means to the individual seeking it and whether, without a serious probing into the whys of this, it can be taken at face value as an adequate and self-explanatory reason for becoming a religious? Has anyone, in fact, ever explored the reason for this need for the common life among the younger applicants to religious orders? Is it a value that is seen by us in the light of our tradition, or do we need to examine it nonjudgmentally in the context of today as, in fact, we also need to examine the growing phenomenon of religious seeking to live alone?

It seems to me that even if newer members want community,

it would, nevertheless, be naive and at best premature to suggest that our return to the common life—having a plethora of women or men living together—would solve our membership problem. Why must it be, as Johnson citing Doris Gottemoeller suggests, that "true" community can only tolerate living alone as an "exception,"[43] and where is the data establishing that those who choose to live in what some have come to call "nonresidential community," are in fact less involved with congregational matters and the mission and are, therefore, "in a different category" from those who live "under the same roof and interact daily"?[44]

The questions which Mary Johnson in her *Review for Religious* article of March–April 2000 wants to keep separate might need to be kept apart for a peaceful discussion, but, if we are to look at "community living" honestly, holistically, and in a nonaccusatory way, these are precisely the kinds of questions that need to be explored *together.* We may wish to recall the earlier reference to Parker Palmer's remarks about conflict as necessary at times if we, indeed, are to further the truth among us and to stretch each other. Whether "the daily interaction" possible in a common life situation is "life-giving or death-dealing" has enormous probative value in the examination of our life if we are, in fact, looking for the actual reasons for the changes in our mode of being together and of witnessing love in a world that so desperately needs it. It is my experience that the diversity in our living situations that seems to have evolved from the grassroots and is, at this point in history, a real aspect of our being together cannot be ignored or rejected high-handedly. It happened precisely as a result of individuals responding to concerns that the group did not want to address, and because of it the whole tenor today of what used to be called "community life" has changed. This is the reality addressing us today as is the fact of our ever depleting residential community settings. Neither of these realities can be addressed without the other.

Clearly the hunger today is for relationship furthered by a common vision. This is not unique to new members. It calls for a standing together, a being there, a sustained love which, although it can be found, and often has its beginning, in physical togetherness, can also transcend it.* I do not argue with Johnson's questions at the end of her essay in *Review for Religious*[45] and laud the suggestion that they be explored collectively by all. I fear, however, that her assumption that the concept of community disintegrates when it is expanded beyond life under one roof and that this is, in fact, a serious problem for us,[46] is founded on a bias which in itself would prejudice the very discussions she invites.

How the legitimate need for intimacy and depth relationship can be responded to in religious life today is a much deeper question than reflections on the need to return to residential communities. It is a question that addresses all of us in the most authentic sense of our "belonging" to one another, a question that connects us deeply to the mission of Jesus, to the wholesomeness and health of the members of his Body called to celibate life in a congregation founded in his name. Whether life in common fosters growth and allows for intimacy, how it needs to change if it does not, what other creative lifestyles might be explored to further our life in mission such as it is today, as well as to nurture our needs: these are all questions that need unbiased attention in the revisioning of our life.

Perhaps it is true that only intimacy allows for intimacy. When our communities, however they are created, become our homes, and we can be for each other without fear and in nonjudgmental ways, intimacy may become less elusive and we

---

*I refer the reader to appendix 3, an essay I first wrote for *Sisters Today* in honor of my friend Pat Underhill, S.C., whose life and death bears powerful witness to this.

may begin to see it as a natural and healthy part of our being together, a normal phenomenon of maturation. "Fear," Henri Nouwen tells us, "prevents us from forming an intimate community in which we can grow together, everyone in his or her own way," where we can "confess to each other our sins, our brokenness, and our wounds," where we can "forgive each other and come to reconciliation."[47] Intimacy, on the other hand, allows for space to grow, for littleness and vulnerability and honesty.

Our Homesickness for God

In his book *Inner Loneliness*, Sebastian Moore makes the bold suggestion that the desire that can make people desperate enough to move into addictive behavior of whatever kind is really deep down the desire to have their nagging emptiness filled by unreserved, unconditional, unending love, in other words, by God.[48] "In the depths of my ultimate loneliness," he says, "where none can reach me, I want there to be Another whose very 'to be' is 'to be for me,' whose selfhood is not a selfhood into which he [or she] must ultimately retreat leaving me to mine." I want someone "constitutionally involved with me, and constitutionally other than me. And this *is* 'what all call God.' "[49] Moore contends that human loneliness for the ultimate, because its intensity can often be quite unbearable, frequently gets displaced. "People try to fulfill *with each other* the insatiable requirement of inner loneliness, to be totally entered and led forth into the whole ecstasy of existence. That there *is* this need for God in us is shown by the fact that we demand of each other to *be* God for us."[50] The history of human loving is one of unquenchable thirst.

Men and women religious here, as in all other aspects of the human condition, are very much part of history. We might have hoped that joining a community of adults for adults as adults would allow us to escape the pain of misplaced expectations of intimacy and even addictive emotional dependency. This, however, simply is not the case. Adulthood, as we all know, does not imply maturity. The latter, as the spiraling process it is, has a tendency, regardless of the pain, to bring us over and over again into our own past in order to move us toward ever deeper levels of integration. This is a difficult concept to appreciate in a culture where "having it all together" once and for all is the sign of integrative excellence. In my own work I often tell people: "Having it all together means knowing that you don't and accepting this fact with equanimity." This is the truth of maturation as journey. It is generally messy and excruciatingly on its own time.

It may help to know that with regards to "inner loneliness" and the possibility of displaced affect, contemporary religious as a group are in a particularly vulnerable situation. To begin with, as Charles L. Whitfield, M.D., estimates, "from 60 to 80 percent of today's men and women religious come from dysfunctional family settings."[51] Many of us, therefore, belong quite readily among Alice Miller's "Prisoners of Childhood": Women and men who because of their parents' inability to parent and to be for them what they desperately and rightfully needed learned early in life to reverse roles, becoming "well-behaved, reliable, empathic, understanding, and convenient child[ren]," who for the most part, however, were never really allowed to be children at all, and who now spend a good deal of their adult life seeking their lost love.[52] Alice Miller writes her book primarily for therapists who by their sensitivity and care for the feelings of others have, in fact, developed the virtues of their affliction but not without pain: the pain, namely, of facing, of grieving, of mourning, and ultimately of letting go what never was for them and never really will be.

Many religious, in this respect, are very similar to therapists.*
They developed in the earliest years of life concernful attention to the needs of their elders in order to get what little love
they could. Their legitimate needs, however, were never met.
They became like sponges absorbing the pain of others while
their own longing for love remained like an open wound. Their
ministerial concern for, and awareness of, the needs of others
today (gifts of their deprivation, as it were) frequently speaks
of the neglect they suffered in their childhood. They too now
need a forum where they can come to see the futility of seeking
in their adult life what they were deprived of as children and
what will never be theirs in human terms. They need to mourn
it and to let it go.

It would, of course, be ideal if these issues were dealt with
prior to entry into religious community. The recommendations
for counseling certainly help our newer members in this regard. The truth is, however, that their "novice director" may
be dealing with the same pain and all its affective struggles still
and so might the regional and even the congregational leaders,
and so will the newer members as they journey through life,
for it is a life issue that rarely gets cleared up quickly. There
really is precious little one can do about the human condition
except acknowledge it and support others in it, hoping for the
same from them. This is what I have tried to say "vowing to
love one another in community" is all about. Letting-go, as
final as it may sound, is not a once-in-a-lifetime decision. We
die daily at ever deeper levels of surrender.

A second factor to be considered as we reflect on the particular vulnerability of religious in community today is the fact

---

*The deprivation we are talking about here is not necessarily the result of our parents'
willful neglect. Dysfunctionality can be the result of violence in the society, war, poverty,
youthful ignorance on the part of the parent, death. The parents in these situations are
victimized too and often have no evil intent.

that the vast majority of active religious in our congregations are dealing with the growth issues of the second half of life. It is particularly during the "second journey," as Jungians call it, that the need for inner integration takes hold of us and our individual stories need literally to be re-membered into our lives. Intimacy needs which may not have been consciously felt or acknowledged before, or which we may never even have known we had, frequently surface during this time with frightening acuteness. As the authors of *Chaos or Creation* see it, there are a variety of reasons for this:

> The growing sense of mortality that creates the common "last chance" mentality; the recognition of my destructive capabilities that may drive me to long for the one perfect, integral relationship; the emptiness of my personal relationships, or my prayer life (or both) that leave me lonely or empty, and longing for fulfillment.[53]

And, as was already suggested, there are the deprivations of childhood which have finally broken through the taboos that caused repression of their memory and which now come to haunt me, together with struggles to forgive and deep feelings of isolation and inadequacy. These are only a few. The emotional turmoil and confusion and the agonizing recognition of needs can at times be almost unbearable. It is not uncommon, therefore, that often deep emotional attachments are formed to help weather the storm; sometimes also, perhaps, to avoid it or postpone it. Religious may quite literally experience the "falling in love" which they never expected for themselves. This can be a real learning experience for them if the support and environment are right, but it can also come as a great surprise and sometimes even as a severe shock. To add to their confusion, they may also discover that the gender of the beloved seems often of little relevance to the feelings they have. The pain and guilt of this experience especially if it takes genital expression can frequently be as acute as the fascination is exhilarating. Although someone more advanced in the integration process may, as Moore points out, quite readily see here an infatuation which ultimately points beyond itself, it usually is of little use to suggest this until the person involved can hear it. It may be true, as scholars tell us, that "the sexual drive and the unitive drive (or the religious impulse) in human beings is the same."[54] The discovery of this, however, in one's incarnate being is a long and arduous process.

Nevertheless, religious, trying to make sense of their relational struggles, might at least draw some consolation from the fact that the maturation process and the life-force within us, in spite of the emotional chaos through which we may pass in our experience of it, has an ontological momentum toward the transcendent. Gerald May, echoing Moore somewhat and speaking here very much within the context of the holistic paradigm discussed in chapter 1, suggests that all emotional experience is grounded in the same kind of "root" energy of the spirit and toward the whole. He points out, however, that the expression and use of this energy may be distorted because of *insufficient awareness of this.* Referring to the "transmutation of energy" he says:

> The experience of emotions as manifestations of raw energy can shed considerable light on the relationship between sexuality and spirituality. If the energy that fires both sexual and spiritual feelings is indeed a common "root" force, the distortions of sexuality and spirituality...can be seen as resulting not only from confusions about the *nature of longing* but also from primary *misdirections* in the processing of emotional energy. Any given stimulus may become connected with either spiritual or

sexual associations and thus acquire a sexual or spiritual label. . . .

To some degree, individual intentionality or choice can affect the processing of an initial burst of emotional energy. The extent of this influence is directly proportional to one's *clarity of awareness* of the process of emotional formation.[55]

May's insight may make it less difficult for us to understand why seemingly self-possessed religious, in moments of more acute vulnerability and loss (such as, but not restricted to, the mid-life crisis), seem to lose equilibrium at times and may need particular sensitivity and care. What they experience acutely is the sexual or erotic aspect of the same basic life energy moving through each one of us and more or less capable of being focused, differentiated, and channeled or being misdirected and misused on our part. Our presence to each other during such times needs to be one of compassionate sensitivity and mature friendship.

It is clear that, in an age of sexual idolatry such as ours, blindness to the appropriate use of life-energy is prevalent. The dualism of our culture makes awareness of the holistic momentum of our "root" energy extremely difficult. The resultant exaggeration and distortion which in past decades may have come to the fore as "angelism" or Victorianism is today expressed in eroticism and the immediate satisfaction of all cravings. "It must be right because it feels so good," is our culture's slogan as it seeks fulfillment through instant gratification. It is here where the counter-cultural stance of one called to consecrated celibacy can be extremely significant. It witnesses to a world where the genital expression of love virtually excludes all other relational expressions and where sexuality is degraded by its absolutization. It claims that there *can* be other modes of loving, that there can be intimacy without the exploitation and manipulation to which "appetite" so frequently reduces relationship, that sexuality belongs to an embodied wholeness wherein its expression is holy but need not necessarily be genitally manifested at all times. It speaks of inwardness and of human yearning beyond the human, of emptiness endured to make room for the sacred.[56]

The fact that religious in the past have rarely, if ever, discussed or addressed their own sexual nature with any kind of seriousness or depth can, of course, be a disadvantage to their witnessing potential here. It has crippled many of us in our own differentiation and channeling of primal energy and frequently prevents us even now from being able effectively to celebrate and enjoy the powers of celibate loving. We live, as I mentioned already, in an age of sexual promiscuity and confusion. "Sexual liberation" for many means precisely the opposite: compulsive surrender to every genital urge. The notion of celibate freedom often seems to escape us as we are haunted by intimations of neurotic repression, sexual frustration, and even deviance and abnormality in a culture which has mechanized sexuality and devalues intimacy on virtually every available billboard and television commercial. Teresa Bielecki of the Spiritual Life Institute in Colorado, when asked how members of her community deal with physical desire, offered some interesting observations concerning the experience of celibate freedom:

> First of all, obviously, you recognize what's happening. You see it in terms of your ultimate commitment to celibacy, and you don't hate yourself for it, because sexual desire is normal and human; it is a power and a gift. Then you deal with it creatively. *You have to recognize that you are free to choose. This is why celibacy has so*

much to offer our culture. We are *free to choose*. People need to know that, because a lack of genuine freedom is killing our culture, killing sexuality, killing marriage, killing love. People feel that every time they experience desire, they have to act on it. There are *other* ways to act on it besides genitally.[57]

With May, Bielecki believes that "sexual energy is the life-energy at the heart of every human person. We can choose to exercise that human potential genitally or not."[58]

Some time ago while I was teaching at the Athenaeum of Ohio, a young man in his fourth year of theology at the seminary stopped into my office for a little self-reflection. He shared with me that day his thoughts and concerns regarding celibacy: "On the day of ordination," he mused, "I do not want to be asked about promising celibacy. I want to be at the point where I can volunteer it: 'Oh, Bishop, and by the way, I choose celibacy as my way of living out ordained ministry.'" Somehow this young person saw a lack of integrity in being forced into celibacy for the sake of a ministry. For life to be significant *we must freely choose it*. No doubt, he will have to make his life's choice over and over again, as all religious serious about their vocation do also. Forced celibacy, at best, is meaningless; at worst, it demeans both the person and the creative energy that flows through him or her. Consecrated celibacy embraced freely points beyond itself and bears witness to human interiority. This, most likely, will never be totally without struggle. As Kavanaugh rightly points out:

> The pains of relinquishment can be frequent and intense. The physical incompletions felt in intimacy without genital orientation or expression are filled with difficulties, purifications, and an aching vacuum close to the bottom of one's physical life. Care and carefulness are difficult to

express in an integral way, and the sequential struggles found in a life of celibacy are as trying as the struggles in married love.[59]

There is also always the temptation to fill one's emptiness with surrogate loves. Moore's "addictions" can be plentiful. We can easily spend a lifetime as exemplary "celibates" whose sexual abstinence cannot be faulted but whose displaced affective energy hankers after "things, possessions, games, professionalism, achievement and the collection of trifles,"[60] not to forget the unavoidable "additional member" of every household: television and its countless flights into unreality. Affection that is displaced rather than transformed has us live shallow and dehydrated lives surrounded by the inconsequential. We lack the passion of the real.

A tragic fantasy assails me on occasions of reflection such as this to remind me of my own weakness in this regard: I see myself on my death bed haunted by the indescribable agony of a single regret which can be phrased quite simply in one sentence: "Too late have I loved Thee." Our freedom as consecrated celibates is a serious business. Our lives are destined to point all human longing to its ultimate fulfillment in the Heart of God, to give special visibility to what Nouwen identifies as the "inner sanctum," the "holy empty space in human life,"[61] where intimacy with God awaits all our loneliness and yearnings. We come to an in-depth realization of this, our vocation, only slowly, sometimes all too slowly, and often very painfully—in the stripping of our own lives and the searing of our own hearts to which loving in community exposes us. Our initial motivations go, therefore, through innumerable levels of fine-tuning, agonizing purifications, betrayals, and rededications.

In these last several pages I have tried to reflect on the particularly acute vulnerability of religious today. It is my sense that perhaps precisely because of it, as wounded witnesses, we are called to stand for the "priority of God in all relationship,"[62] to give testimony to the ultimacy of the Holy, the inadequacy of all human loves, and our fundamental homesickness for God. Our prayer must be that at all times "God's strength is made perfect in [our] weakness" (2 Cor. 12:9). Thus, we experience our utter dependency on God and it is here that we ultimately find our freedom. Living into this destiny of ours, like living into the sacrament of matrimony for others, is, as I mentioned already, a life-long task, not an accomplished fact on the day of profession. But it is *our* task. Our call is to embrace it in gratitude and freedom.

Questions for Focus, Reflection, and Discussion

1. What are the gathering priorities in your community? Is religious life for you centered around celibacy and its defining characteristic or do you focus on charism and how it might be expressed today? Are these issues clear for you or do they need further reflection?

2. How comfortable do you feel about broadening the notion of membership beyond the defining characteristics of celibacy? What do you think of Transformative Element 8 (see p. 110)?

3. How comfortable are you with our post–Vatican II diversification of ministries, or ways of living together?

4. Can you identify with the *Gesellschaft* model of togetherness described in this chapter? Have you experienced it? Where in your religious life have you experienced *Gemeinschaft*? Do you relate to the Parker Palmer model

adapted here for us? What are your thoughts about the characteristics he identifies for an authentic community?

5. Is your experience of community one of women or men *for* women or men *as* women or men? What does this mean for you?

6. How can our ways of bonding be liberated from the sometimes coercive or prescriptive models we use to create community?

7. How comfortable are you with the idea that living celibate chastity is a life-long task, not an accomplished fact on the day of profession? (This, of course, would apply to the other vows as well.)

8. What are your primary feelings and emotions as you move into living your celibacy relationally—fear, anger, confidence, joy, hope, anxiety, discouragement, etc.? Why is this so?

9. What has been your experience of friendship in community? Have you felt empowered in your experience of intimacy and have you empowered others? Do you experience friendships as a positive element in community interrelations?

10. Has your appreciation of consecrated celibacy been enhanced through mature and serious discussion about sexuality and the channeling and focusing of life energy? If not, would you see this kind of discussion as useful in helping you effectively to enjoy and celebrate the powers of celibate loving?

11. How do you see the connection between solitude and creative relationship? What about loneliness—does it exist in community? If so, what do we learn from it?

12. Do you see residential community as mandatory for religious life? If so, why? If not, why not? What is your reaction to religious living alone? Do you live alone? If so, how do you see your connectedness with the congregation? How do you see yourself as a "community member"? What are your learnings?

13. What are the values and the difficulties of living together? Does physical proximity guarantee "presence"? What is "presence"? Does life together empower you for the mission? If so, how? If not, what would have to happen for you to feel empowered?

14. "Our unwillingness to see our own faults and the projection of them onto others is the source of most quarrels, and the strongest guarantee that injustice, animosity, and persecution will not easily die out." What do you think of this observation?

15. What has been your experience of "learning" intimacy? How do you see the connection between celibacy and freedom?

Chapter Five

CREATIVE FIDELITY

A dear friend of mine some years ago told me that in his view the most creative word ever uttered in the history of humankind was the *fiat* of the Mother of God. A powerful insight, this; yet, sad but true, for some of us, especially for women today, to experience the full power of it and appreciate its depth may not be possible. When we hear statements of this kind, in fact, they may at first evoke discomfort and perhaps even irritation in us rather than awe. Though many among us still remember the heritage of May processions and crownings, of sodalities and October rosaries recited during early school years, our relation to the young girl in blue whom we almost worshiped then has undergone some serious questioning. The Mary of those years has become somewhat of a stranger to those of us who have come to experience a certain one-sidedness, unwholesomeness in the "feminine" meekness, mildness, weakness, and gentleness with which Mary was idealized during our youth. With Carolyn McDade we are working hard to have this myth die, so that the fullness of personhood, the strength and wholeness of God's Mother, and, by extension, our own potential for wholeness, might finally appear, flourish, and be celebrated.[1] To hear of the *fiat* as "creative," therefore, may initially evoke memories of dualistic fantasies glorifying the submission and passive resignation we hope to have grown beyond and would rather do without.

Elsewhere I have reflected on Ann Belford Ulanov's observation concerning the virtual silence in theological literature and certainly in liturgical worship when it comes to celebrating "Mary as a figure of fierce aggressive capacities who singly held herself open to God's presence, without support of reason or conventions of her culture,"[2] and whose *fiat*, one might add, came only after she dared press an angel for explanations (something for which Zechariah was struck dumb). In recent years I have discovered that this same ecclesial silence also applies to much of our tradition's interpretation of obedience. In many respects our estrangement from Mary as "woman on the pedestal" has come hand in hand, I believe, with a certain questioning and experiential reevaluation of our church's traditional interpretation of this virtue and of the vow we embraced many years ago. In a church where oaths of loyalty are required of pastors and theologians alike, where obedience to the supreme pontiff needs to be promised constitutionally by religious congregations, and where thinkers who dare to express differing views from the magisterial status quo are silenced often without anything even remotely resembling due process, "fierce aggressivity" and a questioning stance are the last qualities one would ascribe to obedience. The present-day official view of this virtue seems to speak much more readily to Baumgarten's interpretation in the 1927 edition of a then highly respected theological lexicon which states: "Very few people are capable of achieving a wholeness of life; thus no better use of their freedom can be imagined than for them to relate to some existing whole and to associate with those above them who have achieved wholeness."[3] This kind of position leaves most of us today alienated and angry. The lexicon sees obedience as "submission to authority, full compliance without questioning motives, the simple telling and presenting of holy things rather than the endless asking and answering of questions."[4] We, however, of contemporary times, seriously wonder what such an interpretation has to offer educated adults who see thinking and questioning as necessary for the meaningful encounter with all aspects of their lives and would, in fact, consider neglect in this area as irresponsible and disrespectful.

Perhaps no other vow stands more stressfully at the crossroads of the "turning point" in our culture's self-understanding than does the vow of obedience. Perhaps also no other evangelical counsel is interpreted still (and especially in our present magisterial setting) with as much dualistic rigidity, resisting the challenge and opportunity of creative rethinking.[5] Perhaps no other virtue is exalted with such absolutism, evoking individualistic reactionism in kind and, therefore, closing off all avenues for dialogue and transformation. There seems to be little doubt that obedience in our church is crucified in the intersection of both the archaic vertical and the present-day horizontal modes of relationship. It is the victim par excellence of a hierarchism that cannot as yet yield to the wisdom and sacredness of the community, of a "head" that cannot permit itself to trust its "body" and therefore runs the risk of losing itself in heavenly fantasies of grandeur rather than being rooted in reality, with its feet firmly planted on the earth.

Facing the Crisis

In order to situate ourselves specifically and directly in this crisis point of obedience today, it may be of value for us to recall briefly the two major paradigms of spirituality which we identified in chapter 1 as having been present in our tradition from the earliest times. The more pervasive of these, we will remember, originated out of the metaphysical dualism which we as church inherited primarily from the prevailing Greco-Roman culture of our early missionary encounters. Its structure even to this day is hierarchical, accenting comparatives in its view of reality. The "better than," "higher than," "holier than," and "more real than" dominates in this worldview over the "lower," more material aspects of reality. That which is closer to the spirit, hence closer to perfection and, therefore, more "godly" must be sought after and deferred to. Dualism thrives on perfection priorities. There exists a chasm in this spirituality between God and creation, God and man, and, most definitely, between God and woman.

Though the metaphysics of Greek thought as it had permeated the Roman empire in the time of early church expansion was largely responsible for the pervasiveness of dualism in our tradition even to this day, Sandra Schneiders assures us:

> Even among the Jews whose God was close to them in covenant love, a chasm existed between the human world and the divine, between the profane and the sacred prior to the Incarnation. Humans bridged that chasm by various forms of consecration. They took profane realities such as space, time, objects, and persons and separated them from profane use in order that they might become go-betweens or mediators between an inaccessible God and common humanity. This separation made these human realities superior to their profane counterparts. The Sabbath, the Temple, the sacred vessels, the priests, the animals for sacrifice, and the Law became— by consecration—sacred rather than profane and superior to ordinary places, times, things, behaviors, and persons.[6]

No wonder, then, that the vision of Jesus was revolutionary! We discussed in both chapters 1 and 2 its egalitarian rather than hierarchical emphasis. In it lay the charism of the early Jesus movement, the "discipleship of equals" in love covenant with one another and mutually empowered: "I no longer speak of you as slaves.... Instead, I call you friends.... Love one another" (John 15:15, 17). Though, except for its earliest moments, never dominant in the church, the spirituality of this second paradigm, nevertheless, was never quite lost throughout our tradition. In chapter 1 we reflected on the message of mystical thought that, though sporadic and often misunderstood and persecuted by a hierarchical system, preserved the insight of a lover God, of universal holiness and wholeness, of human equality and cosmic celebration. Today, also, persons interested in wholeness and justice—those concerned with the liberation of the oppressed, with the emancipation of the feminine, with ecology—point to this vision and call our culture toward transformation.

As we attempt to situate obedience in the intersection of these two paradigms, it becomes clear that critical reflection here may be profoundly unsettling. We discussed in chapter 1 the trauma of crisis and the unwillingness of civilizations to let go of the perspectives through which they have achieved their glory. Rigidity, mistrust, and persecution usually precede all paradigm shifts. Today's obsession with "loyalty" and the present magisterium's virtual rejection of all invitations to dialogue can easily be understood as a case in point. But, as in all other crisis situations of human and cultural maturation, stagnation, the unwillingness to grow, and the intransigent conservation of the past for the sake of "tradition" will only lead to regression and decay. It is time that we face the "drought" of obedience in our church; that we enter into "our quiet little house" and pray for the rain of creativity and new insight lest we wither in the dry spell and die of dehydration.

Authoritarian Obedience

In her classic work *Beyond Mere Obedience,* the noted German theologian Dorothee Sölle identifies the obedience of a dualistic, hierarchical society as generally authoritarian.[7] Its chain of command is linear and one-directional, moving from the one who speaks, who gives the command and is presumed to have the insight, to the one who listens, obeys, and is not only presumed, but in fact exhorted to be, if not ignorant of, then at least blind to, the significance of the action commanded. He or she is, therefore, for all intents and purposes, not responsible with respect to its consequences. The one who gives the order is seen to be the superior; the one who obeys it, his or her subject. Diligence, speed, and accuracy in receiving and carrying out the command are prized in the subject, while the content, circumstances, and possible consequences of the action are left to the consideration and wisdom (by the grace of state) of the superior.

Sölle introduces this model of obedience by citing an autobiographical account written by a German Catholic born in 1900 and raised in a strictly Christian tradition:

> I was brought up by my parents to give due respect and honor to all adults, particularly older persons, no matter which social classes they belonged to. Wherever the need arose, I was told, it was my primary duty to be of assistance. In particular I was always directed to carry out the wishes or directives of my parents, teacher, pastor, in fact of all adults including household servants, without hesitation, and allow nothing to deter me. What such persons said was always right. *These rules of conduct have become part of my very flesh and blood.*[8]

As a child, this writer tells us, he "was brought up to *obey every command without question,* to be neat and orderly in all things, and to keep scrupulously clean."[9] In Sölle's view:

"Obedience to the voice of command," learned early in life, "subordination to authority," practiced until it becomes habitual, "complete submission of one's own will to the will of another which demonstrates itself in action," in short, obedience as the cornerstone of religious education and as the key concept of the entire Christian message, is a commonly accepted Christian principle.[10]

Though the biographical example cited above has its origin in German Catholicism, Sölle suggests that Protestants and Catholics alike fostered this model of obedience. The author of this example was Rudolf Höss, the director of Auschwitz from 1940 to 1943.[11]

Without succumbing to any simplistic cause and effect theory linking German Catholicism to Nazi atrocities, we have to admit that Sölle presents here a serious indictment of a view of obedience which can no longer be tolerated with impunity. Stanley Milgram's behavioral study of obedience conducted in the 1960s at Yale University,[12] as well as brutalities executed on command against innocent citizens in the war-torn countries of so-called civilization everywhere, attest to the fact that concentration camp violence under orders is not unique to the German psyche. Neither nationality nor ethnicity creates blind obedience, only a certain abnegation of responsibility and unwillingness or inability to assume personal autonomy and to balance external orders with one's own conscience. Sölle is right when she observes that it is up to historians and social scientists to determine the level of influence Christian training in obedience had in creating these behavioral monstrosities.[13] Nevertheless, the theologian of this century may no longer look at the notion of unquestioning obedience with innocent eyes, let alone hold it up as virtue—not, at any rate, if she or he lives with any authenticity in history.

I suspect that we Christians today have the duty to criticize the entire concept of obedience, and that this criticism must be radical, simply because we do not know exactly who God is and what God, at any given moment, wills. It is no longer possible to describe our relationship to God with a formal concept that is limited to the mere performance of duties. We cannot remove ourselves from history if we wish to speak seriously about God. And in our Christian history, our history of the 20th century, obedience has played a catastrophic role. Who forgets this background or conveniently pushes it aside and once more naively attempts to begin with obedience, as if it were merely a matter of obeying the right lord, has not learned a thing from the instruction of God called history.[14]

Any kind of interpretation of obedience that refuses to understand culture, history, sociological data, and social responsibility is today simply unconscionable. One may not hold on to, and certainly not recommend, what clearly can lead to dysfunctionality and irresponsibility. Nor does the free choice of blind obedience in the name of humility or for the sake of "God's glory" alleviate the seriousness of betraying one's own mandate to mature behavior.

It is a known fact that blindness to the total picture—to the implications and ramifications of the act involved—ultimately results in blindness to the authority who commands the action as well. If content is ignored, anyone can command me, and, whereas this may at one time have been considered desirable (in religious communities, parishes, or dioceses where humble acceptance of whatever superior "God had ordained for me" was lauded as virtue and was, in fact, very convenient to the system), in the broader sphere of human behavior and the development of attitudes, this blindness to Christian superiors easily leads to the same with respect to military, political, or economic superiors. What I am suggesting, in other words, is that, since the emphasis is on the structure of the act rather than the content, religious authority is easily replaced with state, party, market force, or any other system which follows along the same principle.[15] The easy acceptance of totalitarian rule by some of the most Catholic countries of our century speaks for itself. And in America the simplistic (albeit often unconscious) identification of culture with God and all that is holy, which blindly rejects any criticism of American values as unpatriotic, is a blatant indication of the malformation of conscience which blind and unthinking acceptance of our "heritage" and its rules of conduct has led to. My fear is that the Oliver Norths are not an exception here as much as they are a symptom of something much more prevailing. North's popularity among the masses would seem to confirm that in his basic stance he is not alone. Jim Wallis puts it well when he observes:

> In the U.S. churches, it is not the kingdom of God that is at hand; it is the American culture that is at hand. It is the social, economic, and military system of the United States. ... Our conformity to the culture has made the fullness of the teachings of Jesus incomprehensible to many.[16]

The Consequences of Authoritarian Obedience

Conditioned blindness, whether for the sake of God or simply out of fear of punishment or the desire for reward, also invariably leads to lack of self-esteem and ultimate self-deprecation. Looking for one's center always outside of oneself inculcates a basic sense of unworthiness, distrust of self, as well as subservience to those "better," "more qualified," "older," "male," or, quite simply, "called" to be above, to be superior, and therefore to counsel and to guide. It may in some cases even be doubtful whether, after lengthy exposure to the conditioning effects of blind subservience, there remains a self to distrust. Authentic growth demands "movement from an orientation toward heteronomy [finding the law outside] *through autonomy* [having an inner law] in order to reach an ultimate mature, free relationship to God" and the human community generally.[17]

I suspect that one of the reasons why the community of adult friends we discussed in the previous chapter is still such a challenge and so difficult to come by in religious life today is quite probably the lack of authentic autonomy from which many of us are still suffering. Nor is the counter-movement of today's carefree society, which has so often raised its children without any boundaries in the name of freedom, any better off. Any movement "against" is generally caught up in that against which it stands. No boundaries can be as debilitating, therefore, as too many since the inner center is missing in both cases. Truly and genuinely to have found our inner law is more than having attained independence from the demands of superiors or even from each other. It means for us, above all, having encountered our past and faced there the unfulfilled needs as well as the voices of our childhood: those inner authority figures that haunted us deep into adulthood and, for years, simply spoke to us through our superiors or allowed themselves to be displaced onto the people around us. Authentic autonomy comes when we can acknowledge the extent of our capabilities and accept our essential co-being hand in hand with our uniqueness. When, in other words, we experience interdependence.

That conditioned blindness was very much part of our religious "formation" prior to Vatican II will probably not be denied by anyone. To be sure, it affected some of us more so than others, and particularly sensitive personalities steeped in it for years may even today be incapable of retrieving the personal center and inner authority so necessary for healthy adult interaction. These persons are "victims" of the system of coercion which, though freely chosen, nevertheless stood against the very meaning of freedom. Today they walk the halls of our community houses looking for someone to give them permission. Any opinion proffered by anyone asked becomes their dictum and often even their order, their "obedience." They agree with anyone and dialogue or argument confuses them. A "good" religious, after all, does not disagree. Strong-willed persons easily control them. They suffer much.

But we do not have to look for such extremes to find the consequences of authoritarian obedience in our lives. They can be much more subtle and infiltrate our modes of thinking and acting when and where we least expect them. We might, for example, quite honestly find ourselves among those strongly attracted to more holistic paradigms of obedience for today; we might even try to live accordingly and to form community by their standards. But what happens to us when the "crunch is on" and difficult decisions need to be made? We might test ourselves then to see how readily we revert to the old phrases: "But if I were *really* obedient, I would do what I am asked to do. If I were *really* obedient, I would do what is more difficult or what I don't want to do because others, authority, my community ask me to." It is one thing for us to give intellectual assent to more holistic models of obeying; it is quite another to have a "conversion of consciousness" and to live actively that way, seeking out leadership which will empower us to move from the model of primary family, discussed in the previous chapter, to a mature standing within the integrity of our own being, to say to a leader, "We want you to empower us toward the depth of our own responsibility, to empower us to be about what we as a group—in chapter or in our yearly assembly— have committed ourselves to be about," instead of, "We want you to tell us what to do, to lead the way in these difficult times, to model for us the life we are to live, to show us the direction we are to take."

Reactionism is probably the most subtle result of oppression and a sign of unresolved authority issues. When persons have been kept at childhood levels of responsibility far beyond the chronological limits, a dam of unresolved but potent energies breaks forth once oppression is lifted. Blindness to all legitimate authority can easily follow, and communal chaos is its consequence. Most of us have become aware during recent years (when the experimentation phase after Vatican II had lasted long enough for us to identify valid results) that governance in many local residential communities is in serious crisis. When everyone among us decides everything, nothing may get decided. It seems obvious enough that consensus is not necessary concerning every mundane detail of our existence. Yet, how upset some of us get when even minor decisions are made in our absence. We waste much time and energy by our unwillingness or fear to call forth our sisters and brothers to serve in leadership according to their gifts. The near paranoia with which some of us approach the issue of community decision making leads one to suspect that our visions and expectations of leadership, despite our outward appearance of independence and maturity, are often clearly still authoritarian (heteronomous) in style, and that a true experience of interdependence has not as yet graced us. We may want to recall our discussion of chapter 2 concerning a holistic approach to leadership, seeing it as a "needed gift wherever people are gathered together toward a common end."

Co-authority and Co-obedience

After this rather painful reflection on authoritarian obedience
and its consequences, it is refreshing but also sobering to refer
to Sandra Schneiders' "to the point" observation:

> What the religious does then, in vowing obedience, is to
> commit himself or herself without reserve to the seeking
> of the *will of God* in all circumstances and to fulfilling
> it with wholehearted dedication not only because one's
> own holiness lies in this total obedience to God but also
> in order to extend the reign of God in this world.[18]

It is clear that the universal call to wholeness experienced in a
"community of friends who are co-disciples in ministry" cannot be linear and one-directional. As a "discipleship of equals"
who are in love-covenant with one another, we are all responsible for actively seeking the will of God and fulfilling
it wholeheartedly. Speed and blindness in carrying out commands need to be replaced, therefore, by the virtue of listening
and mutuality, as we become aware in ever deepening ways
that God reveals God's self unconditionally to the attentive
heart and that all of us are expected to listen to the message
and to respond to it. Authority, which formerly was seen as
the guardian of responsibility, is thus embraced as co-authority
and responsibility for choices and decisions made is shared.

Sölle sees the holistic model for obedience as trinitarian in
nature, operating within the interconnectedness of, first, the
one who asks obedience (always God); second, the one who is
obedient (the individual, community, and designated authority); third, the content of obedience itself. Living responsibly
in the world implies sensitivity to the situations demanding
action on behalf of God's reign. This sensitivity is at all times
in a discerning posture with regards to content. It is impor-

tant for a serious appropriation of the holistic paradigm to recognize that authentic obedience on the part of all people involved embraces the dual responsibility for answering the one who asks for the action and taking ownership of what one is asked to do. To overlook this and to regard obedience simply as monolinear—directed only to the person "representing" God—means reverting back to dualism and consequent irresponsibility. The will of God is discovered within the situation. It can be found nowhere else.

Holistic obedience exhibits concrete involvement in the lived reality of the moment. This implies the totality of circumstances and can in no way isolate the action and its urgency from the ones who ultimately perform it, as if the health, disposition, gifts, and talents, as well as general condition of individuals were irrelevant. Hesitations which, in the past, were so frequently dismissed as "weakness of faith" to be surrendered to the instant remedy of the ever present "grace of state" are taken seriously and explored together when co-authority becomes co-responsibility. God asks neither the ridiculous nor the impossible. Watering sticks in the blind faith that leaves will sprout, like scrubbing floors with a toothbrush, may appear desirable in a system that values blind submission (be it religious "formation" of the past or military training even today), but neither practice fosters responsible obedience for the sake of justice and wholeness. Nor do any of us today benefit from having such practices or their like held up to us as laudatory examples of obedience in the founding days of our congregations. If the spirituality of that time made such actions possible, the virtue of patient endurance in the face of unjust oppression, much more likely than authentic obedience, should be reflected upon.

In our days the remnants of this sort of oppression may still creep into our discernment, whether we know it or not, every time we choose to overwork someone as well as ourselves for the sake of just one more need; every time we ask persons and even ourselves to live under excessive stress for the sake of "filling" a community house or saving on transportation; every time a decision is made about someone *without* that someone. When resentment is the response to these kinds of actions, it is not the individual who has the problem with authority. A *Gesellschaft* may operate that way; a community of equals simply does not. Though working for the reign of God may quite readily involve sacrifice, the sacred is not designed to be excruciating or to be accepted without personal and holistic discernment. There is in the disposition which comes with holistic spirituality the "calm, arcane assurance that the grace for the next step in the Spirit is already there, given."[19] Thus, we gather to explore together the reality of the situation and how, as well as by whom, God's reign might best be furthered in joy and peace.

Autonomous Obedience

Already in the Hebrew Scriptures we find that content—the act and the situation which elicits it, its circumstances and consequences—is most important. In Micah 6:8 we read: "You have been told . . . what is good, and what the Lord requires of you: Only to do right and to love goodness and to walk humbly with your God." The primary mandate for our obedience is doing justice and loving goodness. Sölle assures us that "in the Old Testament obedience is always related to justice. Under no circumstances is it related to the ruler in a completely authoritarian manner."[20] The ruler's task was to do justice and to empower others to do the same. Prophets warned him if he betrayed his calling. Theirs was the task of calling him back to his own integrity, to the obedience he owed to the voice of conscience within, to autonomous obedience. We are dealing here with something profoundly creative that has nothing to do with blind submission to orders and everything to do with personal responsibility. "The obedience requested of people is directly concerned with shaping the world entrusted to humans," making it into "a human society in which justice is realized."[21] Biblical obedience is transformative, not preservative. Its energy lies in process. It is future directed. "Where the world is understood biblically, that is, as moving toward an end, a goal, an authoritarian obedience cannot adequately express the will of God for the world. It is interested solely in the preservation of order and consequently displays hostility toward the future."[22] It threatens and destroys all that arises out of the creative center of authentic human autonomy.

Authoritarianism and the obedience which it demands arise from what I have come to call "serpent consciousness": the direct result ("punishment") of original sin.[23] It thrives on subjugation and control for the sake of nothing but the stagnation of the status quo, often misleadingly referred to as "law and order." A consequence originally of a state of "un-centeredness" (of dis-obedience, i.e., being scattered in one's listening, hence being unable or unwilling to hear the law within and acting on it; being, therefore, out of focus, harmful to oneself and others), this "serpent consciousness" is obsessed with externally enforced rules requiring heteronomous obedience. The curse of the serpent was to be crushed. Unredeemed dissipation, which knows no other law but outside control, experiences this crushing. It may even hold it up as necessary, since it has never encountered its deeper self, inner directedness, and strength—the freedom, as it were, of the children of God. Both ego-enhancement (the will to power) and the self-deprecation flowing form this dissipation further the "crushing" of the curse. The latter needs it to get direction;

the former, to build itself up as ruler, superior, chief. The freedom of redemption, on the other hand, calls us home to the
law written in our own hearts and found in centered listening—in the autonomous obedience modeled for us by Jesus
and called for, already before him, by the prophets throughout
Old Testament history.

In modern times perhaps no greater testament to the glory
as well as the paradox of Christian freedom, to the inner
autonomy to which all of us are called, can be found than
Dostoyevsky's parable of "The Grand Inquisitor."[24] This man
would have enslaved all in order to give to all the benefits
of the prison of security. When he encounters Jesus revisiting his church centuries after its founding and in the midst
of its inquisitorial excesses, he brands him a heretic bound
on disturbing the status quo for which his church had la-
bored assiduously during the centuries after his death. The
crime for which the Inquisitor condemns the founder of Christianity consists of reintroducing freedom, of forgetting that
humans prefer "peace, and even death, to freedom of choice
in the knowledge of good and evil." The Inquisitor admits
that "nothing is more seductive for [someone] than his [or
her] freedom of conscience, but nothing is a greater cause of
suffering."[25] In his accusations against Jesus he raves on:

> And behold, instead of giving a firm foundation for set-
> ting the conscience of [humans] at rest forever, Thou didst
> choose all that is exceptional, vague and enigmatic....
> Instead of taking possession of [human] freedom, Thou
> didst increase it, and burden the spiritual kingdom of
> [humankind] with its suffering forever. Thou didst desire
> [a person's] free love, that he [or she] should follow Thee
> freely, enticed and taken captive by Thee. In place of the
> rigid, ancient law, [humans] must hereafter with free heart

decide for [themselves] what is good and what is evil, having only Thy image before [them] as their guide.[26]

The redemptive "crime" of Christ Jesus, according to Dostoyevsky's Grand Inquisitor, was to model for us the freedom of autonomous obedience, to ask us to listen to the law of the heart and thus to open us up to the turmoil of our own conscience. For this he was bound and imprisoned; for this his tormentor planned to burn him at the stake the following day. Yet, paradoxically, precisely for this also, and because of Christ's mandate that all of us embrace our freedom, even if by it we betray him, Jesus lovingly and without condemnation moved toward his oppressor while they were facing each other in the prison cell and, after he had gently kissed him on the lips, walked back out into freedom, leaving him to his own responsibility.

Even if we would reject him, Christ would have us free. As the free victim of our freedom, he stands at the center of authentic human existence. He is the living truth about freedom as the necessary condition for God's creative love realized in human history. The Christian philosopher Nicholas Berdyaev explains the paradox presented as follows:

> Free goodness involves the freedom of evil; but freedom of evil leads to the destruction of freedom itself and its degeneration into an evil necessity. On the other hand, the denial of freedom of evil in favor of an exclusive freedom of good ends equally in a negation of freedom and its degeneration—into a good necessity. But a good necessity is not good, because goodness resides in freedom from necessity.[27]

Any interpretation of obedience that turns Christianity into coercion betrays the truth which is Christ. And yet, "enforced goodness" has been part of Christendom almost from its inception. The "crushing" of the curse is very much part of our history even to this day, and here we too can respond only with a "kiss," for counter-oppression is oppression also and does not serve our freedom as children of God.

For anyone who gives these considerations the serious attention they need, it soon becomes clear that the inner freedom with which Jesus embraced the truth of his own integrity is easier to reflect on than embrace, yet in this lies above all else our way home to God. The nature of God's creative love demands of us that our response be free, for love dies when freedom ceases. This is what the kiss of Dostoyevsky's Jesus symbolized. Far from indicating weak niceness in the face of unkindness or cruelty, it came from a disposition of inner strength and quiet self-directedness. It was the kiss of freedom that allowed others their responsibility. Given by the God-man, it would bless even the Inquisitor's unfaithfulness rather than coerce his loyalty. It would not protect him, however, from its ultimate consequences. The "kiss" was given for the sake of a greater good, namely, love which, without freedom, could not be.

Creative Fidelity

To live into the truth of this can be agony. Only a deep centeredness can endure the pain. It seems to me that often, perhaps because of this pain, many of us spend our time at the periphery of obedience, worrying about its structures and allowing ourselves to be oppressed there, rather than moving into its depth. I do not wish to deny the importance of our concerns with matters of governance and the proper chain of command and the like. I wonder, however, why they seemed to play such a minimal part in the obedience of Jesus. As Sölle remarks: "Neither the traditional reflection on the how of obedience nor the direct relationship between the one who demands obedience and the one who obeys plays an immediate role" in his life and in his teaching.[28] Whether persons making the request were duly appointed authorities or not was never as important as the inner authority with which they spoke and out of which they lived. Jesus, himself, is our primary example here. Was he not simply the carpenter from Nazareth? Yet power went out from him. People "were spellbound by his teachings, for his words had authority" (Luke 4:32). I cannot help wondering whether, especially for those of us vowed to evangelical obedience in religious congregations, the inwardness of Jesus' obedience will not have to receive a much stronger focus than it seems to have up to now if we are to survive the "crushing" experience of ecclesial traditionalism. A quiet centeredness that draws from inner strength can, I believe, weather arbitrary high-handedness much more effectively than angry demonstrations for the sake of "making a point." Autonomous obedience may even at times require heteronomous disobedience for the sake of God's reign, which always includes the well-being of humankind. In all this, however, centered listening, communal discernment, and a sincere desire to follow the movement of the Spirit in our lives and in history are the test of authentic freedom. Institutionalism and the worship of law and security are not. "The law was made for humans, not humans for the law" (Mark 2:27).

It seems to me that, once the cultic interpretations of patriarchism have been removed from the redemptive designs of Jesus,[29] there is precious little left of the preordained and fixed. The obedience of Jesus was much rather a listening-in-process than an accurate following of orders or of a preexisting ground plan. As such it was futuristic, creative, and so must ours be. "Where the divine will is thought of as fixed, that which is considered divine is of necessity misunderstood as anchored in the past—an establishment, a homeland, a right of possession,"[30]

tradition, and holy customs. Life lived holistically does not ignore the past, of course, but it will not allow itself to be lost
there, not even by the demands of a "holy rule" or of a magisterium. Only when we respond creatively to the will of God as
it is revealed to us in the existential situation of the concrete
moment does obedience become alive in us. Then we can listen
with excitement to the possibilities for the transformation of
the world which reveal themselves to us for our response.

> If person[s are] restored to freedom through the liberation
> of Christ, [they] will not merely accept responsibility for
> the order of the world; [they] will engage in transforming
> the world. The power [they need] to change things, to
> discover, to invent, to set things in motion, is spontaneity.
> This spontaneity in turn inspires new freedom. Persons
> who grow up in this life cycle are *not trained to find their
> place in a given order,* but to practice freedom.[31]

The spontaneity of creative freedom ought, in no way, to be
misunderstood as a free-for-all. Creative fidelity to the will of
God revealing itself in the lived reality of the here and now
requires, rather, acute sensitivity: the readiness of the "pru-
dent virgin," the fastened belts of servants waiting to serve.
Freedom without obedience is not freedom. It becomes license
instead. The depth disposition of listening openness requires
discipline and a willingness not only to give of the self at any
moment for the needs of the situation, but also to wait and to
serve the silence; to endure the darkness of that moment until
insight on how to act graces us. The power of authentic obedience lies first and foremost in the depth and surrender of the
human heart sensitized by patient endurance. Once again, this
is not something we resolve to "do" in one flash of inspiration.
It is rather a call whose growing edge usually remains a good
distance ahead of us.

Unifying Force for All Three Vows

The reflections of these past several pages may appear foreign in many respects to an age that values accuracy and expeditiousness. What does "listening-in-process," after all, have to do with practical efficiency? There seems, however, no way around the fact that what energizes our spontaneity for the obedient freedom exemplified in the Gospels is nurtured not so much by feverish planning and doing as by humble waiting. The "active" life of Jesus followed only after thirty years of this waiting. Is it not possible and even probable, given especially the drought of our time and our radical need, in so many respects, to gather ourselves in and "pray for rain," that the answers of contemporary revelation lie much more likely in deeper questions—in the mandate to stand radically in the service of truth as mystery and to endure the pain?

What if for each one of us today obedience meant first and foremost attentive openness to the signs of our time and faithfulness to our own integrity as it unfolds? What if the practice of obedience were today more frequently found in the courageous encounter with doubt and with the possibility of faith experienced therein than with staunch declarations of certitude followed by clear-cut actions? What if obedience meant for us the patient standing in the tensions of seeming moral opposites and enduring the agony of ambiguity? What if we found ourselves, for the sake of the Gospel, having to choose against all our heart's desire and having to bear the pain in silence because no one would understand? What if obedience pointed to bitter endurance of the void, listening into the silent darkness of contemporary faithlessness and letting oneself go in hope, unconditionally, into the questions that seem to have no reply? I have already suggested that in an age of technology, of quick as well as accurate replies, it is immensely difficult to assume an attitude of waiting, of standing in the pain of the questions and not demanding a resolution, of reverencing the unfathomable. It is difficult, even more it is agony, in fact, "to face the issues of our time and to wait in humility for the proper questions wherewith to address them."[32] Yet it is here, precisely in this difficulty, where the paschal mystery opens up for us, where the sacrifice which is Gospel living, far from the hair-shirt and chain mentality of previous times, blossoms forth from the inside and heralds redemption. It is here also, I believe, where depth obedience becomes the unifying force for all three vows, and where authentic Christian community lights up for us as a possibility.

> How can we possibly know *poverty* as "solidarity with the poor," for example, unless we *wait* in reverence and in pain for the revelation of that poverty which permeates our very beings: a poverty which opens us up to humble listening and serving and prevents us from engaging in works of pity instead of mercy? How can we live relationally as celibates... and, therefore, counterculturally, unless we can allow ourselves to face the uncomfortable questions concerning our own inner darkness; unless we can face the mysteries of the contra-sexual tendencies present in each one of us... and admit to our ever ready willingness to project these upon those whom we encounter? Finding the truth concerning our inner selves as cobeings means living the questions toward the deeper insight of further questions encountered in our reflective being together with others.[33]

It means being in community. It means being obedient.

Authentic obedience requires poverty of spirit. It means self-sacrifice: that "act of total responsibility" we discussed in chapter 3, "whereby we take complete hold of ourselves and place ourselves at the disposition of the whole" in order to " 're-present' the whole."[34] Through self-sacrifice autonomy is safeguarded in its integrity. It does not deteriorate into egocentric individualism but sees at the center of human interiority a deeper law that points to our oneness with all of humankind, with our earth, with the cosmos, and ultimately and intimately with God.

Authentic obedience also requires the emptiness of "virgin motherhood," the *Vacare Deo* reflected on in chapter 4, the vulnerability that can acknowledge need and let God be God in us. If we lack emptiness and are full of answers to every situation and for every problem, we cannot possibly be released enough to listen, neither to one another, nor to God. There is too much noise inside of us to hear the gentle breeze of the Spirit. We have the answers before the questions are asked and find ourselves unable to endure the creative tensions of possibilities. For us obedience would be too risky, too painful, and, conscious of it or not, we, therefore, prefer to oppress or be oppressed.

Fiat People

It is interesting that Jesus, the obedient one, the free listener who spoke and acted with inner authority, was most at home with the *anawim*, "the truly and utterly poor before God,"[35] who were poor and knew that they were poor, who, therefore, could also be obedient—empty receivers of the Word, of the energy of God. Their emptiness allowed for "virgin motherhood," for bearing God to the world, because it pointed them to the source of their power and, in their poverty, they abandoned themselves to God. Their justification did not come from doing the proper thing promptly, but from being vulnerable before God and from solely depending on God's power to work itself out in their surrender. They were *fiat* people, involved in what Sandra Schneiders calls "a kind of existential humility,"[36] which counted on nothing other than the infinite mercy of God, and in turn walked this earth with compassion, never judging nor condemning, let alone deciding for anyone. Because of their profound sense of littleness and brokenness as well as their experience of the unconditional acceptance and love of God, the *anawim* through the ages have known that, though the law can be useful, obedience to the law does not make for holiness. Holiness comes with openness to the "Spirit of wisdom, prayer, love, pressing zeal, the very Spirit of Jesus.... It is not the law which will tell us what is good (or that we are good); it is our constant seeking of the good which will enable us finally to discern what, in our human affairs, is truly God's will."[37]

Authentic, Christ-liberated obedience flows out of the willingness to let go—a willingness with which we are gifted when we encounter ourselves as *anawim,* as God's poor. As long as we have our talents, strengths, intelligence, position, and power to hold on to, we will continue to compare ourselves and set standards for ourselves and others. Only by embracing and allowing ourselves to be embraced by the radical emptiness of Jesus can we let God be God for us and in us. In this lies our redemption, our homeward path. It is the path that leads to the recognition of our utter incapacity to do anything good by ourselves, and to our acceptance, at last, of God's unlimited love. It is the path that expresses the truth of the human condition as *loved* and as *free.*

Lately I have wondered whether the twentieth century, which revealed itself to us as so utterly without answers, as the age of alienation, where none of the "old" ways seem to work anymore, as the age of despair and nihilism, may not also ultimately have prepared us for a future that invites us to the most radical Gospel obedience. Perhaps for the first time now, when ready-made solutions simply no longer work, when answers prove as many times ineffective as they prove effective, when radical doubt has replaced radical certainty, perhaps now we will be driven by our sheer inability to do much else than to *abide in the question and to wait,* to have the question lead us to the depth of inwardness so that we might dwell there in humility and in hope for the birthing of God in our lives.

In the light of these considerations it may now be possible to reflect once again on the *fiat* of God's Mother, which we mentioned at the beginning of this chapter. It may have become clearer now that, far from being a word of passive resignation and meek submission, Mary's yes unleashed extraordinary power. It allowed God's energy to become flesh. Her *fiat* was the testament of her obedience, of the creativity which flows from self-emptying. It gave witness to her courageous surrender to unspeakable difficulties, innumerable questions, and to her utter trust in God who would see her through. Mary is a model of the incredible daring which obedience demands. Through her yes the Christification of the cosmos was made possible; the Word was made flesh and history became significant. Her obedience was powerfully creative, a hallmark of freedom. Yet she had no need to speak of it or even to justify herself in the face of possible rejection. She quietly held these things in her heart in utter releasement. The *fiat* of the Mother of God is for the strong. This means, paradoxically, for those vulnerable enough to give their lives for the transformation of all things in Christ.

Some Reflections on Our Existential Situation

The paradoxes which reveal themselves to us when we probe the depth of obedience are staggering: vulnerability is strength; surrender opens us to freedom; creativity lies in fidelity; obedience must sometimes be disobedience. Powerful insights these, but for many of us frustratingly "useless." It seems that speculations into their practical significance for our lives as religious in the twenty-first century will yield few tangible results. Paradox, it is true, is peculiarly impractical, as well as hopelessly nontheoretical; and when it graces us, it usually reveals nothing until it has moved us to a different kind of "order." One way to learn from it here may be to direct ourselves very intentionally once again to the "drought" of our times and to remember what the rainmaker of Kiaochau modeled for us. As the story goes, the Catholics, the Protestants, as well as the Chinese all had their solutions for the drought, but none of them brought rain. Then the dried-up old man gathered himself into a quiet little house and "waited." Obedience, more than any other virtue, is first and foremost disposition. In Kiaochau the Catholics, the Protestants, and the Chinese spend a lot of energy "doing." The Catholics "*made* processions," the Protestants "*made* prayers," the Chinese "burned joss-sticks and shot off guns." The dried-up old man, however, *waited* and through his waiting brought them rain. To wait means to listen, to be open, to be vulnerable, to be poor, to know dependency and, therefore, to point beyond. Often when we wait we are visited by pain, by longing. Waiting implies humble expectancy, creative receptivity, obedience. To wait means to pray.

Prayer

We remember Shinoda Bolen's observation that the "drought mentality" of the psyche signifies dis-ease, anxiety caused by a lack of inner order, a feeling of isolation, of separation from the whole. In an extroverted world where action needs to bring results and anxiety and worry run high, where few have time enough to move inward, let alone stay there, viewing our vow of obedience as commitment to prayer-filled centering for the healing of the human family can be very significant.

So often, it seems to me, we also *do* too much when we pray. We "say" our prayers. Even when we come together, we "make" prayer—someone always gets to *do* the prayer service. Personally I often feel quite guilty when I become aware of how bored I get during the fifteen or twenty minutes before every gathering when we *do* our praying.

When prayer services replace the Eucharist we work especially hard to make them symbolically significant. There is something about ritual, however, that seems to move between the old and the new and shuns too much variation all at once. Ritual that is too original and, therefore, foreign to many of the participants, tends to distract and move us outward, away from ourselves and even, sometimes, from each other. Women especially, I believe, are caught in their prayer together between the oppression of a system that will not allow them to choose from among themselves someone who will preside at the ancient rituals of their faith (and that, for dearth of its own ordained ministers, frequently cannot provide them with someone adequate to do it for them), and the need to worship together and to express their togetherness in Christ. In this dilemma it may help to remember that when we gather to pray, not everything needs to be ritualistic. Ritual has its place, but so does quiet gathering.

Prayer that is obedience is listening prayer: the prayer of stillness, of simplicity, of doing and saying nothing, of being with but not of clutching. It is the prayer of "waiting." Though it is true that in many of our prayer services a time of quiet reflection is built in, for many (especially for introverts) the invitation to share which usually follows this tends to make the silent period more like rehearsal time for what needs to be said when one's turn comes than one of quiet listening. I wonder what it would be like if religious today gathered more frequently with the express intention of listening, if prior to our congresses or chapter meetings we came together not only to praise, but also to listen for the silent Word of God in our midst speaking to us out of the concrete moment. I do not mean here the time for reflection which many of us provide at moments of communal discernment when all of us can run off into the garden or the chapel to be quiet for a while. I mean *taking time to be alone while being together,* in order to listen to and experience what John of the Cross calls:

> Silent music
> Sounding solitude
> The supper that refreshes, and deepens love.[38]

Prayer that is obedience "is not preoccupied with thought but with the ground of being from which thought takes its origin."[39] It nurtures and prepares us for thought and speech. In it, William Johnson tells us, "lies the true self,"[40] and I would add: in it also can be found depth communion with others. Energy flows through our midst—a sacred presence that lies deep at the core of our togetherness—when we are all gathered to listen. No words can adequately describe this. One moves intensely inward and, the deeper one goes, the more one feels alive, connected to every living being; the more clearly also one opens up in compassion to all the pain in the world.

Healing also happens in our silent solitude-together. It is a healing that is energized from the center where accusations and judgments melt into forgiveness. It is a healing that moves us from our individual and congregational concerns through the pain and suffering of humanity, the agony of the cosmos, into wholeness. No reports can be given of insights gained during our silent time together. No reports need be given, for the energy will be felt by all and the insights will follow—in God's time.

Obedience That Touches the Universe

The prayer that is obedience needs, of course, to be part of us at all times. Our silent moments together remind us of it. This kind of prayer marks our vow as primarily and essentially disposition—an attitude of concernful presence and openness to all things. Our struggles with aging and with diminishment know the depth disposition of obedience with particular acuteness; but so does all authentic movement into maturity and wholeness. The mid-life journey and second half of life generally with their moments of yearning for intimacy and generativity, their particularly sensitive encounters with the contra-sexual within, and their need to withdraw projections and face transference call the majority of active religious into a great deal of patient waiting—into obedience.

A dear friend of mine sees reflected in the agony of our personal journeys the odyssey of all of humankind. Her view may be particularly helpful in having us understand that the holy waiting, the patient endurance that is our obedience, is of much broader significance than merely our personal concerns. We embrace the pain of our journey for the salvation, the conscientization of all of humankind. The obedience to holistic growth accepts responsibility for the "Christ" in our title of "Christ-ians." The struggle into maturity, the quest for human integrity, to which each one of us surrenders out of our own unique sensitivity to the commitment of our vow, has repercussions that are cosmic in scope. We will recall Gerald May's observations in the previous chapter concerning the "transmutation of energy." Though our specific concerns centered there around the erotic aspects of life-energy, the principle here is the same. "Agape" energy is the basic life-force of the universe,[41] the Spirit moving us and all of nature into the fullness we call Christ. Conscious surrender to this process is what I see first and foremost as authentic obedience. Through it emerges for us not just our own personal holiness, but the Christification of the universe as well. It is, therefore, not just individual in nature but communal as well, and this in the deepest sense of the word. An exhortation of Lao Tsu comes to mind which captures well this disposition of creative releasement that touches the universe:

> Carrying body and soul and embracing the one,
> Can you avoid separation?
> *Attending fully* and becoming supple,
> Can you be as a newborn babe?
> Washing and cleansing the *primal vision,*
> Can you be without stain?
> Loving all . . . and ruling the country,
> *Can you be without cleverness? . . .*
> Understanding and being open to all things,
> Are you able to *do nothing?*
> Giving birth and nourishing,
> Bearing yet not possessing,
> Working yet not taking credit,
> Leading yet not dominating,
> This is the Primal Virtue.[42]

Without attempting to dissect so profound a meditation, we can, nevertheless, quite readily see here poetically expressed much of what we have already touched on: a stress on the incarnational that avoids the temptation of dualism and is open, able to bend, and, therefore, ready for new life like a newborn babe. The attentiveness here proposed harkens for the primordial, seeks for depth perception, for original innocence. It loves universally and does not need to be shrewd or to impress with self-sufficiency. It knows the strength of creative passivity and can give and let go. It does not seek praise or power. It leads because it has touched the inner center of all things whence direction flows. It does not need to control because power comes from within.

Authority

With deep sensitivity Lao Tsu blends into harmony for us what in the dualistic tradition has always stood in opposition: listener and leader, obedience and authority. It is clear that in the holistic paradigm only the one who can wait, the listener, who has touched the heart of life and learned from it, can lead. Leadership is never something one "deserves," no matter how hard one has worked or how many committees one has been part of. It worries me in any situation, but particularly in religious life, when elections replace discernment of gifts and when politicking, no matter how pious, enters our leadership process. Subtle as this may be, elections (no matter how democratic they are), because of their affinity with the power plays of contemporary politics, too easily lend themselves to an interpretation of authority which is dualistic. Furthermore, democracy, even at its best, still only displays the "will" of the people. It may have precious little to do with the reign of God.

Religious ought not to win elections. They ought to "experience call." To be sure, this call cannot be purely an external imposition, as most of us experienced it prior to Vatican II and as church structures still foster it, with slight but insignificant modifications, in parish and diocesan settings. The call to leadership emerges out of the recognition within the community that authentic authority is present in an individual and is needed for the growth and wholeness of all. As was mentioned already, inner authority has little to do with "position" ("state"). Discernment within a community, however, does well if it aims at linking the two. This is not, of course, so that, when this happens, we can revert to seeking all our answers and expecting the solutions to all problems from those "who were chosen to lead us." The word "authority" (Latin: *augere*) means to give increase, to empower, to build up, to edify.[43] As such, authentic authority leads us to the threshold of our own vision and empowers us there. This is what we must come to expect from it. This is what we must seek for in our discernment processes.

The task of authentic authority is primarily to listen to the depth pulsations of the community of which it is a part. Bernard Boelen puts it well when he points out that "mature authority not only has to obey the authority of those who obey, but also has to obey its own authority."[44] It can do this because it knows the meaning of listening and the benefits of waiting, because, on its journey through the dyings and risings of religious life, it has experienced the power of prayer.

On the practical level, "obeying the authority of those who obey," means assuming responsibility for calling the community to be about what we have said we are about, that is, challenging us ever to be who we are. This is by no means always an easy task. It involves, in particular, listening intently to the whole group and differentiating what might be the proclamations of a few possibly strong personalities—perhaps even one's own—from the spirit of the whole. It also demands a blend of compassion and radical honesty. The "kiss" of Dostoyevsky's Jesus is a solemn reminder that autonomous obedience is built on freedom. It is built, however, on honesty as well. The need for approval ought not prevent a leader from saying what must be said. Often timing is of the essence, of course. The crucifixion of leadership more often than not is found in the agony of waiting.

Elsewhere I have suggested that leadership in contemporary times, instead of trying to supply answers, ought much rather model the asking of questions. Its authenticity emerges in its attentive openness to the signs of our time, in its "passionate waiting (with all the pain that this implies) for the questions which radically address our age."[45] Its primary mandate is surrender to truth unfolding. Truth, however, reveals itself always as enigmatic. Clarity of personal vision is precisely that: personal. No amount of certainty regarding my own or even a group's correctness will preclude the possibility that someone else's perception may not add something that has simply escaped me (us) and that will, therefore, quite possibly alter the picture. This does not mean, of course, that total indecision is, therefore, inevitable. Decisions, however, and the actions flowing from them are open-ended, not absolute or final. Laws are written in human hearts, not on stone tablets. They are ever respectful of the collective wisdom of the group as it is evolving.

Only when authority closes its eyes to issues at hand, refuses to probe deeper and to ask us to do the same, does indecision and lethargy set in and empowerment cease. Obedience ceases then also and a life dedicated to attentive listening turns into aimless drifting. Instead of challenging ourselves and the way we live to greater authenticity corresponding ever more clearly to our pronounced commitments around our charism, we begin rather to move unthinkingly into lifestyles or behaviors of one kind or another only to find ourselves at some point down the line renaming our situations to suit the status quo without ever seeking to know how we got there. It may be true that at any time or in any situation few of us experience the ideal we envision, but can we with authenticity avoid striving for it and trying to live into its meaning for us today? What is our vision for religious life today? What will happen when, because of indifference or thoughtlessness, most of us have lost the vision? Who then are we?

These are the questions of authentic authority. They rarely are asked by those who "won the election" by "running a good campaign" and who may now be too busy maintaining their popularity to challenge us into authenticity. They are asked only by those who are obedient to the whole for the sake of the Holy. These are the poor in spirit who work without "taking credit." "Understanding and being open to all things," they bear yet do not posses; they lead yet do not dominate. They practice "the Primal Virtue."

Conclusion

I fear that the reading of this reflection on obedience may prove disappointing to some. In a time when many among us are struggling with true oppression by the forces of autocracy, it may not appear helpful to hear about obedience as "surrender to the depth of one's own integrity." What do we do with actual oppression which bars some from ministries for arbitrary reasons and denies dialogue and mutual reflection to others for the sake of unilateral control? I must sadly confess that I have no answers here save, once again, the "kiss" of Dostoyevsky's Jesus and the silence of the man of the Gospel who knew the origin of power (John 19:11) and was centered there. This did not prevent his crucifixion, of course (nor does it and will it prevent ours), but it preserved his integrity, and God raised him up.

As followers of Jesus we must work for God's reign and be obedient to its mandates. This will at times mean speaking out against oppression even if we will suffer for it, but, as a community and as individuals, this also means intense discernment lest we ourselves succumb to the very practice of oppression which we are called to transform. Our journey depends on our commitment to holiness in our own lives, in our church, and in our world; our integrity lies in our hunger and thirst for justice

Questions for Focus, Reflection, and Discussion

1. How have you experienced authoritarian obedience in your life? How has it affected you? What feelings does this concept evoke? Do you still see it as your major paradigm for obedience? If so, why? If not, Why not?

2. "Any kind of interpretation of obedience that refuses to understand culture, history, sociological data, and social responsibility is today simply unconscionable." Is there a danger of this in our society? Might we today fall victim too of blindly accepting the status quo? If so, in what areas of our life?

3. How is it that "conditioned blindness" with respect to obedience can lead to lack of self-esteem, self deprecation? Can you explore practical examples here?

4. What does the statement: "Authentic obedience leads toward transformation, not preservation" mean to you in your life?

5. Do you see us as communities embracing the trinitarian model of obedience? Has this worked to our advantage or disadvantage? How so?

6. How have you in your life come to understand "obedience for the sake of justice and wholeness"?

7. What is your response to the interpretation of disobedience as being "scattered in one's listening, being unwilling and/or unable to hear the law within"? How does one find the law within? What does it effect in us?

8. What is your reaction to the "crushing of the curse" as part of Christian history to this day and to the observation that "counter-oppression is oppression also and does not serve our freedom as children of God"?

9. Can obedience, at times, mean dis-obedience? If so, how so? If not, why not? How does this observation relate to the insight that "freedom without obedience is not freedom. It is license instead"?

10. "The power of authentic obedience lies first and foremost in the depth and surrender of the human heart sensitized by patient endurance." Have you experienced this?

11. How is it that depth obedience is the unifying force for all three vows? Do you agree with this insight?

12. Have you ever experienced "silent solitude-together"? If so, was it effective for community discernment? Did it bring about healing?

13. What is your response to the observation that the agony of our personal journey reflects the odyssey of all humankind; our struggle into maturity, our quest for integrity has cosmic repercussions?

14. What do the following statements mean to you? Have you experienced leadership as described here?

    • "Only the listener who has touched the heart of life and learned from it can lead."

    • "Leadership is never something a person deserves."

- "Religious ought not to *win* elections. They ought to *experience call.*"

- "The call to leadership emerges out of the recognition within the community that authentic authority is present in an individual and is needed for the growth and wholeness of all."

- "Authentic authority leads us to the threshold of our own vision and empowers us there."

- "Mature authority not only has to obey the authority of those who obey, but also has to obey its own authority."

- "Authority needs to be about challenging us ever to be who we are."

Chapter Six

CONVERSION TOWARD INCREASE

We began our reflection on living the vows in today's world with a story: the message of the rainmaker of Kiaochau. Stories can be powerful change agents. Once we have heard them, they have a tendency to stay with us, to accompany us and to call us back to themselves whenever the need arises in order to help draw us in from being too scattered, from being lost in "outwardness"—at the circle's rim. We can dwell in stories. They neither force us to concentrate unnecessarily, nor rush us. They capture us instead and fascinate. Joseph Campbell, reflecting on Jung's respect for stories and myths, tells us that when we are too outward oriented and have lost touch with our inner energies, myths and stories are the means of bringing us back in touch with ourselves. "They are telling us in picture language of powers of the psyche to be recognized and integrated in our lives, powers that have been common to the human spirit forever, and which represent the wisdom of the species by which [we have] weathered the millenniums."[1] If we take stories seriously and dialogue with them we can learn much and "come to terms with the greater horizon of our own deeper and wiser, inward self."[2] Good stories tell truths but rarely threaten or frighten us. Jesus used stories, we know, as his most successful way of teaching, because stories bring us home to our own integrity. John Shea claims that for Christians, ever since Jesus, the perennial strategy has been to

"1. Gather folks. 2. Break bread. 3. Tell the stories."[3] This has worked so well because storytelling has, in fact, been an addiction for humans since the beginning of creation. "No matter our mood, in reverie or expectation, panic or peace, we can be found stringing together episodes. We turn our pain into narrative so we can bear it; we turn our ecstasy into narrative so we can prolong it. We all seem under the sentence of Sheherazade. *We tell our stories to live.*"[4]

And so it seems fitting to begin these considerations—concerned with the possibility of new life in religious congregations today but also shadowed by the very real probability of death—with just one more story. It is a story with which many of us may already be acquainted.[5] Like all good stories, it has universal significance. In my sharing it here, however, I want to claim it specifically as ours, for it speaks very sensitively to the whole picture: the pain, the discouragement, the yearning, the sharing, the hope, and the promise that is religious life today. It is a story about grace and about the responsibility with which grace always gifts us. It is a story about silence, about wonder, about reverence, about trust, and ultimately about new life.

> There was a famous monastery which had fallen on very hard times. Formerly its many buildings were filled with young monks and its big church resounded with the singing of the chant, but now it was deserted. People no longer came there to be nourished by prayer. A handful of old monks shuffled through the cloisters and praised their God with heavy hearts.
>
> On the edge of the monastery woods an old rabbi had built a little hut. He would come there from time to time to fast and pray. No one ever spoke with him, but whenever he appeared, the word would be passed from monk to monk: "The rabbi walks in the woods." And, for as

long as he was there, the monks would feel sustained by his prayerful presence.

One day the abbot decided to visit the rabbi and to open his heart to him. So, after the morning Eucharist, he set out through the woods. As he approached the hut, the abbot saw the rabbi standing in the doorway, his arms outstretched in welcome. It was as though he had been waiting there for some time. The two embraced like long-lost brothers. Then they stepped back and just stood there, smiling at one another with smiles their faces could hardly contain.

After a while the rabbi motioned the abbot to enter. In the middle of the room was a wooden table with the Scriptures open on it. They sat there for a moment, in the presence of the book. Then the rabbi began to cry. The abbot could not contain himself. He covered his face with his hands and began to cry too. For the first time in his life, he cried his heart out. The two men sat there like two lost children, filling the hut with their sobs and wetting the wood of the table with their tears. After the tears had ceased to flow and all was quiet again, the rabbi lifted his head. "You and your brothers are serving God with heavy hearts," he said. "You have come to ask a teaching of me. I will give you a teaching, but you can only repeat it once. After that, no one must ever say it aloud again."

The rabbi looked straight at the abbot and said, "The Messiah is among you."

For a while, all was silent. Then the rabbi said, "Now you must go."

The abbot left without a word and without ever looking back.

The next morning, the abbot called his monks together in the chapter room. He told them that he had received a teaching from "the rabbi who walks in the woods" and that this teaching was never again to be spoken aloud. Then he looked at each of his brothers and said, "The rabbi said that one of us is the Messiah."

The monks were startled by this saying. "What could it mean?" they asked themselves. "Is Brother John the Messiah? Or Father Matthew? Or Brother Thomas? Am I the Messiah? What could this mean?"

They were all deeply puzzled by the rabbi's teaching. But no one ever mentioned it again.

As time went by, the monks began to treat one another with a very special reverence. There was a gentle, whole-hearted, human quality about them now which was hard to describe but easy to notice. They lived with one another as men who had finally found something. But they prayed the Scriptures together as men who were always looking for something. Occasional visitors found themselves deeply moved by the life of these monks. Before long, people were coming from far and wide to be nourished by the prayer life of the monks and young men were asking, once again, to become part of the community.

In those days, the rabbi no longer walked the woods. His hut had fallen into ruins. But, somehow or other, the old monks who had taken his teaching to heart still felt sustained by his prayerful presence.

We tell stories to live. Perhaps no other concern haunts religious today more than the question of declining life in their congregations and the future of religious life. Somehow what we are about receives encouragement when we know that others are joining us in the same effort, that we are not alone. There is a sense of worthwhileness that is enhanced when new membership gathers around us because of our mission. It

is difficult to experience diminishment, death, and painful to
question into it and to ask "why." Teilhard de Chardin speaks
of the diminishment of physical death with great insight:

> God must, in some way or other, make room for Himself
> [Herself], hollowing us out and emptying us if [God] is
> finally to penetrate into us. And in order to assimilate
> us in Him [Her], [God] must break the molecules of our
> being so as to re-cast and re-model us. The function of
> death is to provide the necessary entrance into our inmost
> selves.[6]

Perhaps religious congregations today are experiencing this
necessary "hollowing out," this emptying which will ultimately make room for God. It may be disconcerting for some
of us even to conceive, let alone admit, that institutions ex-
pressly formed for the consecrated life need "hollowing out."
Yet perhaps this is where our questioning will lead us. Death,
says Teilhard, "will put us into the state organically needed if
the divine fire is to descend upon us."[7]

I have already pointed out, and students of human development assure us, that the maturation process of the human
person passes through a number of deaths and resurrections—
crises—that can quite readily be paralleled with the turning
points of cultures and systems as they move toward their own
fulfillment. What is characteristic of every crisis or turning
point is the death or disintegration of the dominant mode
of perception that is always necessary before anything new
can appear. In chapter 1, I discussed the natural resistance
to this letting go, the danger of intransigence, and the subsequent "calcification" of one's mode of seeing and behaving
into which one can slip in order to avoid the pain of death.

It is natural for persons in crisis situations to pass through
prolonged periods of desolation and darkness after the initial

experience of death. For individuals this period may consist of several years. A culture, however, paralleling this experience, may need to endure it for decades or even centuries.[8] Institutions such as ours may be in transition for a very long time also for, as I suggested already, we are inextricably connected with the movements and processes of our time. During these periods one (the individual with respect to his or her own life, as well as with respect to institutions and cultures) experiences the previous, comfortable mode of perception and behavior to have disintegrated completely, but nothing as yet to have taken its place. One feels oneself in absolute darkness, in the desert of utter need, an ocean of nothingness with no direction to follow: no past to revert to, no future to hope for. The great temptation during such times is to give up instead of learning from the signs of the times, to despair and to make decisions accordingly. By this, however, one forces the process into one's own direction and runs the risk of aborting it. The silent waiting of the rainmaker and the prayer of the "rabbi who walked in the woods" alone prepare the way of redemption.

And when redemption comes, it rarely does so with great noise and tumultuous change. Perhaps this is the paradox of it all. During a silent night in Bethlehem a Child was born, and only the poor noticed. Cannons and swords can bring about change but rarely effect transformation. A little babe in swaddling clothes and, later, a silent carpenter held within himself the energy that would forever alter perception and make all things new.

It is interesting to note what happened to the old monks "with heavy hearts" after the rabbi's message was imparted to them. The story tells us that they were startled, that they wondered, but that they never mentioned it again. Like Mary, they kept these things each one in his heart. They let their hearts teach them and slowly their vision was transformed:

"They began to treat each other with a very special reverence" which was "easy to notice," but hard to describe or talk about and had certainly never been programmed or planned. People were attracted to them once again because they prayed with longing and lived lives filled with purpose: *The Messiah was in their midst.*

We have here a very powerful message for ourselves and our future. Since Vatican II we have spent a great deal of energy and talent addressing the vocation issue. Almost no other program in religious life has received equal attention, planning, discussion, and worry; almost no other program has been revised and rediscerned as frequently as "formation." Yet our houses remain empty, and the talented people we train for "formation" all seem underemployed. Why is this so? Are we perhaps, in spite of our good intentions, asking the wrong questions, having outdated expectations, making unrealistic demands? Are we truly moving into the center of this issue, or are we in fact staying dangerously close to the rim, forever spending our energies at reforming our programs instead of surrendering our hearts to the rabbi's message and allowing *ourselves* to be transformed?

Expectations and Assumptions

Some time ago a student of mine in a lay ministry training program with which I was associated informed me that she was putting her house up for rent and moving in with a local community of women religious to live with them a life of simplicity and to share community. She is a mother of several grown children, divorced, has worked for a number of years, and now felt a call to simplify her life and a desire to experience the companionship of other women working in various and diverse ministries in the church.

Needless to say, I was pleased with her decision, fascinated particularly by the fact that she had really no immediate interest in joining the community as a vowed member, but simply wanted to live-with and share, to com-panion—"break bread with." Her story led me to reflect about new movements in religious life, new avenues of response to the vocation crisis, new life in the midst of apparent death. It led me also to probe into the kind of expectations we continue to have, the demands we continue to make.

In *Wrestling with God* (part 3) I addressed the topic of alternative forms of membership, a hope that Transformative Element 8 (reflected on in chapter 4) envisions for us. Perhaps a few additional remarks on the topic of diversity, as well as on our apparent assumptions with respect to membership, may still be in place.

To begin with, it is clear to anyone who takes the trouble to observe that our newer members, though few in numbers, show great diversity with respect to almost every aspect of their lives. Age, ministry background, interests, education, relational experiences, culture, and race can all be quite different for each. Furthermore, few religious congregations still accept young girls or boys into their "formation" programs, so that persons discerning a religious vocation for the most part tend to be at least young to middle adults if not older. (The oldest "newer" member I ever taught in the Studies for Spirituality Program designed for them was seventy-two years old.) We expect them to behave according to their age. Our philosophy is, and rightly so, that a person needs to have navigated at least the major phases of adolescence in order to appreciate the implications of religious commitment. We hope that our new members will have experienced life, dated, worked, become professionally competent, self-directed, responsible.

What continues to puzzle me, however, is why, in spite of

our awareness of all this and our well-grounded policies concerning the admittance of candidates, the response of many congregations to those who come to explore our lifestyle frequently continues to seem out of touch and obsolete. If the men and women coming to us are indeed as mature as our policies expect them to be, why do we not treat them that way consistently? Why do our assumptions, in fact, appear in many cases to be still those of years ago? If these women and men, on the other hand, are not as mature as our policies expect them to be, why do we encourage them toward incorporation in the first place?

A member of the leadership team of a large religious congregation recently shared with me her puzzlement at the fact that newer members were being attracted but somehow, after a period of investigation, did not stay. "We draw them, but we cannot seem to keep them," she said. The reasons for this can, of course, be many and in some instances there may even be a "lack of vocation." However, might one of the reasons not also be our expectations and demands of them once they enter— demands, I might add, which few of us live up to ourselves? Adults notice inconsistencies and are not edified by them.

It is clear that no woman in America *needs* to enter religious life today to improve her status. Men who see ordained ministry as a status symbol may still on occasion seek entrance into religious community to obtain orders. But generally men do not *need* to enter community to improve their status either. Education and advancement in the professional sphere are now open to all women alike and certainly to men. I do not by that fact imply that improvement for all women and for minorities is not warranted regarding this issue in the society at large, but only wish to make the point that membership in a religious community will certainly not bring this about for anyone. Men and women who enter, therefore, in America at least or in other countries of similar economic standing do not seem to do so for social status. And, as I have mentioned already, although they may identify ministry as one of the major reasons for coming, it is not their prior incompetence in ministry and consequent need for training by religious, but rather their desire to *minister together with others* joined in a covenantal commitment around charism that has them seek out religious life.

Those who come to join us also do not as a whole need training in the social etiquette requisite for a professional, i.e., proper manners and general demeanor. They are not ignorant (in need of advice from any and all "older" professed). Frequently they do not require ministry discernment either and will not necessarily need to be exposed to every single ministerial option the congregation can offer them. Many of them have their ministry already chosen and, if not, are quite capable of looking around for themselves, of exploring, asking questions. They, more often than not, can on their own, without preprogrammed "mini-ministry experiences," seek the opportunities they need for discernment, provided these are offered them, as they are in fact offered to most of us, through our ministry offices. They are, after all, adults, and it is on that premise that we have invited them to be with us. Mature adults naturally ask questions when they need information and resist problems being solved for them. They find it difficult to be given answers to questions they have not even asked yet.

Once again, I am not suggesting that the men and women coming to discern religious life will not need advice and help. I am merely proposing that we will need to respect their right to seek it and allow them the opportunity to do so in their own time. The Messiah is among them too. Rushing their insight, no matter how sure we are of what is "good for them," only violates the process of emergence. That this may be frustrating for some of us goes without saying. The difference between the functional (*Gesellschaft*) mode of dealing with persons that springs from dualism and the personal way of relating with others which evolves from the holistic attitude of a *Gemein-schaft* discussed in previous chapters is precisely in our ability to wait and to let be. It seems to me that some of the greatest frustration points in our life together as a community generally lie precisely in our attempts to "make each other over" into our own image and likeness. The hardest part of being together for many of us, and perhaps one of the main reasons why we ought to invest quality time in getting to know one another, is learning to "let be" and trusting enough to "let God," without, however, sinking into indifference. There is a fine balance here between concern and control, and one that needs particular attention in our interactions with newer members.

The Stress Factor

My almost seventeen years of experience teaching them in the various spirituality programs arranged for them throughout the country leave me no doubt that much of the unhappiness our newer members experience in their initial years of religious life revolves around control issues as well as policies requiring frequent mobility. Having already experienced one major stress factor in the life-change they have chosen to make, it is of little help to them that so many congregations propose numerous changes in living situations and ministerial explorations during their discernment years. This, furthermore, is of questionable value from the perspective of community discernment as well. Too much change and undue control, besides preventing any possibility for establishing meaningful relationships, tends to bring out regressive tendencies in even the healthiest adult. Hence, if some of our newer members seem to exhibit "dysfunctional relational patterns" (as one "formation" team pointed out to me) or discover within themselves problems with authority, sexuality, and, sometimes, chemical dependency or other addictions, the stress we often put them under by overplanning their lives and moving them from one "formation" site to another can certainly be counted as a contributing factor.

Dr. Jackie Schwartz, management consultant and family therapist, in her work *Letting Go of Stress* cites stress factors conducive to illness. Among them I counted a significant number applicable to persons entering religious life. Not least of these are changes of residence, major changes in social activities, changing to a different line of work, changes in responsibility at work, changes in living conditions (group living, climate), revisions of personal habits (dress, manners, personal associations, cultural expectations, diet), changes in number of family get-togethers, and others.[9] Citing Lisa F. Berkman and S. Leonard Syme's nine-year study on stress, Schwartz emphasizes the need for an adequate support system to maintain good health:

> Every time I found evidence of disrupted social relationships, I found evidence of some sort of negative health outcome. And the range of disease outcomes is very broad indeed. For example, people with interrupted social ties exhibit more depression, unhappiness, and loss of morale...higher morbidity rates for such illnesses as gastrointestinal upset, skin problems, arthritis, and headaches.[10]

A large number of symptoms indicating excessive amounts of stress can be detected among many of our newer members. Besides the general irritability, hyperexcitation, or depression so frequently present, one often can observe impulsive behavior, emotional instability, the overpowering urge to cry, the loss of the *joie de vivre* with which they came, emotional tension, high-pitched laughter, hypermotility, loss of appetite or overeating, increased smoking, increased use of legal drugs and alcohol, and other substance abuse.[11] The danger of misdiagnosing stress-related symptoms as indicative of problems in the personality of the newer member is clear. Instead of addressing the cause of the stress, reducing stress factors wherever possible, and arranging programs of initiation to suit the demands and needs of the times, as well as of the individual, we often place the onus entirely on newer members and question their capacity for adjustment to situations which may be entirely unnecessary and totally unrelated to the essentials of discernment. Quite often the programs we create for them—often without them—are for our convenience rather than theirs. We bring them together from near and far so that we only will need one "director" and can also save on facilities. We do not even fathom that a contemporary program of welcome and mutual discernment, if creative and inclusive of other members of the congregation, might be able to do away with both. Does one have to draw the conclusion that we prefer to impose the stress on the newer member rather than to challenge ourselves to new and innovative ways of welcome?

It may be that for many of us stress is one of those things one grins and bears. To introduce it here as a significant factor to be taken seriously in the discernment of vocation may strike us as an exaggeration, even "sissification" of the process. *We* had no such consideration. Yet, true as this is, many of us are also here to manifest the consequences of such neglect. Perhaps a greater sensitivity to stress-related dysfunctionality could raise our own levels of compassion both for ourselves and others and enhance our communal life considerably. As Richard M. Stein points out: "Stress has been studied objectively by scientists for less than forty years. In that same period of time, the ramifications of modern technology have contributed new sources of stimuli and stress which were unimaginable when the scientific study began."[12] We live in times of change. We need to take these times seriously if we wish to be viable witnesses of God's compassion and mercy.

Drawn to Prayer and to Community

I believe it to be generally true and an accepted reality that contemporary men and women seeking religious life are also persons attracted to prayer and community. Being adults, many of them were probably drawn by someone among us with whom they have shared prayer and with whom they have interacted on a personal level. When they come to us, therefore, many of our newer members already pray and commune. Like us, however, they cannot pray with everyone equally well and, because of the theological divergence in community generally, they can perhaps not pray with some sisters or brothers at all; but, then, neither can we. Like us they will want to look for a compatible community. Their education, background, interests, and needs cannot be satisfied equally well in all of our residential or nonresidential communities, nor should our "formation" of them demand or expect this. In fact, I wonder whether, within the holistic paradigm we are called to embrace today, we ought to "form" anyone. The entire notion of "formation" is Aristotelian-Thomistic at best and does not speak of our contemporary understanding of person, which resists "mold" and "form" and honors the emergence of inner capacities and strengths, given proper environment and empowerment. The term "novitiate" also seems questionable, and I find it disrespectful of the adults we hope to attract. Etymologically it refers to the "uninitiated," those in need of guidance and "training," not to men and women seeking the companionship of adults for adults as adults, not to mature persons drawn to community because of an inner sense of call to minister with, to pray with, to share.

It is my sincere conviction that the women and men who want to walk with us and break bread with us in religious life today do not need "formation." Like us, they will need and they will ask for spiritual direction and guidance. They will request it of those among us or elsewhere who inspire them and empower them toward further growth. They may not always ask it of their "formation" directors. The policy of receiving spiritual direction from someone whom the system, as it prevails to date, still sees as primarily responsible for assessment and evaluation is administratively "unclean" and, as I mentioned already, can be psychologically, as well as spiritually, damaging. It opens up the possibility for mistrust and even dishonesty.

Like any other adult, the men and women drawn to community will need to be able to discern the place and the group with whom this community can be experienced. It is clear that being new, they will need our help and suggestions in doing this, and the communities involved need to dialogue and discern as well. What no one today needs, however, is the orchestrated environment of a community set apart for "formation." It may be true, as we already observed, that contemporary community situations are in the process of change and are developing in diverse ways. That, I am sure, needs to be addressed and cannot be avoided while we propose Band-Aid solutions to "formation" problems or unilaterally hold up the traditional as the ideal. Those coming to discern their call to religious life are coming to join *us*. They are seeking an active, ongoing lifestyle of ministry and relationship. They are looking to meet the women and men with whom they will spend their lives. They do not need a preprogrammed package of what they may never experience after they have taken their vows. If we cannot meet them where we live and as we live, perhaps we should not encourage them to come.

Nor does the rationale of having all newer members live together for purposes of bonding hold up anymore. To begin with, few religious congregations experience that great an influx of newer members that a viable community situation can be formed for any stable length of time to enable bonding and relationship in a realistic sense of the word. Secondly, the individuals coming may quite possibly come from diverse areas of the country, from diverse cultures and even countries. They may vary greatly in age and interest. To assume that, because they are all new in the congregation, they will automatically bond with each other and form the "support system," the "band," we all had, is to look for something which may no longer be real for them. They should not be asked to live community without, like us, being part of discerning its direction and composition. They should not be asked to live community at any cost, in any setting, especially a prearranged one. In other words, they should not at any time be expected, as they so often are even today, to "grin and bear it."

Unless an adult model of interaction is encouraged right from the start, adult behavior cannot be expected. This can, of course, be a considerable challenge for us as we struggle with the very real relational issues discussed in chapter 4. Facing the question of new membership in the midst of our own acknowledged brokenness is indeed difficult, but it can no longer be swept aside or passed on to a few "well trained directors of formation." If we want increase, we (all of us) will have to surrender to the conversion that is asked of us. This means opening not only our houses but also our hearts to those who seek incorporation. They will not forever knock at the doors of our already existing friendships to seek inclusion. They yearn to live with, be with, suffer with, and celebrate with us, to work out their journey with its history, its brokenness, and its future with us, and to be there for us in our journey as well. But they cannot be asked to do this in the vacuum left after we go off to be involved with our well-established relationships weekend after weekend, night after night. We need to include them in the reality of our relationships and our lives. We have no ivory tower setting to offer them. Our reality needs to be offered honestly: a group of struggling, loving women and men who invite them into our midst to join in the journey home, to minister and be ministered to, to help and be helped.

As I mentioned already, the men and women who come to join us these days are very much products of this age. They will want to experience with us in diverse ways how to be effectively lovers of God's *basileia*. The counter-cultural stance of celibate loving may be new to many of them. We can share our dreams, our visions with them. They, on the other hand, may bring new energy, new hope to tired hearts. Their life-experiences—very different from ours, especially if we entered young—can be of great value to us. Their style of communicating, of confrontation and interaction, may be very helpful for our explorations into new forms of relating and being with one another. We might learn much from them, not only from their experiences, but also about us: about our charism, about our willingness to learn, as well as our willingness to share. In turn, we invite them to learn. They are invited, not programmed. Our interaction with them ought to be mutual and open-ended. We invite them to move with us in shared responsibility toward our charism—the Christian message particularized in our covenantal reality. Their communion with us flows from our already existing communities. It is not forced in stereotyped group sessions with other "young professed" on programmed weekends or at study days which they all "must" attend because *we* feel it is good for them.

Organic Incorporation

Adults today, if they respond in an adult way to an adult congregation, may, as I mentioned already, wish to commit themselves in varying degrees: for several years, for one year at a time, forever, or in varying types of membership. They may wish to be ministerially bonded only or may wish to contribute financially. They may be communally bonded but work in what some congregations may still regard as "secular" professions and minister for justice there. Their discernment with us in all this should be open-ended and dialogical, in the spirit of mature interrelationship where the needs of all are considered and respected and where concern for the congregational charism is primary.

Incorporation that is oriented to diversity must be "organic" rather than "institutional. By this I mean a "being drawn" which is natural rather than formal: adults attracted to a particular local group get invited to share in that group's activities or ask to become a part of them. In that group they pray, commune, share their resources, and discern membership even while membership is already going on. They move into the larger group as the spirit directs: slowly, through visits to the provincial house, congresses, assemblies, and the like. They reach beyond the local community when the need presents itself and shared discernment directs it. The community, including all its members, evaluates the situation of that community, not only of the new member. There is a general recognition that the Spirit gifts each member with various insights concerning the whole.

Organic incorporation means that the women or men inter-

ested in our lifestyle are simply invited to be the women or
men *they* are, among the women or men *we* are, with all the
risks that growing together implies. They, no doubt, will want
and need a contact sister or brother: someone who walks with
them and can share our history with them. The congregation
will need someone trained in coordinating the various modes
of membership, to make resources available and give support.
Most of all we will need community-life facilitators: those who
are trained to help diverse communities in their personal interactions, conflicts, and general relational issues, those who can
help all of us become aware of the demands of intimacy which
are beginning to emerge among us and are inviting us beyond
professionalism to depth relation and generativity.

We all know that there is enough neurosis and dysfunctionality in our midst, that we do not need a new influx. In
order to prevent this, the vision of organic incorporation I suggest here will need much thought and prayer. But it will also
need generosity and the willingness to risk. It will certainly not
guard us against mistakes but, then, neither has the model of
"formation" most congregations have followed up to now.

I have experienced both excitement and resistance to this
possibly new vision toward increase when I have presented
it to various groups. The excitement frequently came from the
men and women now in "formation," but also from those who
knew interested persons but saw them as too mature for the
structures of incorporation presently in use in most religious
communities. They found themselves hesitant to recommend
sometimes even their own congregations to these individuals.
Positive response has often come also from religious working
in areas away from the unit or congregational center, away
from large numbers of their own sisters or brothers. For them,
communal relating with other women and men is part of their
own support system. They treasure these mature interactions

and would welcome more organic ways of connecting their friends with their congregations.

Among the negative reactions, mistrust in one's own ability to deal with newer members and a desire to leave this to the experts is certainly one. Some have pointed out to me that newer members are not always as mature as I seem to imply. I hasten to point out that neither are we, and that the maturity we are striving for is there to be aspired to by all of us. The organic approach is unquestionably one of risk. It disrupts old, well-oiled methods designed for step-by-step progress and eventual closure to a process of incorporation that connects the individual forever with the group. It can, therefore, make us very nervous for, among other things, it will not provide us with the certainty of a "job well done." Thus it is quite probable, for example, that knowledge and appreciation of the vows will be difficult to measure when discernment is individualized and spans years, when the "religious" emerges out of each newer member slowly, and stamps the congregation each time with originality. It may be difficult and at times disconcerting for some of us to experience in the lived reality of our newer members that vows are not once and for all entities which we "take," at a fixed moment in time, forever. We may commit ourselves forever, but the substance of our commitment deepens and may in a very real sense change as life teaches us the reality of our promise. This, I have suggested throughout these pages, is true for all of us, not just for our newer members. When one is "formed" in a dualistic paradigm, however, as many of us were before Vatican II, expectations of closure die hard. It is difficult to accept that few if any of us know fully what we vow when we vow it; that our commitment is surrender to the mystery; that, organically speaking, having only a glimpse is really all that can be expected at any given moment.

We spend most of our lives living into the vowed experience, altering our motivations frequently, hopefully ever toward greater depth. We are all "a risk." The intensity of the vowed experience lies ever in the yearning. Knowledge, as well as the ability to articulate, is really secondary. To feel this yearning in all humility is grace; to speak about it, on the other hand, may be one of the riskiest attempts of all. I know, therefore, that moving into "organic" modes of incorporation is more easily suggested than carried out. To feel the necessity for it within us is one thing; sensitively to witness it unfolding in our newer members may be quite another. It requires above all compassionate being-with, patience, sisterly and brotherly love which, more than anything else, knows the power of releasement. It requires persistent obedience to one's own integrity. It requires the knowledge of the "rabbi who walked in the woods."

What we have to offer is precious but, like all things precious, it must be handled gently in open hands and with hospitality and trust, out of a sense of sharing rather than bestowing, or else it will be broken or lost. Our trust and hospitality, no doubt, will bring us suffering as it did to our founders, but it brought holiness (wholeness) as well. It brought women and men of vision; it brought increase.

Questions for Focus, Reflection, and Discussion

1. "We tell our stories to live." How does the rabbi's message gift religious congregations with life?

2. Does Teilhard de Chardin's meditation on death (see p. 204 above) have significance for religious life as you see it? Do we as congregations need to be "hollowed out" to make room for God?

3. Do you experience resistance to the letting-go required for the sake of new life? Are we as congregations realistically facing the possibility of death? Are we in the "desert of need"?

4. What is your attitude toward, and what are your expectations of, the newer members of your congregation? Are you willing to share your life with them?

5. What, do you think, are the reasons why "we draw them but cannot seem to keep them"?

6. What does religious life have to offer today? Why would a man or woman want to join your congregation? What model of life would you like to live and would you propose for our newer members?

7. Do you agree that "some of the greatest frustration points in our life together as a community generally lie in our attempts to 'make each other over' into our own image and likeness"? Does this apply to our attitude toward our newer members as well?

8. What is the difference between "letting-be" in order to "let God," and indifference?

9. Can you identify stress factors in the life of our newer members? What do you see as the solution to the seemingly excessive amounts of stress experienced by them?

10. "If we want increase, we (all of us) will have to surrender to the conversion that is asked of us. This means opening not only our houses but also our hearts to those who seek incorporation." What is your reaction to this observation?

11. How do you respond to the varied ways of membership suggested in this chapter? How has your congregation acted in this area up to now?

12. What would you add to this chapter's reflection on "organic" incorporation? How practical is it? How risky? Is it worth trying?

EPILOGUE

Just as I was nearing the end of writing these reflections, a list of questions and concerns was sent to me by members of a major religious congregation to help me prepare an address for their yearly assembly. Among these there are several, I believe, that are particularly important for us today:

- I believe religious life is dead. Community as we have lived it and as we continue to try to live it and structure it does not work. Can we start talking about this and come to a point of shaping the future rather than have it shape us by default?

- When will we get to the point of discussing our vision of the future without fear?

- Why do we stay in religious life? What are our dreams? How are we together in community?

- Our first concern needs to be how we live together and how we are together.

These questions are not new for any of us. Some of us hold them quietly in our hearts; others, more boldly, want them addressed at yearly assemblies; all of us ask them. There is much sadness in many of these questions, sometimes even desperation. They are the questions of the "turning point"—the crisis of our way of life and, although solutions to the difficulties they raise will probably never come by way of clear-cut formulas or constitutional reformulation (many of us have spent hours already in vain trying to make this happen), in a certain sense, and encouragingly so, an answer to them is already emerging *in the very asking of the question*. Awareness and recognition—the intentional exposure of oneself to the darkness and (like the rainmaker) to the "drought," in spite of the pain that this involves—are the beginning of vision.

We will remember, however, that vision when it emerges will not be our achievement. (The rainmaker did not do anything; he merely surrendered to the Tao.) True vision always is a gift. When it graces us, therefore, we do not experience "sight" as much as we experience "being sighted," being drawn, being enticed into depth. Our answers, then, will emerge out of that depth. The struggle with formulas, decrees, and properly stated resolutions concerning our life and our mission, important though these may be, will be quite secondary, for our actions will flow from an inner encounter with our deepest self and, through it, with all of humankind.

For the activists among us the invitation to creative waiting, to quiet watchfulness and passionate surrender, may seem quite useless. None of what I have suggested, however, implies inaction or quietism. When Paul pointed out to the Romans that hoping "for what we cannot see means awaiting it with patient endurance" (Rom. 8:25), he was not recommending passivity, but merely exhorting them to recognize their own limits as they work toward establishing God's reign, to give heed and to surrender to a greater power. The invitation given by Rahner and cited in chapter 2 comes to mind:

> Give deeper realities of the spirit a chance now to surface: silence, fear, the ineffable longing for truth, for love, for fellowship, for God. Face loneliness, fear, imminent death! Allow such ultimate basic human experiences to come first. *Don't go talking about them, making*

up theories about them, but simply endure these basic experiences.[1]

Religious life today finds itself in crisis. The time has come, therefore, to draw inward together and alone, to embrace the depth questions of our vowed life, and to put ourselves "back in the Tao," so that the rain may once again come. Before we do any more, we need to be: to face and endure the darkness. The preceding pages have attempted to help us in this; to open up the issues and suggest possibilities without attempting to give solutions; to invite all of us to keep asking, to keep exploring, to keep risking. Crises, as we know, are not solved. They resolve themselves in their own time, in God's time. Ours is ever the task of obedient listening even as we wait passionately and creatively for "the grace of a better dawn" (M. Heidegger).

Appendix 1

CONVERSION OF CONSCIOUSNESS

It happened on Saturday of Holy Week during the liturgy's proclamation of the Gospel. You will recall that the reading for that night tells of women who went to the tomb of Jesus to anoint his body. As they arrived, however, they did not find Jesus. They were met, instead, by two angels who asked them this startling question: "Why do you seek the living among the dead?" Here it was that I experienced a special breakthrough, where, for a moment, my attention drifted away from the rest of the proclamation, and I was struck by the incredible challenge of that question, as well as by its relevance for religious life today.

Why do we in so many ways persist in looking for the living among the dead? There is no doubt that religious life today is in crisis. We, along with the culture that in many respects birthed our mode of living the evangelical counsels, are experiencing a monumental paradigm collapse. Nothing seems any longer what it used to be. Entire structures appear to be imploding before our very eyes and the word is out, though it is at times vehemently rejected, that we can't go back to the way it was, no matter how much we loved it.

The substance of this essay was first published in *Religious Life: The Challenge for Tomorrow* (New York: Paulist, 1994), chapter 2. It is included here to provide the reader with some added information regarding human and cultural development as foundational to the transformation of consciousness to which we are being called today.

Now, students of culture and social consciousness assure us that when paradigms collapse the only worthwhile and creative thing to do is to start from point zero.[1] They suggest that all attempts to rearrange matters—to rectify old views and fit them into a newly emerging vision so that no one will feel hurt, so that tradition will not be violated, and that all will remain orderly—only serve to distort things and to de-energize, if not destroy, creativity. When paradigms collapse, the only creative thing to do is to let go, so that free space is created for the new to emerge.

This is extremely difficult since, among other things, not all of us are aware of the death of our primary paradigms at the same time and, therefore, we keep holding on; we keep looking through outdated lenses. Our vision becomes blurred, but somehow we keep plodding along and keep thinking that if only we strained our eyes a bit more things might get back into focus. We lack "releasement," but somehow we think that not letting go is "being faithful to our founders," that holding on is "walking in their footsteps." We keep looking for the living among the dead and, as a consequence, the resurrection escapes us.

The words of Carl Jung come to mind: "No one can make history who is not willing to risk everything for it, to carry the experiment with his [or her] own life through to the bitter end, and to declare that his [or her] life is not a continuation of the past, but a new beginning."[2] This, I believe, is what it means ultimately to be "resurrection people." This is also what it means, in the truest sense, to be faithful. Faithfulness, more than anything else, revolves around creativity, around depth listening that blossoms into hope-filled spontaneity. Being faithful to our founders is, therefore, being true to the life-giving approach that they brought to their here and now. They saw a situation of need and responded to it radically.

Loyalty to that kind of tradition means, first and foremost, seizing the present moment and responding to it in creative obedience to the now. It does not mean obsession with what appears to me to be an ever more debilitating past. It does not mean holding on to the good ideas of our founders without checking for their relevance today. It does not mean looking for the living among the dead.

"No one," Jung tells us, "can make history who is not willing to risk everything for it." History, however, and with it its cultural expression and authenticity, is directly proportionate to the development of consciousness on the part of the individual persons shaping that history. The opening up of awareness—human transcendence—directly influences human depth and transformation, and it is here where I see the relevance for religious in the years to come. It is here where I see unbelievable need and, therefore, limitless opportunity. It is here where I see *call*.

In a work entitled "Problems of Modern Psychotherapy," written just two years after his previously quoted observation, Jung has this to say about Western culture: "Our civilization is still young, and young civilizations need all the arts of the animal tamer to make the defiant barbarian and the savage in us more or less tractable. But at a higher cultural level we forgo compulsion and turn to self-development."[3] It is my contention that the time to take ownership of this "higher cultural level" has dawned upon us and that we will not succeed in shaping any tomorrows for ourselves personally or institutionally, and above all and most importantly for our culture and ultimately for our globe, unless each one of us accepts this challenge in our individualized and communal lives, and in this way enables our civilization to embrace it as well. What does this mean?

Religious are not new to pioneering, to creating the new

where others could not or would not. The virgin territory, however, into which we are asked to venture at this crisis point in
Western civilization is not, as I see it, geographic; it is psychic. It will not demand the conversion of swamps and forests
into arable land to provide for our boarding schools and hospitals. It will ask, instead, for personal conversion, for inner
transformation. A transformative future, furthermore, will not
require that we work hard at changing other people's lives. It
demands, first and foremost, our own transformation and our
subsequent living into, and witnessing to, a new way of seeing, of interacting, of holding ourselves in relationship with
others, with God, with the universe. It asks for a new ethos, a
new way of dwelling on earth.

Perhaps a bit of specificity will help us get a handle on what
is required here. It is a well-known fact that all changes in
a person's or in an institution's life grow, of necessity, out
of a change in this person's or institution's vision of reality.
Our vision, however, depends on our consciousness, which, in
turn, is radically connected to the consciousness of the culture
in which we find ourselves. Unless we, therefore, understand
at least somewhat the momentum of awareness in human
culture, we will find it difficult to understand the *why* of
the shifts in vision that are asked of us and of the need for
change.

Religious life, as we said already, finds itself today, along
with the culture in which we live, in the pain and confusion
of radical change, of disintegration, of disorientation, of "lostness," of the dark night, of crisis. We are in a major turning
point of our own journey, and being a religious today can,
therefore, be extremely difficult and disconcerting. It is important during this time, however, to remember that, although
crises are not pleasant experiences in anybody's life, and cultural crises are generally wrought with turmoil and confusion,

we ought not to overemphasize the pain of this moment and might try to understand our era in history, instead, as a holy opportunity, as a cosmic groaning, if you will, for redemption, as clearly part of the Gospel event of dying and rising.

I believe that if we cannot get ourselves to see this, we will miss a precious opportunity for new birth. Karen Schwartz said it well a number of years ago when in *Review for Religious* she pointed out that "new paradigms emerge out of old truths and are the result of gradual letting go of traditional assumptions, prejudices and ways of thought. . . . We do not know where we are going. . . . A deep faith and a lot of listening will mark our way forward."[4]

The word "crisis" comes to us from the Greeks and means "turning point." Philosophers as well as psychologists and spiritual writers assure us that everything aware of itself experiences crises—moments of transition—in its own consciousness. Crises of consciousness are, therefore, not unhealthy but are, in fact, signs of normality and health even though experiencing them can be extremely unpleasant.[5] Furthermore, just as individuals are ontologically designed toward expansion of consciousness and go through specific developmental phases of awareness, so do groups of individuals and, in fact, entire cultures. As their phases of awareness climax, that is, reach their inherent perfection, they begin to disintegrate. Yet in this very disintegration lie the seeds for the breakthrough into a still deeper level of awareness. The disintegration, therefore, is the painful but necessary part of the turning point of growth. We generally identify the term "crisis" with this painful aspect. Thus, we tend to miss the fact that crises are creative moments of tremendous import that carry within them also great excitement and joy.

Simply put, we might say that every ontological crisis or turning point in maturation has six parts to it:

1. There is the reaching of perfection or climax in one particular level of awareness. This is understandably accompanied by a sense of well-being and accomplishment, of "having arrived."

2. This period of fulfillment is generally followed, however, by an overall feeling of boredom, of "is this all there is?" along with disenchantment and disintegration.

3. Next comes a period of lostness, the desert experience of the "dark night." One does not know where to turn. Sometimes individuals, institutions, and even cultures make a lot of noise during this time. I call it the phenomenon of "whistling in the dark as one walks past the cemetery." A lot of activity tends to make us forget momentarily the experience of desolation with which we seem to be afflicted. As congregations, we hold strategic meetings, make all sorts of plans, make numerous declarations about new beginnings. Individuals may talk much, laugh loudly, and bluster. They may also drown their crisis in work. Psychologists call this "being in denial."

4. The desert, if endured and suffered through, however, eventually gives way to a new vision. It will do this, of course, only in its own time. Vision is gift. It is not something we strategize or plan for; neither is it deserved or earned. It is dawn after the darkness. It comes when it will and as it will: sometimes gently, sometimes exuberantly. It is pure grace—like the bridegroom in the middle of the night.

5. There follows a period of experimentation and exploration with the new vision. Sometimes it is extreme. Always it is exciting and energizing.

6. Finally, after enough experimentation and celebration has taken place, a general integration of the new level with previous levels of awareness takes place.

Now, although individuals, institutions, and civilizations all pass through ontological levels of awareness and the crises that accompany them, they obviously do not all pass through them simultaneously. Furthermore, whereas individuals are called to pass through these levels in their particular lifetimes, institutions and certainly civilizations can take centuries if not millennia to do the same. It can be readily surmised, therefore, that when individuals are more advanced than the cultures or institutions in which they live, they can suffer much. They are also often called to prophetic witness, to social transformation, to martyrdom. It is my sense that the difficulty and pain we find ourselves in today is as acute as it is because of the intersection of levels of awareness and of crisis experiences. The table on the following page may help to clarify what, upon first reflection, may appear unduly complicated.

In *Where Two or Three Are Gathered* I drew a parallel between the levels of human consciousness as discussed by Bernard J. Boelen in his book *Personal Maturity* (column 1)[6] and Beatrice Bruteau's theory of the evolution of cultural consciousness, from the "paleo-feminine," through the "masculine," into the "participatory" (column 2).[7] I have also suggested that parallels can be drawn in the evolution of religion from animism and magic, through the systematization of the mystery and a general deductive approach to theology, to induction, experience, and an overall praxis as well as depth-oriented religious consciousness that draws away from dualism to wholeness (column 3).[8] Similar evolutionary patterns are discussed by Richard Tarnas in his book *The Passion of the Western Mind* (New York: Crown/Harmony, 1990), and Desmond Murphy in *A Return to Spirit: After the Mythic Church* (New York: Crossroad, 1997). An even bolder approach is posited by Genia Pauli Haddon in her book *Body Metaphors: Releasing the God Feminine in Us All* (New York: Crossroad, 1988).

LEVELS OF CONSCIOUSNESS

	1 HUMAN CONSCIOUSNESS	2 CULTURAL CONSCIOUSNESS	3 RELIGIOUS CONSCIOUSNESS	4 INSTITUTIONAL CONSCIOUSNESS
	Personal Level Self Interdependence Wholeness	*Holistic Level* Union in Diversity Inclusion Coniunctio Participation	*Experiential Level* Unity in Diversity Accepting of Polarities/Paradox The Whole/Mystical Union Induction/Praxis	*Inclusive Level* Diversity in Membership Society of Equals Communion Hospitality/Welcome of Others
		COMMUNION		
	Functional Level Ego Emergence Opposition to Significant Other Independence Uniqueness	*Masculine Consciousness* Separation from the Whole Emergence of the Hero Abstraction, Objectification Isolation/Focus	*Dualism* Idealism/Materialism Systematization of Mystery Speculative Theology Theory: Intellectual Assent	*Caste System* Sacred/Profane Exclusion Bureaucracy Hierarchism Administration Functionalism Institutional Involvement
		SEPARATION		
	Biological Level Coenesthesis Symbiotic Union Dependence	*Paleo-Feminine Level* Tribal Unity Ostracization Meant Death	*Mystery Religions* Animism Magic	*Clan* Blind Obedience Total Group Identification Dependence
		UNION		

MID-LIFE CRISIS IV ←

NEGATIVE ADOLESCENCE CRISIS III

AUTONOMY CRISIS II

BIRTH CRISIS I

Personal Maturity

As the table indicates, we can identify at least three levels of human maturation. Within these, Boelen sees four ontological crises marking distinct shifts in awareness during which disintegration of previous perspectives and ultimately their reintegration on a deeper or higher plane occurs.

The first level can best be understood as biological. It is ours during our sojourn in our mother's womb and remains with us even after the birth crisis during the period of coenesthesis and overall at-oneness with our mother. It is the level of dependence—a state of undifferentiated cosmic unity where the general sense of my existence arises from the sum of my bodily impressions. Recent research in fetal psychology, especially by such pioneers as Stanislav Grof and Frank Lake, identify this rather forgotten period of our existence as tremendously influential for subsequent psychic development.[9]

The second level might best be identified as the level of functionality and of independence. It happens upon us during the period of *ego*-emergence (often known as the "terrible twos" and identified by Boelen as the crisis of autonomy). It is marked by a general stance of over-againstness and a need for separation and the acquiring of a separate identity. One recognizes oneself in one's difference from others and takes an individualistic stance vis-à-vis life and one's surroundings. Mutuality and sharing are not yet recognized as viable and commendable modes of interaction. The functional level, especially in its later phases, is marked by competition and ambition. Its values are in the calculable, in what can be measured and compared. It is the level of the rational, during which we are moved toward higher and higher abstraction even as we experience an ever growing alienation from our own embodiment. Its institutional parallel can probably best be understood by the term "bureaucracy"—so well described by Patricia Wittberg in her book *Creating a Future for Religious Life*—and still a powerful mode of official interaction in religious congregations at present.[10]

The functional period climaxes for the individual during the objectifying phase of negative adolescence and ultimately gives way to the third level of consciousness, marked by interdependence and an acceptance of, in fact, a craving for, the interpersonal. The third level is by far the longest and contains within itself numerous sublevels. In Jungian terms, the entire second journey of life is experienced on this level. There we encounter the wider horizons of the self, and our ego as locus of activity, functionality, and primary identity yields center stage to the deeper dimensions of human existence.

Once again, it is important to emphasize that no level yields readily to the next. There is, especially during the more mature crises of human growth, confusion, pain, disorientation, alienation, the experience of desolation, of "sickness unto death," and intense resistance. But the pain is necessary to facilitate the letting go and to stimulate the process of conversion. And often when the night is darkest, and all hope seems to have dissipated, the moment of insight breaks through. There comes, as pure gift, a gentle breeze—revelation dawns and light appears at the end of the tunnel.

But with conversion comes the mandate to embrace the gift, to surrender to the new, to cease seeking for the living among the dead, and to let one's life be transformed. The conversion of authentic maturation presents one with insights that affect one's entire way of being. There is marked change in one's disposition, one's value orientation, one's actions. Insight moves toward radical depth.

It is clear, of course, that this depth event is not something we cause or effect on our own, but rather something to which we are summoned and in the face of which even our response, although it is free, takes on the form of surrender-as-gift rather than planned execution. Individually and culturally, as well as institutionally, this call can always be shunned, and one can fixate wherever one finds oneself. This choice is, however, not effected without great loss of personal and cultural as well as institutional integrity. It is the betrayal of one's birthright and, within the Christian context, of one's baptism into the Christ event and the Christification of the cosmos for which all of us were created.

Cultural Maturation

As will be noticed, the second column outlined on the table identifies the movement of our culture. It is, as I already mentioned, also divided into three levels. We recall Jung's observation, that our culture is still very young and that we still seem to need much time for the taming of the barbarian within. It is my hope, of course, that most of us at this point of our development do at least recognize the barbarian and, therefore, no longer project the shadow within upon our neighbor or other nations and cultures. Watching the news and monitoring our nation's international activities frequently discourages me, however. Jung's suggestion to forgo compulsion and turn to the development of the self seems to be going largely unheeded. And it is here, precisely because of this general apathy, that I believe we as religious need to risk all and put our lives on the line for the shaping of history.

It would seem to me that, as a culture, our developmental level overall is probably somewhere in the negative phases of the functional level, or what Bruteau calls the "masculine" level. Though our national and international rhetoric often would have us believe differently, the confrontational style still seems to be our predominant mode of operation: we build weapons to threaten others into peace while our inner cities fester in poverty, degradation, and violence. Bigger is still better for most of us, and having or "making" it takes precedence on almost all counts over *being*. Our foreign aid is largely in arms, and, even if we work toward development, it is frequently in the giving of things to raise others' standard of living for our economic advantage, not in the nurturing and empowering of their own cultures. There is general boredom or ennui about life among many of our young people, and despair among the old. We seem to find ourselves, therefore, in an atmosphere of upheaval. What used to be is no longer. Old values appear to have perished. Our heroes have died and, with them, much hope and enthusiasm.

In order to get a more accurate picture of cultural development, it is helpful to parallel it more specifically with Boelen's individual progression from dependence through independence to interdependence. What Boelen identifies as the biological level, Bruteau, with reference to our culture, sees as the paleo-feminine era. It came to an end sometime around 3000 B.C.E. after it had held us within its womb for what is estimated to have been over twenty thousand years. It is surmised that the paleo-feminine era was marked by tribal unity and an almost symbiotic bonding with the clan. Nature enveloped the early human with its overpowering presence. Religion was animistic and tribal; ostracization spelled annihilation.

Just as each individual's infant phase is marked by universal at-oneness with his or her surroundings, so for the paleo-feminine consciousness there is cosmic unity and an almost total sense of absorption. Though its primary influence disappeared with the advent of the second level of consciousness, it cannot be denied that vestiges of it remain even to this day. The intense group identification and stress on blind obedience in religious congregations prior to Vatican II, for example, which so often resulted in thwarted ego development and regression to childishness and moral irresponsibility, situates this lifestyle quite readily on the clan level of consciousness paralleling the paleo-feminine.

It is clear that the mode of consciousness of ancient culture imposes severe limitations on progress and individual maturation. Though the paleo-feminine had its in-built securities, during its dominance freedom as an essential human dimension had not adequately evolved yet. There emerged, however, in due time among the people of the tribes those willing to "risk everything for the sake of history"; those who would steal fire from the gods; those who, as the Greeks would tell us, destroyed the domain of Mother Earth and erected their kingdom in the heavens. They were later called the heroes, for they brought consciousness out of enslavement by the clan into individual awareness. They claimed for humans their power to reason, and, as the centuries moved on, they developed it.

As I mentioned already, Bruteau calls the level of consciousness earned for the human race by these heroes the "masculine" form of consciousness. Like the functional level of Boelen, it developed because of its propensity to separate, to objectify, to take apart and analyze, to put over-against. It stressed diversification, abstraction, and independence as a way of salvation from the tribe. Its strength lay in its capacity to focus, to set apart, to confront, to subdue, to overpower for the sake of progress. It established itself in claiming "difference from" rather than "union with."

Few of us will find it difficult to recognize the mode of consciousness described here as that of our age. Few also would want to argue that in our time its implosion, because of its waning relevance in our quest for meaning, seems imminent. Fixation here can, of course, also be possible and, with fixation, invariably regression to the barbaric and self-destructive. If it is true that individuals who do not allow themselves to be moved through the ontological crises never reach fullness of personhood and thus betray themselves as well as their history, then it is equally true that cultures that fail to embrace higher forms of awareness and of interrelationship than the ones in which they find themselves and to which they have become accustomed also betray themselves.

Participatory Consciousness

Bruteau offers a third form of consciousness. It parallels Boelen's "personal level." She insists that it cannot authentically arise through rebellion or the overthrow of an old oppressive order. Rather, it must emerge through conversion, through a genuine revolution of consciousness that transcends the dualistic and divisive modes of perceiving reality and, taking up within itself the lessons learned during previous levels of awareness, aims at wholeness without absorption. In "participatory" consciousness, as she calls it, inclusion rather than exclusion will be viewed as strength. Interdependence—the union of levels one (dependence) and two (independence) on a higher plain—will be valued. In this new paradigm the stress will be placed on unity in diversity rather than either conformity (as in the clan phase of awareness) or individualism (as in our collapsing paradigm of today). It will be a gathering together of both the functional or masculine and the paleofeminine modes of awareness and will effect a moving of both into a deeper mode. Instead of over-againstness, confrontation, as well as competition, this deeper form of consciousness, to which we as individuals and as culture are called in the building up of our history, values mutual affirmation and trust. One does not find one's identity in comparing oneself negatively with the other; one rather sees oneself as loved and as good and, therefore, knows the other as loved and as good also.

If we surrender to this call to conversion, our task will be to empower one another individually and, ultimately, internationally as well, rather than yielding to the temptation of overpowering and dominating. If we surrender to this form of perception, we will no longer experience the need to "preserve ourselves," to maintain a defensive posture. Our stance, rather, will ever more become one of self-possession; hence, we can lose ourselves. From ego-enhancement we will be moved to embrace the mystery that we are. Just as ego-consciousness— along with its ability to abstract, isolate, deduce, control—was necessary at one time in the evolution of human beings from clan existence (and its emphasis on ancestral "memories") to rational and discursive thought, so now the time has come to allow humanity not only to honor its head achievements (its strength), but to embrace its heart (its vulnerability) as well, and to seek creativity there.

It is clear, of course, that we are not talking of returning to the emotionalism and superstition that may have characterized the time before the emergence of reason. We are rather pointing toward a synthetic gathering together, a movement from isolation to incorporation, a conversion of consciousness that takes up the contributions of the previous levels into itself and converts them into a deeper, more truly human form of awareness out of which authentic human relating can then flow. Many of the transformative elements envisioned by the Leadership Conference of Women Religious and the Conference of Major Superiors of Men in 1989, mentioned in chapter 4, speak to this mode of relating.

Nevertheless, the skeptics among us might easily see this vision as a dream of impossible magnitude. This, of course, is not so. What we are describing here is a way of seeing modeled for us some two thousand years ago by a carpenter preacher in Palestine. He was, it is true, crucified for it by the representatives of the functional forms of consciousness prevalent at that time. *But he was raised up.* We live in the fullness of time—in the fullness of his resurrection. The vision, therefore, is already here. The revolution has already claimed its first hero. He dwells now in our midst and calls us to conversion. It is for us to claim our heritage. And it is here where I see the future of religious life today.

Because of our vision statements and chapter acts, because of the ideals we set forth in many of our documents, it would be too easy to delude ourselves into thinking, however, that the vision is already realized in our midst. This, no doubt, is one of the reasons why so many of us are puzzled by the seeming lack of interest in our life together and the lack of response to our attempts at gaining new membership. But for us, as for all Christians of good will, the reign of God is here and also not yet. Our future, then, lies in striving for what is not yet. It seems that proposals about what religious life might do, what works and causes we might involve ourselves in, are not difficult to find. Our documents abound with objectives and plans. It is more difficult to find it within ourselves, however, to reflect on, and to abide in, the questions as to what we might *be,* what we are called to strive for inwardly, to allow for conversation to touch our inner attitudes, our way of being.

There is, of course, a certain complexity and a need for much honest discernment in what I am claiming here. Perhaps a point by point identification of my position will make the task a bit easier:

First, it is clear that religious, like all other human beings, are called to depth maturation or holiness, and that the third level of consciousness ought, therefore, to be their quest, as it is indeed for any other maturing person.

Second, it cannot be ignored that religious, like all other persons in their culture, are also *affected* by their culture—are the products of their culture—no matter how much they would see themselves and their lifestyle as almost automatically counter-cultural.

Third, religious institutions, as well, are culturally influenced. What Patricia Wittberg, S.C., so eloquently describes as the bureaucracy of our communal lives speaks accurately to our preoccupation with functionality and its effectiveness. Our concern for our survival, our endless drawing up of objectives, our actuarial studies, our persistent fears about retirement funds, our five-year plans, our various mission statements, and our stacks of paper sent out annually and faithfully filled out and returned to headquarters for still another self-study of one kind or another all manifest what seems to be a feverish holding on to what is slipping from our grasp. It comes with an inability to face death, and thus to ready oneself for a new, but also perhaps radically different life.

Fourth, hard as it may be to face, religious life as predominantly institutional is dying. Our convents and our schools are closing. Our hospitals are largely lay administered. The good works for which we were founded are being performed by numerous other wonderful people. The boundaries between the sacred and the profane are disappearing, and those who come to join us because they still see relevance in our life are calling us to radical Gospel living.

Fifth, to live the Gospel today requires third-level values. In the third and fourth columns of the table, I have attempted to outline the development of consciousness through which religious institutions are progressing. Much of this outline is explained in detail in my book *Where Two or Three Are Gathered* and does not need to be repeated here. Suffice it to say that I see us in a variety of places within the three levels. As I mentioned already, the transformative elements articulated in 1989 clearly speak to the vision of level three. So also do the voices of many among us working with the disenfranchised of our culture. In many respects, however, our words and our lifestyle and policies do not connect, and how we relate to each other, as well as to those interested in bonding with us around our charism, lacks much of the relational justice that we proclaim for the world beyond our institutions.

Honoring diversity of culture and inclusivity in our membership cannot be achieved by the year 2010, as the transformative elements envision, unless behavior, and the vision that induces it, opens up today. The clan values, still pervasive among us, and the caste-like nit-picking concerning the diversity that is emerging among us as well as regarding who belongs and who has not yet done all that is required for full membership, who may attend certain meetings, and who is not invited (all in the name of tradition and of honoring our heritage), need to be addressed candidly. Their relevance for today needs to be questioned, and the hidden and often unconscious motivations for the perpetuation of such concerns needs to be explored.

It is my experience that creativity here is often sadly lacking. We can so easily reject the call to inner transformation by pointing out that religious ought to be dealing with bigger things than worrying about regressive attitudes and behavior in their midst. But the sad fact remains that unless our life together empowers us through justice and love, our modeling of it in our ministry will eventually appear hollow as well. The need to address the injustice in others can easily become compulsive if it is not balanced by the awareness of personal sin and an earnest attempt to address the latter. Jung's warning that "at a higher cultural level we forgo compulsion and turn to self-development" can be dismissed as a luxury that we can-

not afford in a world of injustice, oppression, and cruelty only
at our own peril.

Often the resistance to examining our mode of being together and of accepting others into our midst comes from a
fear that if we finally address it, we will be forced to return to
pre–Vatican II models of co-habitation, to what Sandra Schneiders identifies so accurately as the primary family model of
group living that reduces all of us to infantilism and invariably
brings about psychological regression.[11] It is my suggestion,
however, that the unexamined life exposes us to many more
serious dangers.

Witnessing to the third level of consciousness to which, I
believe, we are called in this age of cultural crisis demands that
we explore the unhealthy patterns of fixation and regression
in our midst. This, without question, demands great personal
and communal courage and a genuine return to the holiness of
our founders, as well as the pioneering spirit of our forefathers
and foremothers. Our journey in this regard, as I pointed out
already, will be primarily psychic and will open us up both
to our collective strength as well as to our darkness. This can
indeed be frightening. I do not believe, however, that we have
any choice if we are to remain true to our call to wholeness.

Great holiness demands great sacrifice. "No one can make
history who is not willing to risk everything." This is the tradition passed on to us by our founders. It asks us to liberate
hitherto unknown, because unconscious, energies and to trust
that the Spirit of God, once more as always, will move over
the chaos of our lives and make all things new.

PARADIGM SHIFT

Throughout this book we have been claiming that our culture and, therefore, also religious life are in crisis, that we are in the throes of a major paradigm shift. Appendix 1 suggested that as religious, as ministers of the Gospel, we need to be on the forefront of the transformative process which this paradigm shift is announcing. The following reflections are intended to clarify and contextualize these observations.

1. We will explore briefly the foundations of the "modern" worldview that appears to be imploding at this time and, in its demise, inviting the new.

2. We will follow this by identifying foundational perspectives of the paradigm that seems to be taking its place.

3. Last, we will attempt to point to the impact the new foundations might have on our religious self-understanding.

If much of what is happening in our times seems disconcerting to us, it may be due to our unawareness of the foundations of many of our values and of the origin of our worldview. We may have accepted both as givens, not knowing that they, like all things human, are grounded in a context. When the context changes, much of what was accepted as unquestionable also changes. Getting a grasp of this, although it may not make things that much easier, will at least help us understand the *why* and enable us to get a bearing in the here and now.

The scope of an appendix does not permit a detailed account of a vast and complex body of knowledge. These reflections are, therefore, condensed and sketchy at best. They are offered simply as an aid in situating us in the present moment.

Foundations of the Modern Worldview

Students of the history of culture and of thought tell us that the values and the vision of the world we are living in were founded primarily on the Greco-Roman cultural perspective, on its metaphysics, and especially on its dualism. They received their strongest impetus, however, during what is now referred to as the "modern" period of thought, the time of Francis Bacon (1561–1626) and his scientific method, of Cartesian philosophy (René Descartes, 1596–1650) and its emphasis on reason and certitude, and of Newtonian physics (Sir Isaac Newton, 1642–1727) and consequent "reductionist materialism."[1] The major views inherited there were:

A. From the Greeks we learned to divide the world of reality into two categories—that of spirit and that of matter (dualism). The first was governed by the principle of permanence and the second by the principle of change. The first was seen as real and the second as unreal; the first as reliable and the second as unreliable; the first as good and the second as evil; the first as generally masculine and the second as feminine. Given this view, change gradually began to be viewed as fickle, false, and illusory, and the perpetual, indelible (and, in ecclesial thinking, the dogmatic—declared *ex cathedra* and forever) was seen as good, as laudable, as the truth.

With dualism the hierarchical worldview can be explained, since that which is viewed closer to the spirit, what is good and real, is easily identified as better than that which is closer to the material, what is evil and unreal. (Within that division also can be found the religious rationale for masculinism and its effects on our self-understanding.)

B. The mechanistic universe came to us from Descartes—a clear inheritance, therefore, from what is today referred to as the "modern" era. The Greeks and the people of the Middle Ages still saw the world as living—with soul as the animating principle. With Descartes and modern rationalism as well as its dualistic counterpart, empiricism, the world became machine-like, governed entirely by universal mathematical laws. A mechanistic theory of nature became the foundation for our view of technological progress, scientific advancement, and medicine, with its approach to the human body and to the person. The machine became the central image. There was and still is today a life-denying, soul-less, purposeless dimension to this perspective. Things are pushed by causes, not drawn by their own inner direction or goals.

C. Newton provided the laws of motion for the mechanistic universe. Matter was unconscious stuff made up of inert atoms. Nature was determined, predictable, controllable, and knowable by mathematical reason. Objectivity implied certainty and could be attained by detached reason. This was understood as attaining the truth.

D. Bacon gave us the scientific method—universalized to approach all knowledge.

"Modern" thought gradually and almost imperceptibly (primarily under the influence of empiricism) took the Greek emphasis on spirit and shifted the focus of its dualism to the material world, although the trust in reason continued with the belief that eventually all of reality would be explainable and could, therefore, be controlled.

The Values of This "Modern" Worldview

Truth in this worldview is understood as truth only if it is objective, permanent, definable, and can, therefore, be equated with reality. It is obtained through detached observation. Certitude is primary. Predictability is essential when serious decisions have to be made, and risk should at all times be avoided. Control (being on top of things) is prized highly, for it brings about order. Change is seen as advisable only within the boundaries of predictability. Measurability is a high value in running a successful organization. Conservation and preservation are necessary for true progress.

Not only did the "moderns" approach nature out of this context, but they also approached themselves—human interactions—that way. The latter became increasingly mechanistic and confrontative—overpowering, bureaucratic, controlling, detached, uniform. The "humanities" also—history, philosophy, literature, theology—all were affected by the mechanistic worldview, for it became the only valid perspective, representative of reality as such.

If truth was identified with certitude, objectivity, and eternity (permanence) then the *definition* became primary in arriving at understanding, and one's capacity to define something became proof of knowledge. If we apply this view to our religious way of life, we can see its effects in most of what we do even to this day. Objectives are high on our list of priorities; predictability, order, and organization are valued. We define ourselves, our goals, our very charism. Our interactions with each other and with the "outside" world, therefore, also speak to its norms: anything whose reality is clearly definable becomes by definition exclusive of that which does not fall within its limits. Group identity, therefore, revolves around who is in and who is not. The group's value and status depend on its difference from others, not its at-oneness with others. We understand inclusion by exclusion, belonging by identifying who does not or cannot. Many of our policies on membership, on where and how and with whom one should live, on what practices, especially with respect to prayer, are essential to our life, and what we should do with those who do not see it our way, on who can come to our meetings and who will not be invited find their place here. So also do our difficulties in understanding, let alone envisioning, anything other than what has always been the norm.

The close connection of religious life to the Catholic ecclesial model of governance and our dependence on church approval perpetuate dualism in our midst, although, since Vatican II, valiant efforts have been made by many of us to protest it and modify our way of making decisions. It seems that official Catholicism is almost by definition dualistic, exclusive, and triumphalistic in its policies and self-understanding. The strange moral reductionism and almost obsessive need for uniformity and doctrinal absolutes, the fear of change, and the sacralizing of permanence have its effects on all of us and forever threaten to invade and restrict any creative movement and innovative thought.

Discoveries and Theories of Post-"Modern" Science

With this as our background it is understandable that the implosion of this worldview—the basis for the structures of our life and the foundation, in many respects, for the interpretation of our faith—can be very upsetting. When one view has been accepted as clearly the way things are and always have been, it can be disturbing, to say the least, to find out that the discoveries and theories of modern science see things very differently and, therefore, offer a different worldview.

Today scientific research suggests that truth, instead of being objective, might really much more accurately be understood as *relational*. Consciousness and the physical world are really not separate entities, we are told, but, in fact, form one whole, one fundamental area of awareness. The word "omnijective" rather than either objective or subjective fits this phenomenon of "truth-as-encounter" much more readily. There is an open-endedness to truth. It grows, as it were. The categories of permanence and "define-ability," therefore, do not adequately speak to what is more readily experienced as an *event* than as a static *thing*—"graspable" and limited.

When truth is defined, scientists tell us, it loses contact with reality, which cannot be limited that way. Open-endedness defies limitations. Definitions, therefore, become obsolete as soon as they are formulated. We "create" our reality, as it were, for it responds to us according to our expectations. Truth is attained, therefore, through involvement rather than by detached observation. Reality is best seen in terms of dynamic events rather than as unchanging substances. It does not respond to the expectations of certitude and permanence since the only thing permanent is, in fact, change. There is an interplay of law and chance in all of reality. Predictions can, therefore, not readily be made.

Modern science warns against the setting up of closed systems. They run down, we are told, because they are deprived of the new. Open systems, on the other hand, receive constant input from the environment. This allows them to thrive. Reality, rather than being seen as mechanistic, is better understood as organic. As such it is an "undivided whole" that transcends space and time* and is in fact "in perpetual dynamic flux." Holography teaches us that every part of reality contains, in fact, the whole of it. All is interconnected, interwoven, one.

---

*Space and time are human constructs to help navigate our sojourn here on earth.

The "desirables" of modern science might best be understood as open-endedness, as respect for the mystery that underlies reality, as participation and relationality, as process.

Implications for Religious Self-Understanding

An extraordinary sense of freedom can open up for us with this new information, if we allow ourselves to move into the insights presented here and begin to see the bigger picture. Both in *Wrestling with God* (the chapters on "Creative Courage," and "In Search for the 'Why' ") and in *Prayer and the Quest for Healing* (all of part 3) I have tried to identify the possible impact of contemporary scientific discoveries and theories on our life and on the choices we make. I do not need to repeat these thoughts here. By way of closure, however, let me suggest the following:

(a) Certainly our concern with our identity in terms of difference from the rest of the world will have to yield to a deeper understanding of community. A profound sense of responsibility for, and interconnectedness with, the other would do much to change our priorities.

(b) Our holding on to permanence as superior to change, especially evident in our theology of commitment, will need reconsideration.

(c) The values of preservation and conservation as sacrosanct for every aspect of a system whose nature is constantly and dynamically to change become obsolete. (The word "system" here includes both our congregations and our way of life.) Our stress on preservation and conservation was based on a fixed world order. Our response within its context was to protect what *was*, therefore, with all the strictures that this necessitated.

The importance of preservation and conservation in our ecclesial tradition was enhanced, furthermore, by empirical decrees, once Christianity became the official religion of the Roman Empire. What we even now theologically consider unchangeable and sacrosanct—the indelible marks, the *ex cathedra* statements, the perpetual vows, the priesthood forever—were largely the result of an attitude that fostered this for empirical convenience and control. Today this needs to be reexamined on its own ground and within a very different perspective.

(d) Clearly in our interactions external influence (control) must yield to respect for the inner dynamics of growth and development. *Overpowering*—even with the gentlest of demeanors and always, of course, for "sister's or brother's own good"—must yield to *empowering.* That this shift will have major implications for our theories of formation and human development needs little comment. "Formation" as a concept, in fact, may need serious reconsideration as it implies the molding of inanimate matter into a preconceived form by an external efficient cause. We simply can no longer confuse control with order. "If organizations are machines," says Margaret J. Wheatley, "control makes sense. If organizations are process structures, then seeking to impose control through permanent structure is suicide."[2]

(e) If, as was mentioned above, reality is altered by observation, and truth, in a very real sense, depends on how one looks at it, this insight could have a considerable impact on the way we view our evaluations of each other, our approach to new members, to different models of membership, to the reality of our situation, to change, to our self-studies. We would have to take seriously the fact that all are affected by our attitude, our hidden or not so hidden agendas. *They are never merely objective.* We help bring about our reality (both positive as well as negative) by the way we interpret our situation and by the choices we make.

(f) Lastly, a consideration particularly relevant for religious congregations in this period of paradigm shifts, of dying, and of refounding: science assures us today that when a system interacts with a great amount of new information, eventually a level of disturbance is reached such that the system experiences a loss of equilibrium and "falls apart" in its current form. What needs to be remembered, however, and is, I believe, of particular consolation for us is that "this disintegration does not signal the death of the system. In most cases the system can reconfigure itself at a higher level of complexity, one better able to deal with the new environment."[3]

1. It is clear that we live in a world that has in most respects changed drastically from the world in which our congregations were founded.

2. For whatever reasons we have in many respects resisted inevitable change and adaptation often for the sake of "tradition."

3. Where this is not true, especially since Vatican II, we now find ourselves having caught up with the modern era (especially in our professional lives, if not in our communal ones) only to see it collapsing in its turn because of the information from the post-"modern," post-industrial, post-mechanistic discoveries (especially in science) that we have been discussing.

4. For us to resist responding to and creatively integrating the information coming our way means almost certain demise. Our greatest danger is in the denial of the collapse of our previous equilibrium and the feverish attempts to get things going again without reconfiguration.

5. Reconfiguration is not a patch job. It does not mean repainting the old. It means radical change toward a higher level of complexity. It means seeing with new eyes. It means conversion and a deep belief that God is in our midst.

Creation is ongoing. God is not finished with us yet. The universe is truly unfolding as it was intended: dynamic, changing, ever alive and transforming toward deeper and holier levels of possibilities. The death and the resurrection of the Christ is a cosmic event, and we are called to be a part of this.

Appendix 3

RELIGIOUS:
A NEW WAY OF LIVING,
A NEW WAY OF DYING

Were not our hearts burning within us?

(Luke 24:32)

I returned from a funeral today. Pat was a very dear friend
of mine, a woman on the cutting edge of religious life, bril-
liant, with vision far beyond the ordinary and a prophetic
stance that could disturb, challenge, as well as excite anyone—
depending on where one found oneself in the cultural upheaval
of our time.

Pat had lived for many years, as so many of us do now,
either alone or with another sister. Her connections with her
congregation were deep. She loved and cared passionately and
had many friends. Choosing a different community style from
what some might consider the "normative mode" of convent
or larger group setting had never prevented Pat from feeling
and being at one with those with whom she had covenanted
her life nor, for that matter, with friends from other religious
communities and with many of her lay colleagues. She was a
woman of great compassion and had an easy style that readily
befriended the great as well as the small—executives as well as

This essay was first published with *Sisters Today* (November 1997) and is here reprinted
with permission. It offers reflections that may be able to further our discussion and may
deepen our appreciation and understanding of the nature of our emerging ways of relating.

groundskeepers, board chairs as well as secretaries. She handled power easily because she saw it as a means rather than the end. Though she was at home with bureaucracy, she used it for the sake of the relational—working with it rather than being of it. She was a modern religious poised for the post-modern era, a maverick who knew the congregational "diaspora" yet never yielded to bitterness. For me and many of her friends she had been a model of integrity, a woman without guile.

Today we buried her, and it is of this and of her dying that I wish to write. Three months ago Pat was diagnosed with inoperable cancer of the stomach and given only a brief time to live. The diagnosis came suddenly and quite unexpectedly during the treatment of a stomach ulcer. Pat was relaxing for a weekend with some of her friends when she received word not only that she had cancer, but also that it seemed to have spread throughout her stomach, and that a serious operation had to be performed immediately. The operation was unsuccessful, and Pat was faced with death.

Because religious have often very clear medical policies for recuperation, for nursing care, for retirement, and even for the end phases of their lives, it would have been expected that Pat move to the large nursing facility at the motherhouse to prepare for her death. In every respect there was the best medical care available for her twenty-four hours a day. After prayerful discernment, however, Pat with her support group of friends decided to die where she had lived—at home in her apartment, cared for by her friends.

A network of caregivers gathered around her to support her and each other throughout the three months that followed. Hospice was engaged for the needed medical assistance. The sister-friend who lived with Pat took a leave of absence from work to be her primary caregiver. Others volunteered to fill in for rest periods. A group of sisters from around the city offered to cook and bring in meals so that those directly concerned with Pat's needs would not have to worry about cooking for themselves. Others offered to do the washing of bed linens and towels.

Those of us who were not of Pat's congregation offered to be of help in whatever way we could. We were amazed at the network of helpers that simply "did what any sister would have done." It seemed to us that in many respects they would have seen themselves as peripheral had Pat been in a nursing facility, but that, under these circumstances, they knew that they were needed and were most willing and enthusiastic to show their love and support tangibly.

We visited frequently whenever Pat's physical condition would allow it and were deeply touched by the genuine hospitality and homey-ness into which we were received. The mood was not only positive but genuinely filled with friendliness and laughter. There were no secrets in this community of friends. They faced the reality of impending death and, together with Pat, looked it squarely in the eye. Pat's dying was a painful process, but she was determined to get all the meaning out of it, to understand what was happening to her, and to choose her options—limited though they were. She was involved in every detail of letting go; she connected with those to whom she needed to bid farewell; she wrote resignation letters to the numerous boards and committees of which she had been a part; she actively took part in planning her own rite of Christian burial and spoke deeply with us of her own spirituality and vision of the hereafter, of her struggle with glib explanations and pieties.

Visits to Pat's bedside were a source of extraordinary peace for many of us. One never left there anxious or even depressed, but always deeply moved and profoundly enriched. It was like sitting at the feet of Jesus, some of us reflected. Pat worked hard at retaining consciousness until the pain became simply too unbearable. Her keen mind did not want to miss a single opportunity for insight, and learning, and love. And she, as well as all of us, learned a great deal. We learned about the homeward journey of a soul centered in integrity. We learned about letting go, gently, with forethought and deliberation. We learned about generosity—caring mementos shared during the Christmas season with friends. We learned about the pain of not being able to give gifts in return. The nakedness of death confronted us, the emptiness that finally beckons all of us back into itself. We witnessed profound religious encounters with the mysterious Other who breaks into the consciousness of those near death and reveals the possibilities beyond. And Pat taught us. She shared so willingly and even, at times, urgently what in life is of importance and what really does not matter; which questions to ask, and which concerns to let go of; what it means to develop gifts and why. There was a serenity around Pat even in her moments of greatest struggle. We carried it with us whenever we left her bedside, and it sustained us during the difficult days of leave taking.

Shortly before she was no longer able to communicate clearly, a group of us gathered around Pat's bed to anoint her and to pray for God's healing love. Pat had, of course, received the sacrament of the church previously, but somehow we felt that the anointing by her friends had a sacred significance all its own. We asked God's blessing on the oil we were about to use and together prayed that peace and strength be with Pat on her journey. We then, in pairs, gently anointed her forehead, chest, hands, and feet, praying over each. We concluded by singing our Lady's song, the Magnificat.

Pat slipped gently into God's embrace when none of her friends who might have unconsciously held on to her were present. A hospice nurse had finished administering healing touch therapy and working especially hard at raising and liberating the energy around Pat's head to open passage for the divine. Pat's friend had just stepped outside for a brief minute to take care of some laundry while the nurse was present in the sick room. Pat took this moment quietly to leave us all. A number of us were on our way to visit and pray at her bedside when we received the call. We gathered, once again, to commend her soul to eternity and to bless her body before the funeral director would need to take it away.

Not long after our final blessing prayers a young man arrived looking for a convent where he was to pick up a sister's body for embalming. He could not understand the apartment setup and was thoroughly confused to find women religious living there. He was even more amazed when Pat's friends went into her room, tenderly wrapped her body into her favorite pink sheet and carried it themselves out to the gurney. With great care, they placed it into the body bag and pushed it out toward his car. At the apartment steps a bodyguard of two groundskeepers, friends of Pat, helped carry it and lift it into the hearse. Those who witnessed this sacred event were awestruck. "I could only think of the women at Christ's tomb laying him to rest after having taken him from the cross," one of them said. "There can be nothing more sisterly than this. We were experiencing the Gospel enfleshed in our very lives."

Pat's funeral at the motherhouse chapel was a joyfully sad experience. The respect and passion for diversity and inclusion that, throughout her life, she had championed in all her relationships was clearly in evidence. We let balloons fly at the grave site and sang all her favorite hymns. And we cried. The love that so many of us had witnessed throughout these months of care seemed almost electrifying as we gathered for our last farewell.

The community that Pat forged through her suffering and

her dying is clearly a testament to a vision that far exceeds congregational boundaries and speaks of sisterhood in the deepest sense of the word. Religious today live in new ways and are bonding in new ways as well. There is no reason for fear here, however, that the loss of the old ways might have eliminated the sense of community and sacred bonding. The experience of Pat's dying reassures me that all the true values can prevail and are, in fact, inviting us into a wider community of Christian love and care. The hospice nurses who became an integral part of this farewell process witnessed friendship quite new and inspiring to many of them. The groundskeepers from the apartment complex, dressed up in their finest, joined us all to pray for their friend at her visitation. Persons from diverse religious congregations felt included in the support group Pat needed, and all of us felt responsible for her care and well-being.

So often when someone spends the last moments of her life in the well-organized nursing facilities of the congregation, many of us can slip into a sense of noninvolvement. After all, there are so many much more qualified persons who already minister to her. Such notions and excuses are not possible when our sisters die at home. The offers of help during Pat's dying process and the clear rallying around specific needs were a wonderful sign of solidarity and care. There was a genuine experience, a felt sense, among all of us that our sister was dying and needed our love. And the love flowed freely and generously. None of us would miss the final farewell either. We canceled weekend commitments and flew home from miles away to be there and fulfill the promise of walking behind the casket and standing tall for our friend. I wonder whether institutional service to our dying sisters, as excellent and well intentioned as it is, does not deprive many of us of the involvement and, therefore, of the sacredness that sisterhood can be; whether our experience with Pat has not opened up a sacred and a new possibility to deepen and authenticate our connectedness.

At the reception dinner after the funeral we shared quite spontaneously of our love for our friend, of our experiences with her during the last three months. We missed her greatly, yet found each other in a new way. And strangely, like that other time in our Christian story, our "hearts were burning within us." Religious have new ways of living today. These also herald new ways of dying. And God sees that it is good.

NOTES

Preface

1. Frederick Franck, *Messenger of the Heart* (New York: Crossroad, 1976), 53.

Chapter One: Turning Point

1. Jean Shinoda Bolen, M.D., *The Tao of Psychology* (San Francisco: Harper & Row, 1982), 98.

2. Frank Moressey, O.M.I., Ph.D., J.C.D., Remarks made as a respondent to keynote address by Barbara Fiand at the National Convention sponsored by the Legal Resource Center for Religious, Louisville, April 17, 2000.

3. Fritjof Capra, *The Turning Point* (New York: Simon and Schuster, 1982), 15, 16.

4. Ibid., 28.

5. Ibid., 26.

6. Martin Heidegger, *Vorträge und Aufsätze*, 3 vols., 3d ed. (Pfullingen: Günther Neske, 1967), 1:28 (trans. mine).

7. Capra, *The Turning Point*, 16.

8. Edward C. Whitmont, *Return of the Goddess* (New York: Crossroad, 1984), 125.

9. Anne Carr, "On Feminist Spirituality," in *Women's Spirituality: Resources for Christian Development*, ed. Joann Wolski Conn (New York: Paulist, 1986), 49.

10. Hence the emphasis among spiritual writers on breathing and posture in relation to prayer. The panting, hurried breather says much about life and his or her attitude—conscious or not—toward ultimate concerns.

11. Carr, "On Feminist Spirituality," 50.

12. Ibid., 51.

13. Beatrice Bruteau, "Neo-Feminism and the Next Revolution of Consciousness," *Anima* 3, no. 2 (Spring 1977): 1.

14. Whitmont, *Return of the Goddess,* 124.

15. Sandra Schneiders, *Women and the Word* (New York: Paulist, 1986), 19 (italics mine).

16. Bernard J. Boelen, *Personal Maturity* (New York: Seabury Press, 1978), 79.

17. John Shea, *Stories of God* (Chicago: Thomas More Press, 1978), front cover and 39.

18. Elisabeth Schüssler Fiorenza, *In Memory of Her* (New York: Crossroad, 1984), 113.

19. Ibid., 119–20.

20. Ibid.

21. Edward Schillebeeckx, *On Christian Faith* (New York: Crossroad, 1987), 17.

22. Ibid., 18.

23. Schüssler Fiorenza, *In Memory of Her,* 121.

24. Schneiders, *Women and the Word,* 41–50.

25. Ibid., 45.

26. Schüssler Fiorenza, *In Memory of Her,* chapter 5.

27. Joseph S. O'Leary, *Questioning Back* (Minneapolis: Winston Press, 1985), 152.

28. Ibid., 152–53.

29. Ibid., 176.

30. Ibid.

31. Ibid., 177.

32. Ibid.

33. James J. Bacik, *Apologetics and the Eclipse of Mystery* (Notre Dame, Ind.: Notre Dame University Press, 1980), 3.

34. Capra, *The Turning Point,* 76.

35. Cited by Aniela Jaffe, *The Myth of Meaning* (New York: Penguin, 1975), 35.

36. Cited by ibid., 31.

37. Matthew Fox, *Meditations with Meister Eckhart* (Santa Fe: Bear & Co., 1982), 16, 18, 32–33.

38. Gabriele Uhlheim, *Meditations with Hildegard of Bingen* (Santa Fe: Bear & Co., 1982), 32, 34, 35.

39. Cited by George A. Maloney, S.J., *God's Exploding Love* (New York: Alba House, 1987), 23–24.

40. Fox, *Meditations with Meister Eckhart,* 22–23.

41. Barbara Fiand, *Releasement* (New York: Crossroad, 1987), 78–79.

42. O'Leary, *Questioning Back,* 176.

43. Fiand, *Releasement,* 5.

44. Matthew Fox, *Breakthrough* (Garden City, N.Y.: Image Books, 1980), 103.

45. Ibid., 67.

46. Ibid., 59.

47. Sue Woodruff, *Meditations with Mechtild of Magdeburg* (Santa Fe: Bear & Co., 1982), 13–14.

48. Ibid., 15.

49. Fox, *Meditations,* 82.

50. Bernhard Welte, *Meister Eckhart* (Freiburg: Herder, 1979), 134.

51. Karl Rahner S.J., *Theological Investigations,* vol. 1, trans. Cornelius Ernst, O.P. (London: Darton, Longman & Todd, 1965), 310.

52. Karl Rahner, *Theological Investigations,* vol. 6, trans. Karl-H. and Boniface Kruger (New York: Crossroad, 1974), 393–94.

53. Cited in Roger Haight, S.J., *The Experience and Language of Grace* (New York: Paulist, 1979), 128.

54. Fox, *Meditations,* 86.

55. Schüssler Fiorenza, *In Memory of Her,* 135.

56. Fox, *Meditations,* 102.

57. Schüssler Fiorenza, *In Memory of Her,* 130.

58. Ibid., 135.

59. For an interesting discussion of the liberating dimensions of Christianity with particular reference to Jewish law, see Terrance Callan, *Forgetting the Roots* (New York: Paulist Press, 1986), chapter 4.

60. Sebastian Moore, *The Fire and the Rose Are One* (London: Darton, Longman & Todd, 1980), 86–87.

61. Schneiders, *Women and the Word,* 46.

62. Ibid.

63. Ibid., 46–47.

Chapter Two: What Matters Is Vision

1. Brennan Manning, T.O.R., *The Wisdom of Accepted Tenderness* (Denville, N.J.: Dimension Books, 1978), 11.

2. Sandra Schneiders, "Evangelical Equality: Religious Consecration, Mission, and Witness," *Spirituality Today* 39, no. 1 (Spring 1987): 61.

3. Ibid., 62.

4. Ibid., 62–63.

5. Ibid., 64.

6. Ibid.

7. Ibid., 64–65.

8. Beatrice Bruteau, "Neo-Feminism and the Next Revolution of Consciousness," *Anima* 3, no. 2 (Spring 1977): 11–12.

9. Bernhard Welte, *Meister Eckhart* (Freiburg: Herder, 1979), 176.

10. Martin Heidegger, *Die Kehre* (Pfullingen: Verlag Günther Neske, 1962), 45 (italics and translation with inclusive language mine).

11. Karl Rahner, *The Practice of Faith* (New York: Crossroad, 1983), 63 (italics mine).

12. Ibid., 63–64 (italics mine).

Chapter Three: Blessed Are the Poor

1. Jim Wallis, *The Call to Conversion* (San Francisco: Harper & Row, 1981), 57–58.

2. Ibid., 58.

3. Petru Dumitriu, *To the Unknown God,* trans. James Kirkup (New York: Seabury Press, 1982), 56–57.

4. John Francis Kavanaugh, *Following Christ in a Consumer Society* (Maryknoll, N.Y.: Orbis Books, 1981), 26.

5. Wallis, *The Call to Conversion*, 64.

6. Dumitriu, *To the Unknown God*, 35.

7. Donald Nicholl, *Holiness* (New York: Seabury Press, 1981), 21.

8. Ibid., 14.

9. Ibid., 16.

10. Ibid., 18 (italics mine).

11. Ibid., 17.

12. Barbara Fiand, *Releasement* (New York: Crossroad, 1987), 15.

13. Ibid., 22–27.

14. Ibid., 26.

15. Nicholl, *Holiness*, 42, 43, 44.

16. Ann Belford Ulanov, *Picturing God* (Cambridge, Mass.: Cowley Publications, 1986), 15.

17. Ibid.

18. Ibid., 17–18.

19. Ibid., 18.

20. Edward C. Whitmont, *The Symbolic Quest* (Princeton, N.J.: Princeton University Press, 1978), 221–22.

21. Sandra Schneiders, *New Wineskins* (New York: Paulist Press, 1986), 181.

22. Ibid.

23. Martin Heidegger, *Discourse on Thinking*, trans. John M. Anderson and E. Hans Freund (New York: Harper Torchbook, 1969), 54.

24. Hendrik M. Ruitenbeek, *The Male Myth* (New York: Dell, 1966), 17.

25. Schneiders, *New Wineskins*, 91.

Chapter Four: Community, Celibacy, and Intimacy

1. Desmond Murphy, *A Return to Spirit: After the Mythic Church* (New York: Crossroad, 1997), 16–17.

2. Ibid., 17.

3. Ibid.

4. Mary Wolff-Salin, *The Shadow Side of Community and the Growth of the Self* (New York: Crossroad, 1988), 78.

5. Ibid.

6. Ibid., 26.

7. Ibid., 23.

8. Murphy, *A Return to Spirit*, 15.

9. Ibid., 16.

10. Ibid., 18.

11. Parker J. Palmer, *The Courage to Teach* (San Francisco: Jossey-Bass, 1998), 102–6.

12. Ibid., 101.

13. Adaptation made from ibid., 102–3.

14. Ibid., 103.

15. Adapted from ibid., 107–8.

16. Ibid., 108.

17. Sandra Schneiders, *New Wineskins* (New York: Paulist Press, 1986), 247.

18. Ibid. (italics mine).

19. Joan Chittister, *Women, Ministry, and the Church* (New York: Paulist Press, 1983), 32, 33 (italics mine).

20. Wolff-Salin, *The Shadow Side of Community*, 8.

21. A modern example of this can be found in Sr. Joyce Ridick's *Treasures in Earthen Vessels* (New York: Alba House, 1984), chapter 2.

22. Karl Rahner, *The Practice of Faith* (New York: Crossroad, 1983), 62.

23. Barbara Fiand, *Living Religious Vows in an Age of Change* (Cincinnati: St. Anthony Messenger Press, 1989), tape 3.

24. See the section "The Primacy of Disposition" in chapter 2..

25. Rahner, *The Practice of Faith*, 63.

26. See the section "Refounding Our Myths" in chapter 1.

27. See the section "Thinking into Our Myths" in chapter 1.

28. Bernard J. Boelen, *Personal Maturity* (New York: Seabury Press, 1978), x, 12, 128, 129. See also appendix 1 of this book.

29. See section "Toward a Holistic Paradigm" in chapter 1.

30. Henri J. M. Nouwen, *Clowning in Rome* (Garden City, N.Y.: Image Books, 1979), 37–58.

31. Sebastian Moore, *The Crucified Is No Stranger* (London: Darton, Longman & Todd, 1977); the entire book is a reflection on this theme.

32. C. G. Jung, *Psychological Reflections* (Princeton, N.J.: Princeton University Press, 1978), 356.

33. Kathryn North, "Creative Solitude," *Desert Call: Spiritual Life Institute* 21, no. 3 (Fall 1986): 22.

34. Ibid. (italics mine).

35. Ibid.

36. Wolff-Salin, *The Shadow Side of Community*, 25.

37. Jung, *Psychological Reflections*, 224, 225.

38. Ibid.

39. For a more detailed discussion on the shadow and ways to encounter it see Barbara Fiand, *Where Two or Three Are Gathered: Community Life for the Contemporary Religious* (New York: Crossroad, 1995), 38–45.

40. Wolff-Salin, *The Shadow Side of Community*, 37.

41. Ibid., 37–38.

42. Mary Johnson, S.N.D. de N., "Bowling Alone, Living Alone: Current Social Contexts for Living the Vows," *Review for Religious* 59, no. 2 (March–April 2000): 123.

43. Ibid., 122.

44. Ibid., 123.

45. Ibid., 126, 129–30.

46. Ibid., 123.

47. Henri J. M. Nouwen, *Lifesigns* (New York: Image Books, 1986), 31–32.

48. Sebastian Moore, *Inner Loneliness* (New York: Crossroad, 1982), 15–16.

49. Ibid., 22.

50. Ibid., 34.

51. Cited by Marilyn Wussler, S.S.N.D., M.S., "Don't Is a Four Letter Word," *Human Development* 10, no. 1 (Spring 1989): 19.

52. Alice Miller, *Prisoners of Childhood,* trans. Ruth Ward (New York: Basic Books, 1981), 15.

53. L. Patrick Carroll, S.J., and Katherine Marie Dyckman, S.N.J.M., *Chaos or Creation: Spirituality in Mid-Life* (New York: Paulist Press, 1986), 122.

54. Ibid., 127.

55. Gerald G. May, M.D., *Will and Spirit* (San Francisco: Harper & Row, 1982), 185–86 (italics mine).

56. For a more detailed development on the symbolic significance of celibacy see Barbara Fiand, *Wrestling with God: Religious Life in Search of Its Soul* (New York: Crossroad, 1996), part 2.

57. As cited by Rick Fields, "Celibacy and Religious Passion," *The Sun* 157 (December 1989): 7 (first set of italics mine).

58. Ibid.

59. John Francis Kavanaugh, *Following Christ in a Consumer Society* (Maryknoll, N.Y.: Orbis Books, 1981), 134.

60. Ibid.

61. Nouwen, *Clowning in Rome,* 38.

62. Ibid., 52.

Chapter Five: Creative Fidelity

1. Carolyn McDade, "Song to Mary," *Rain upon Dry Land* (Plainville, Mass.: Surtsey Publishing, 1984), stanza 6.

2. Ann Belford Ulanov, *Receiving Woman* (Philadelphia: Westminster Press, 1981), 35–36; quoted in Barbara Fiand, *Releasement* (New York: Crossroad, 1987), 68.

3. Quoted by Dorothee Sölle, *Beyond Mere Obedience,* trans. Lawrence W. Denef (New York: Pilgrim Press, 1982), 8.

4. Ibid.

5. See chapter 1, "Culture in Crisis."

6. Sandra Schneiders, "Evangelical Equality: Religious Consecration, Mission, and Witness," *Spirituality Today* 39, no. 1 (Spring 1987): 60.

7. Sölle, *Beyond Mere Obedience,* chaps. 2, 3, 4.

8. Ibid., 7 (italics mine).

9. Ibid., 7–8 (italics mine).

10. Ibid., 8.

11. Ibid., 8–9.

12. Stanley Milgram, "A Behavioral Study of Obedience," in *The Norton Reader,* ed. Arthur M. Eastman, 3d ed. (New York: W. W. Norton & Co.,

1973), 293–307. This study documents "a procedure for the study of destructive obedience in the laboratory. It consists of ordering a naive S [subject] to administer increasingly more severe punishment to a victim in the context of a learning experiment. Punishment is administered by means of a shock generator with 30 graded switches ranging from Slight Shock to Danger: Severe Shock. The victim is a confederate of the E [experimenter]. The primary dependent variable is the maximum shock the S is willing to administer before he [she] refuses to continue further. 26 Ss obeyed the experimental commands fully, and administered the highest shock on the generator. 14 Ss broke off the experiment at some point after the victim protested and refused to provide further answers. The procedure created extreme levels of nervous tension in some Ss. Profuse sweating, trembling, and stuttering were typical expressions of this emotional disturbance. One unexpected sign of tension—yet to be explained— was the regular occurrence of nervous laughter, which in some Ss developed into uncontrollable seizures. The variety of interesting behavioral dynamics observed in the experiment, the reality of the situation for the S, ... point to the fruitfulness of further study."

13. Sölle, *Beyond Mere Obedience*, 9.

14. Ibid., 10.

15. Ibid., xiii–xvi.

16. Jim Wallis, *The Call to Conversion* (San Francisco: Harper & Row, 1981), 31–32.

17. Joann Wolski Conn, ed., *Women's Spirituality: Resources for Christian Development* (New York: Paulist Press, 1986), 11 (italics mine).

18. Sandra Schneiders, *New Wineskins* (New York: Paulist Press, 1986), 140 (italics mine).

19. Brennan Manning, T.O.R., *The Wisdom of Accepted Tenderness* (Denville, N.J.: Dimension Books, 1986), 19.

20. Sölle, *Beyond Mere Obedience*, 19.

21. Ibid, 19–20.

22. Ibid.

23. Wolski Conn, *Women's Spirituality*, 26. Referring to the ideas of Phyllis Trible, Conn suggests that "subordination is the consequence of sin; the curse is upon the serpent, not the woman, in Gen. 3." The serpent, of course, is possible in each of us when we are scattered from our inner center.

24. Fyodor Dostoyevsky, *The Brothers Karamazov* (New York: Airmont Publishing, 1966), book 5, chapter 5, 223–39.

25. Ibid., 230.

26. Ibid., 230–31.

27. Nicholas Berdyaev, *Dostoevsky* (Cleveland: World, 1962), 70.

28. Sölle, *Beyond Mere Obedience*, 23–24.

29. I refer the reader back to the discussion of the holistic approach to the meaning of redemption in the section "Toward a Holistic Paradigm" in chapter 1.

30. Sölle, *Beyond Mere Obedience*, 24.

31. Ibid., 26 (italics mine).

32. Fiand, *Releasement,* 50.

33. Ibid.

34. See the section "Called to Self-Sacrifice" in chapter 3. The quote is from Donald Nicholl, *Holiness* (New York: Seabury Press, 1981), 21.

35. Schneiders, *New Wineskins,* 162.

36. Ibid., 161.

37. Ibid., 164.

38. Kieran Kavanaugh, O.C.D., and Otilio Rodriguez, O.C.D., trans., *The Collected Works of St. John of the Cross* (Washington, D.C.: ICS Publications, 1973), 714.

39. William Johnson, *Christian Zen* (New York: Harper & Row, 1971), 37.

40. Ibid.

41. Gerald G. May, M.D., *Will and Spirit* (San Francisco: Harper & Row, 1982), 172.

42. Lao Tsu, *Tao Te Ching,* trans. Gia-Fu Feng and Jane English (New York: Vintage Books, 1972), 10 (italics mine).

43. Bernard J. Boelen, *Personal Maturity* (New York: Seabury Press, 1978), 158.

44. Ibid., 159.

45. Fiand, *Releasement,* 48.

Chapter Six: Conversion toward Increase

1. Joseph Campbell, *Myths to Live By* (New York: Bantam Books, 1973), 13.

2. Ibid.

3. John Shea, *Stories of God* (Chicago: Thomas More Press, 1978), 8.

4. Ibid., 7–8 (italics mine).

5. The author of this story is Francis Dorff. It has been cited recently in a number of works: M. Scott Peck cites it in the prologue of *The Different Drum* (New York: Simon & Schuster, 1988), 13–15; Mary Wolff-Salin, in her book *The Shadow Side of Community and the Growth of The Self* (New York: Crossroad, 1988), 82–83. She claims to have "heard" the story from Joan Chittister, O.S.B., "Living the Rule Today: A Series of Conferences on the Rule of Benedict" (Erie, Pa.: Benet Press, 1982), 98–99.

6. Pierre Teilhard de Chardin, *The Divine Milieu* (New York: Harper & Row), 61, quoted here from Shea, *Stories of God,* 45.

7. Ibid.

8. For further reflection see appendix 2.

9. Dr. Jackie Schwartz, *Letting Go of Stress* (New York: Pinnacle Books, 1982), 95–97.

10. Ibid., 98.

11. Hans Selye, M.D., *The Stress of Life* (New York: McGraw-Hill, 1978), 174–77.

12. Richard A. Stein, M.D., *Personal Strategies for Living with Less Stress* (New York: John Gallagher Communications, 1983), 3.

Epilogue

1. Karl Rahner, *The Practice of Faith* (New York: Crossroad, 1983), 63 (italics mine).

Appendix 1: Conversion of Consciousness

1. Joel Arthur Barker, *The Business of Paradigms,* Discovering the Future series (Burnsville, Minn.: Charthouse International Learning Corporation, 1990), video cassette presentation.

2. C. G. Jung, *Psychological Reflections*, ed. Jolande Jacobi and R. F. C. Hull (Princeton, N.J.: Princeton University Press, 1978), 147.

3. Ibid., 147–48.

4. Karen Schwartz, "Alternate Forms of Membership in Religious Congregations," *Review for Religious* 50, no. 4, 562.

5. Bernard J. Boelen, *Personal Maturity* (New York: Seabury, 1978). The entire book deals with the essential necessity as well as the health of ontological crises in human maturation.

6. Ibid.

7. Beatrice Bruteau, "Neo-Feminism and the Next Revolution of Consciousness," *Anima* 3, no. 2 (Spring 1977).

8. Barbara Fiand, *Where Two or Three Are Gathered* (New York: Crossroad, 1992), chapter 1.

9. A well-written account summarizing the findings of both of these scholars in this area can be found in June Singer, *Love's Energies* (Boston: Sigo Press, 1990), chapter 1.

10. Patricia Wittberg, S.C., *Creating a Future for Religious Life* (New York: Paulist Press, 1991), chapter 3.

11. Sandra Schneiders, *New Wineskins* (New York: Paulist Press, 1986), 147.

Appendix 2: Paradigm Shift

1. Brian Swimme, *The Hidden Heart of the Cosmos: Humanity and the New Story* (Maryknoll, N.Y.: Orbis, 1996), 95.

2. Margaret J. Wheatley, *Leadership and the New Science* (San Francisco: Berrett-Koehle, 1994), 23.

3. Ibid., 19–20.